FootprintFrance

Languedoc

Dana Facaros
& Michael Pauls

Lozère

Introducing the region

The Gard

Hérault

About the region

Aude

Roussillon

Practicalities

Contents

About the authors

Dana Facaros and Michael Pauls met in a pre-Socratic philosophy class at university and have been travelling and writing ever since, while raising two kids who seem to have turned out all right in spite of having to learn lots of languages, attending school in Greece, Spain, Italy, France and Ireland. Currently reinstalled in southwest France, Facaros and Pauls have written over 30 books while contributing to the Observer, Sunday Times, Independent, Sunday Telegraph, Sunday Times Travel Magazine, the National Geographic Traveler, Wanderlust and other publications. When not writing about travel, Michael plays the musical saw and writes about urban design and restoring the soul of American cities at recivilization.net, while Dana makes and consumes Scotch bonnet hot sauce in industrial quantities, while trying hard not to become too bitter and twisted from constantly losing to her daughter at Scrabble.

Acknowledgements

We'd like to thank Anthony Peregrine, Laura Chanter and Nick Wilcock for their contributions to this book, and to all the tourist offices who patiently answered all our pesky questions. Also a very special thanks to the lovely Lily, who cooked us gourmet meals and painted our shutters while we scribbled away.

About the book

The guide is divided into four sections: Introducing the region; About the region; Around the region and Practicalities.

Introducing the region comprises: **At a glance** (which explains how the region fits together); **Best of Languedoc-Roussillon** (top 20 highlights); **Month by month** (a guide to pros and cons of visiting at certain times of year); and **Screen & page** (a list of suggested books and films). **About the region** comprises: History; Art & architecture; Languedoc-Roussillon today (which presents different aspects of life in the region today); **Nature & environment**; Festivals & events; Sleeping (an overview of accommodation options); **Eating & drinking** (an overview of the region's cuisine, as well as advice on eating out); **Entertainment** (an overview of the region's cultural credentials, explaining what entertainment is on offer); **Shopping** (the region's specialities and recommendations for the best buys); and **Activities & tours**. **Around the region** is then broken down into five areas, each with its own chapter. Here you'll find all the main sights and at the end of each chapter is a listings section with all the best sleeping, eating and drinking, entertainment, shopping and activities and tours options.

Picture credits

Hemis.Fr pages 1, 12, 37, 38, 61, 103, 104, 146, 155, 160: Jean du Boisberranger; pages 6, 24, 51, 56, 60, 61, 68, 71, 128, 145, 166, 167, 182, 183, 216, 270, 276: Jean-Pierre Degas; page 10: Annette Soumillard; pages 14, 17, 57, 63, 89, 120, 149, 157, 163, 165, 195, 243, 247, 250, 252, 253, 279: Franck Guiziou; pages 15, 23, 33, 45, 55, 139, 158, 159, 196, 256: Patrick Frilet; pages 21, 142, 168, 175, 236, 249, 268: Alain Felix; pages 27, 47, 204, 206, 208, 210, 211, 213, 218, 234, 240, 246, 251, 258, 261, 262: Bertrand Rieger; pages 30, 86, 99: Laurent Giraudou; pages 34, 82, 138: Herve Hughes; pages 40, 122: Frances-Wysocki; pages 43, 78, 80, 151, 152, 192: Romain Cintract; pages 53, 76, 88, 96, 98, 108, 114, 117, 189: Jean-Daniel Sudres; pages 54, 222: Jose Nicolas; page 62: Emilio Suetone; page 73: Marc Dozier; pages 90, 95, 130, 194, 209: Christian Guy; pages 93, 171, 178, 232, 277: Camille Moirenc; page 107: Matthieu Colin; pages 110, 235: Stephane Frances; pages 124, 133, 134, 136, 219, 221: Pierre Jacques; page 126: Denis Caviglia; page 127: Gil Giuglio; page 129: Gilles Rigoulet; page 144: Bruno Barbier; pages 156, 176: Herve Lenain; page 187: Managed by Montpellier Agglomeration / Jean du Boisberranger; page 244: Bertrand Gardel; page 170: Philip Lange.

Shutterstock page 13: cyrrpit; pages 16, 75: xc; pages 31, 87: mizio70; pages 21, 84: Elena Elisseeva; page 28: G Beanland; page 36: Philip Lange; page 100: Richard Semik; page 118: macumazahn; page 154: cynoclub; page 172: Claudio Giovanni Colombo.

Alamy page 20: E.D. Torial; page 255: Mark Zylber.

Dana Facaros pages 18, 19, 32, 35, 49, 50, 65, 67, 81, 83, 94, 113, 115, 121, 123, 186, 220, 220, 263, 265.

Tom Jones page 41.

TIPS page 201: Imagestate; page 202: photononstop; page 203: Sunset; page 230: Tommaso di Girolamo.

iStockphoto pages 29, 58: typhoonski; pages 46, 74: mgfoto; page 164: Kodachrome25; page 212: RobertH2255; page 214: cynoclub; page 229: John Woodcock.

Catalan Sports Tours page 267.

Monkey Business Images page 61.

Front cover Canal du Midi, David Noton/Alamy.
Back cover Torero statue, Hemis.fr/Franck Guiziou; nautical jousting, Hemis.fr/ Jean-Pierre Degas.
Inside back cover Provence vineyard, Shutterstock/ Paul Atkinson.

Map symbols

ℹ	l'Information / Information	🚋	Gare / Train station
○	Endroit d'intérêt / Place of interest	🚌	Gare routière / Bus station
🏛	Musée/galerie / Museum/gallery	Ⓜ	Station de métro / Metro station
Théâtre	Théâtre / Theatre	—	Ligne de tram / Tram route
✉	Poste / Post office	🍎	Marché / Market
✝	Eglise/cathédrale / Church/cathedral	✚	Hôpital / Hospital
	Mur de ville / City wall	✚	Pharmacie / Pharmacy
P	Parking	🎓	Lycée / College

Contents

Introducing the region

La Ola Beach Bar, Sète.

Introduction

I t has the same magical light and sunny climate, but there's still a sense that Languedoc-Roussillon is the 'Other South of France' or, as the local expats prefer, the 'thinking person's Provence'. It's the French Mediterranean in relax mode, laid-back, minus the glitter.

What it lacks in glitz, Languedoc-Roussillon more than makes up for with some pretty spectacular things to see and do. Picnic under the Pont du Gard or wander over the mighty medieval ramparts of Carcassonne. Risk vertigo taking the Petit Train Jaune into the Pyrenees, or barge serenely along the Canal du Midi. Ride with French cowboys on white horses in the Camargue, or trek with a donkey over the Cévennes. Climb up to vertiginous Cathar castles, balloon over the gleaming new Viaduc de Millau or kayak down the magnificent Gorges du Tarn. Go tasting – Languedoc-Roussillon has 24 wine areas and as a region makes more wine than any place on earth.

Wherever you go, you're never far from a sleepy old village, the click of the boules or a café dappled in the shade. Peaceful medieval abbeys mark the way to Compostela and outdoor markets tantalize with fresh colours and scents. Long lazy lunches await, and dancing at a fête under the blazing stars – the idyll of *la douce France* – is what Languedoc-Roussillon does best of all.

At a glance

A whistle-stop tour of Languedoc-Roussillon

Languedoc-Roussillon forged its unique identity in the early Middle Ages, when it was the core of an independent, sophisticated Occitan-speaking civilization of courtly love, poetry, chivalry, troubadours and, fatally, a large band of religious dissidents known as Cathars. It all ended with the Albigensian Crusade and Languedoc's annexation to France in the early 13th century. But the memory of that lost world is the glue that binds the region together. Not surprisingly, medieval re-enactments are the rage.

Montpellier has been the capital of Languedoc-Roussillon since the 18th century, and is the place to go to see the future: in the past two decades it's been the fastest-growing city in France, notably as a university city and a centre for agricultural and IT research. The region's other main cities – Nîmes, Narbonne, Béziers, Carcassonne and Perpignan – don't have the same go-getting drive (the region would probably overheat and blow a fuse if they did) but they're rich in history and character, with plenty to see and do, especially in summer when they gear up for the lively festival season.

The rest of the region is happy to putter along in the slow lane, except perhaps the beach resorts in July and August when things can get rather intense. Only an hour or so away by autoroute, however, you can escape into another world altogether, one of pristine nature – the rugged garrigue, the Cévennes, the Corbières or the Pyrenees – where rivers and lakes offer idyllic alternatives to the crowded sands.

The horses of the Camargue.

The lowdown

Money matters
Languedoc isn't as expensive as many parts of France, although admission prices have gone up recently. Excluding accommodation costs, you'll need to budget about €40 per person a day for meals, transport and entrance fees.

Opening hours
In general, museums (and many shops) close on Mondays, and most close for lunch. Sights tend to stay open continuously in July and August, but close for lunch in spring and autumn; by winter opening hours are often curtailed to weekends, national holidays and French school half-term breaks. The more out of season, the more advisable it is to ring ahead to make sure someone's there. Churches often close between 1200 and 1500.

Discounts
Many cities and *départements* offer discount passes; usually you pay full whack at the first attraction, then save money by presenting your pass at other participating sights. Senior citizens, students (bring ID) and children nearly always pay less as well, or go free. Some places offer special rates for families – it's worth asking.

Tourist information
Every town of any size will have a tourist information office, and nearly always someone there will speak English. They all have a web presence, although it may only be in French. Tourist information offices are especially useful for checking current opening hours and accommodation options.

Useful websites
Among other useful websites covering a range of topics are languedoc-france.info, creme-de-languedoc.com and languedocsun.com. The region's official website, en.sunfrance.com, is chock-full of useful information and it offers packages and online reservations, as well as information about events and exhibitions, details on the best ways to get there and tours.

Languedoc-Roussillon is divided into five *départements* of such distinct personality that it makes sense to divide the book accordingly, from east to west.

The Gard
The Gard shares the Rhône and its delta, the Camargue, and its colour-drenched mix of black bulls, white horses and pink flamingos with Provence, but otherwise its soul is pure Languedoc. The capital, Nîmes, is a vivacious little city that loves its ferias, tapas and flamenco, and glows with its immaculately preserved monuments from the early days of the Roman Empire; its water supply, after all, arrived via the Pont du Gard. Down in the Camargue the high walls of Aigues-Mortes, built by St Louis, still bristle, waiting to welcome medieval Crusaders, while just north the Romanesque pilgrimage church of St-Gilles-du-Gard boasts a stupendous sculpted façade.

The towns of the Gard are exceptionally varied: there's arty, laid-back Sommières with its bridge built by Tiberius, or Villeneuve-lès-Avignon, papal Avignon's bedroom suburb for cardinals. Beaucaire, once host to one of the biggest markets in Europe, is now the capital of bloodless bullfights, the *Courses Camarguaises*; and Uzès, seat of the oldest duchy in France, is just lovely. In the north, the vineyards and olive groves that characterize much of the Gard give way to the Cévennes, the lush green mountains where Protestants hid out during the Wars of Religion, and home to the once-important silk industry. The walking here is excellent, and you can even ride an antique steam train.

The Lozère
Further north, and sharing the Cévennes National Park with the Gard, the Lozère is savage and sublime, replete with fresh air and wide-open

Place de la Comédie, Montpellier.

spaces. It's the ideal place for anyone suffering from *mal de civilization* – as Robert Louis Stevenson found out when he invented the long-distance walking tour here in 1879. Its little capital Mende has a medieval core and a giant Gothic cathedral, and you'll find some ruggedly handsome old stone villages and farms scattered over the *département*. For the most part though, Nature in all her magnificent and occasionally quirky glory steals the show here. The stupendous Gorges du Tarn and neighbouring Gorges de la Jonte get the lion's share of attention and tourists, but they're only the beginning. In the Cévennes, Mont Lozère and Mont Aigoual, the sources of many of Languedoc's rivers, offer splendid viewpoints over much of southern France. Vultures, wolves and *mouflons* (wild sheep) have recently been re-introduced, and caves, abysses and swallow holes offer underworldly splendours. The *département*'s very emptiness has attracted some interesting characters since the 1970s, who have contributed to a precocious interest in sustainable tourism. One

of their legacies is a pair of remarkable adventure playgrounds; Le Vallon du Villaret and Utopix. Although it's just outside the Lozère, this chapter also includes one of the newest wonders of France, Sir Norman Foster's sublime Viaduc de Millau.

The Hérault

At the heart of Languedoc, the Hérault is home to the region's feverish capital and its biggest university. Montpellier's beautifully restored historic centre, L'Ecusson, bursts at the seams with elegant *hôtels particuliers*, boutiques, trendy hotels and restaurants, and the region's top art collection is displayed here in the Musée Fabre. Nearby Pézenas, the elegant former capital, takes pride in its association with Molière. There's a long swathe of coast, with the vibrant port of Sète and great shellfish nursery of the Bassin de Thau in the middle, and two hugely popular beach resorts on either end – the bodacious, Jetsons-friendly La Grande Motte and the fashionable Le Cap d'Agde, built near an ancient Greek colony and with museums containing stunning ancient bronzes found in nearby shipwrecks. The Hérault's amiable second city, Béziers, is piled under its enormous cathedral, near the hilltop Oppidum d'Ensérune, the most impressive of the pre-Greek and Roman cities of Languedoc. The most fascinating stretch of the Canal du Midi begins near here as well, before passing through a series of delightful canal ports. The hilly limestone *garrigue* that dominates the northern Hérault is endowed with wild gorges, Minervois vineyards and beautiful villages, such as St-Guilhem-le-Désert, Minerve, Roquebrun and Orlagues.

The Aude

The Aude, as its slogan proclaims, is 'the land of the Cathars' and interest in the area, piqued by bestsellers, has made it quite popular in recent years. Its capital Carcassonne, a glorious fairytale vision, can get so busy that you'll need to carefully time your visit to avoid the crowds. On the other hand, you'll need your walking shoes for the Cathar castles – the ruined, outrageously picturesque last refuges of Languedoc's medieval heretics. Most of these are in the rugged Corbières south of Carcassonne, an area synonymous with red wine.

Château de Quéribus, Cathar castle.

Lovers of bubbly, however, shouldn't miss Limoux. The curious flock to the vortex of French mysteries, Rennes-le-Château; the adventurous go whitewater rafting down the Aude; and the palaeontology buffs visit Dinosauria in Espéraza. The Canal du Midi passes through the area (although for convenience's sake we've included it all in the Hérault chapter), and one of its branches, the Canal de la Robine, transverses Narbonne. This was the Roman capital of Languedoc and once the seat of a powerful bishop, with a stunning cathedral complex to prove it and a museum worthy of the Cardinal's palaces in Rome. One of the greatest religious houses of Languedoc, the Abbaye de Fontfroide, is nearby, whilst just over the coastal mountain of La Clape await a string of beaches and the excellent safari park at Sigean.

Roussillon

Framed by the Pyrenees and the sea, Roussillon (the Pyrénées-Orientales) was part of Catalonia until 1669, and still has strong cultural links with the dynamic Spanish region south of the border. Most of Roussillon's monuments date from its pre-French days, beginning with the cathedral and royal palace in the sunny capital Perpignan; the Renaissance Fortress at Salses; and a bevy of stunning Romanesque churches, including Elne, St-Michel-de-Cuxa and Serrabonne. As elsewhere, wide sandy beaches and salt lagoons rule the coast, only here the Côte Vermeille kicks up a fine stretch of cliff and coves to the south, with delectable Collioure, the town of anchovies and Fauves, as the main allure. The Conflent, the main valley into the Pyrenees, is guarded by Louis XIV's fortified town of Villefranche-de-Conflent. Near here you can climb the iconic Pic du Canigou, go canyoning or caving, or take one of the most exciting train journeys in Europe to the magnificent sun-drenched plateau of the Cerdagne, home to the region's top ski resorts and the world's biggest solar furnace. Alternatively, visit Tautavel and see relics of some of the earliest Europeans, or charming Céret, once a favourite resort of the Cubists, with a museum to prove it.

Best of Languedoc-Roussillon

Top 20 things to see and do

❶ Nîmes

Nîmes has an amphitheatre in better condition than Rome's Colosseum, an immaculate ancient temple to die for, a charming historic centre, and one of the oldest public parks in France. It's also a great deal of fun, especially during its lively street party ferias. See pages 82-89.

❷ Uzès

The first duchy of France, lovely Uzès puts on a class act. Tour the ducal palace in the heart of town, then wander about lanes and squares that embody a perfect intuitive sense of urban design. Come on Saturday morning, when the entire centre is given over to an outdoor market. See pages 97-99.

❸ Pont du Gard

You've seen the pictures, but they don't prepare you for the real thing: an ancient builders' tour de force, the highest of all Roman aqueducts, pirouetting elegantly over the Gardon. Picnic or kayak under it, or get a real insider's view on a guided tour through the water conduit on top. See page 100.

❹ St-Gilles-du-Gard

This town in the Petite Camargue is a bit frumpy but the abbey, where pilgrims from across France used to gather before departing for the Holy Land or Compostela, has three sculpted portals full of verve and emotion that are Languedoc-Roussillon's crown jewels of Romanesque art. See page 105.

❺ Aigues-Mortes

This mighty 13th-century Crusader port founded by King St Louis looms over the Petite Camargue like a mirage, especially as the port itself silted up long ago. The walls are extraordinary, and close at hand are beaches, wetlands for birdwatching and the Camargue's famous black bulls, white horses and pink flamingos. See page 106.

Above: Pézenas.
Left: Place des Arènes, Nîmes.

❻ Gorges du Tarn

The most famous canyon in France, this 63-km gash of turquoise cuts deeply into the austere limestone *causses* of the Lozère. See it best from the seat of a canoe or kayak – the endlessly changing cliffs, cirques and rock formations, the castles and old stone villages, all basking in the gorges' sheltered microclimate. See page 116 and pages 132-133.

❼ Viaduc de Millau

The world record-breaking spirit is embedded in France's DNA, and thanks to Sir Norman Foster's sleek design, this latest example is a compelling silvery beauty. Drive over it, but head down into the Tarn valley to truly appreciate its astonishing dimensions – its pylons are higher than the Eiffel tower. See page 135.

❽ Montpellier

Languedoc-Roussillon's capital has a cracking buzz. Its elegant 17th- to 18th-century centre, L'Ecusson, is crammed with boutiques, cafés and students. It has the region's best art collection in the Musée Fabre, an incredibly romantic Jardin des Plantes, a spanking new aquarium and a free zoo. Not forgetting the great restaurants, the culture and the nightlife – the works, really. See pages 146-156.

❾ Pézenas

Molière himself came to entertain the grandees of Pézenas, a town that rivals Uzès as the most beautiful in the region. From the 16th to 18th century, it was the seat of Languedoc's governors, who filled its cobbled lanes with elegant *hôtels particuliers*, now home to antique shops, galleries and boutiques. See page 158.

⑩ St-Guilhem-le-Désert

Dramatically set in the *garrigue* by the gorge of the River Hérault, this tiny but beautiful village surrounds the medieval Abbaye de Gellone, founded by Charlemagne's cousin after he laid down his sword. There's exceptional walking all around, and swimming and kayaking by the nearby Pont du Diable. See page 161.

⑪ Cirque de Navacelles

The limestone highlands, the *garrigue* and *causses* of northern Languedoc are full of marvels, and this cirque carved by the River Vis is the most breathtaking of all. Ponder it from above, but also take time to wend your way down to the bottom for an unforgettable swim and picnic. See page 162.

⑫ Sète

If Popeye were French, he'd live in this salty, quirky seaport, a gritty Venice with canals, where the locals joust on boats and the summer sizzles with music festivals. Add fresh shellfish from the nearby Bassin de Thau and a bottle of the local picpoul, and life seems just about perfect. See pages 166-167.

⑬ Canal du Midi

Say 'Languedoc' and the picture that first comes to many minds is this evocative, dreamlike masterpiece of 17th-century engineering, recently listed by UNESCO as a World Heritage Site. Even if you can't go barging, cycle or stroll along the old towpaths. Slow travel doesn't get better than this. See pages 174, 178-179.

Above: Canal du Midi.
Above left: Cirque de Navacelles.

⑭ Carcassonne

It's no wonder Walt Disney came to study it: the walled Cité is the perfect fairytale fantasy of what a medieval town should look like. Visit the mighty ramparts and witch-hatted towers, the cathedral and Viscount's Palace, or watch a joust and stock up on plastic armour and toy catapults. See pages 196-201.

⑮ Cathar castles

South of Carcassonne, the savage outcrops of the Corbières host a good half dozen of these ruined strongholds, where the famous heretics held out to the bitter end. Château de Peyrepetuse and nearby Château de Quéribus are the most spectacular, and exceptionally evocative out of season when they're lost in romantic mists. See pages 209-213.

Vinça, at the foot of Le Pic du Canigou.

⑯ Narbonne
Narbonne was the Roman and ecclesiastical capital of Languedoc, and delivers the historical goods with its Gothic cathedral and Palais des Archevêques, home to a pair of excellent museums. Added treats nearby are the magnificent Abbaye de Fontfroide and sandy Gruissan Plage, where the beach cottages stand on stilts. See pages 214, 220 and 221.

⑰ Forteresse de Salses
Built by Ferdinand and Isabella on what was then the Spanish/French frontier, this astonishing bunker was state-of-the-art military architecture in the late 15th century. It was full of endlessly cunning devices to thwart the enemy, but it had luxuries too, including hot baths for the officers. See page 242.

⑱ Collioure
Most of Languedoc-Roussillon's beach resorts date from the mid-20th century, but this old anchovy port piled around the summer palace of the kings of Mallorca is crammed full of charm. Matisse and Derain came for the light, had an epiphany of colour and changed the history of art. See page 247.

⑲ Le Pic du Canigou
Visible across much of eastern Roussillon, this legendary mountain with its Phrygian cap summit is so striking that for centuries it was believed to be the highest peak in the Pyrenees. Anyone who is reasonably fit can reach the summit, where views on a clear day stretch to Barcelona. See page 254.

⑳ Le Petit Train Jaune
The century-old 'Little Yellow Train' is one of Europe's great rides. Starting in Villefranche-de-Conflent, it gaily ascends terrifyingly vertiginous viaducts to reach the Cerdagne, Roussillon's favourite mountain playground. Although tourists have adopted it, it's still a year-round mode of transport and is a great way to reach the ski slopes. See box, page 255.

Month by month

A year in Languedoc-Roussillon

January & February

January in Languedoc-Roussillon is usually surprisingly bright and sunny, if often bitterly cold. That said, there are days when it's warm enough by the afternoon to sit outside at the cafés, especially around Perpignan. After the New Year's holidays, there are a couple of quiet weeks at the ski slopes in the Pyrenees before the French school holidays crank up again in February. Many museums and sights are only open at weekends, but it's a great time to eat cassoulet by the roaring fire or black truffles in Uzès; if you fancy a city break, Montpellier has plenty to see and do, and Nîmes puts on a Flamenco festival, attracting aficionados from around the world.

Because the French half-term holidays are staggered throughout February, you'll find most sights open and the ski areas going full-tilt. Curious age-old bear festivals take place in Arles-sur-Tech and Prats-du-Mollo in the Vallespir, while the most traditional and spirited Carnival celebrations take place in Pézenas and Limoux. Rugby is one of the main topics in the cafés, and in sheltered areas, mimosa and almonds, forsythias and japonicas burst into bloom. Four weeks before Easter (late February-early March) Nîmes holds its first feria, a sure sign that spring is on the way.

March & April

March tends to bring rain (the Cévennes, particularly around Mount Aigoual, is the wettest spot in France) or days and days of strong winds: the Mistral blasts down the Rhône as far as Narbonne, or the Tramontane gusts over the Pyrenees. However, because the winds are dry, they do have the virtue of making the air magically clear. As Easter approaches the land takes on a lush green mingled with wild flowers; herbs and fruit trees start to bloom and bees to buzz. The sights aren't crowded, but you will need a coat and an umbrella.

Skiing in the Cerdagne.

Cherry season.

In April the ski season draws to a close, and the vines that carpet much of the countryside in Languedoc-Roussillon bud and burst into leaf. Piles of asparagus, fresh greens and strawberries show up in the markets. The mild sunny weather, with a few scattered showers, means the start of the tourist season and this gears up in earnest around Easter when French holidaymakers are joined by families from around Europe.

May & June

There are three national holidays in May, and from May to early June Languedoc-Roussillon is in full blooming glory – wild irises line the roads, and wisteria, lilacs, magnolias, sweet broom, poppies, roses and lavender offer a heady explosion of colour and scent. There are so many butterflies that at times they resemble falling leaves. The mercury inches up and by late May it's hot enough to swim in the lakes and rivers, and in the sea (although the currents can still make it cold in

places). Mid-season prices make it a popular time for school groups and coach tours.

Early June is peak cherry season – a good time to be in Roussillon and especially Céret, the cherry capital of France. The spring rains come to an end, and the season for canoeing and walking in the mountains begins as the last snows melt. The festival season begins in earnest, headlined by the Feria de Pentecôte in Nîmes, and St John's Day in Catalan Roussillon, celebrated with torches on the Pic du Canigou and hundreds of bonfires.

July & August

Daytime temperatures soar into the high 30s and even into the low 40s as Languedoc moves into July and high season – with prices to match. Main sights like Carcassonne and the Pont du Gard are elbow-room only, and the beaches are packed. If you're staying in a gîte, you'll need to close the shutters in the morning to keep in the cool air. There's almost too much to do, from a score of

French Catalans dancing the sardana.

major festivals and ferias to hundreds of old-fashioned village fêtes, markets and *vide greniers* (attic emptiers). It's a lovely time to eat, as the markets groan under the weight of fresh melons, peaches, apricots, tomatoes, peppers, aubergines and bouquets of herbs. Once the sun goes down the nights are lovely and warm, and in rural areas like the Lozère you can see a billion stars.

The heat continues into August, the most crowded month of all, when all of France hits the seashore and all hotels and holiday homes have been booked months in advance. Fields of sunflowers blaze yellow, cicadas buzz during the day and crickets chirp into the night. The festival season continues in full swing, the summer clubs are packed and barbecues are lit every night. By

the middle of the month, the first thunderstorms arrive and start to cool things off…and you spot the first billboard advertising school supplies for the *rentrée*.

September & October

September can be glorious in Languedoc; summery temperatures linger, but crowds at popular sights are less daunting as kids go back to school and the French go back to work. Although it depends on the year, the *vendage* (wine harvest) takes place in the last part of September, and as so many tractors are hurtling about the roads you'd best allow a few extra minutes travelling time (especially if you need to get to the airport). It's a great time to spot migratory birds along the coast, and to go on a walking holiday. Luscious grapes, figs, apples and pears fill the market stalls.

October is generally the tail-end of the walking and canoeing season, but the last half of the month in particular, when the trees and vines turn yellow, orange and red, is a gorgeous time to visit. Chestnuts are harvested in the Cévennes, hotels offer good deals and menus switch over to hearty fare – rich stews, and game and mushroom dishes. By mid-month the autumn rains start and they are famously unpredictable, and sometimes torrential: rivers frequently burst their banks. But there are often fine shirt-sleeve days as well.

November & December

Although it may be wet and windy and not ideal for outdoor activities, early November (during the French half-term holiday) can be a good time to visit the cities or see the sights. After the kids are back at school, hotels, restaurants, shops and attractions outside of the cities close down until the Christmas holidays; if they do stay open, their hours are often curtailed to weekends. Snow starts to fall in the high areas. Inland, the cold air from the Atlantic meets the warm southern air from the Mediterranean at the Cévennes and causes heavy autumnal downpours. There are enough evergreens, however, to keep the region from looking too bleak. It's a good time for mushroom hunting, enjoying a warm bowl of pumpkin soup and tasting the new wine.

In December even low-lying areas can have morning frost. The ski resorts in the Pyrenees usually open by mid-month, although elsewhere the mercury can still sometimes hit the low 20s in the afternoons. Christmas markets appear (there's a famous one in Carcassonne), and opera, theatre and concert seasons in the city are in full swing. This being France, the holiday season means feasts – foie gras, plump oysters, game dishes, truffles, wild mushrooms, turkeys and capons.

Above: Pont du Gard. Below: Font-Romeu.

Screen & page

Languedoc-Roussillon in film & literature

Films & TV programmes

L'homme qui aimait les femmes (The Man Who Loved Women)
François Truffaut, 1977

Montpellier was the set for Truffaut's bittersweet autobiographical comedy, starring Charles Denner as Bernard Morane, the philanderer unable to commit, while Brigitte Fossey plays his publisher lover.

37°2 le matin
Jacques Beineix, 1986

This steamy cult classic of love and obsession was beautifully filmed on Gruissan's Plage des Pilotis and stars Jean-Hugues Anglade as Zorg, the cottage painter who has a doomed affair with a waitress, the sulphurous but schizophrenic Betty Blue (Beatrice Dalle).

Jean de Florette and Manon des Sources
Claude Berri, 1986

Although identified with Provence, many of the scenes of these two great French classics (starring Gérard Depardieu, Yves Montand, Daniel Auteuil and Emmanuelle Béart) were actually shot in Languedoc, especially in the Gard and Sommières.

Cyrano de Bergerac
Jean-Paul Rappeneau, 1990

Depardieu again, in this definitive film version of Rostand's classic play. Many of the town scenes were shot in Uzès.

Robin Hood: Prince of Thieves
Kevin Reynolds, 1991

Carcassonne lends several authentic medieval sets to this lively swashbuckling take on the Robin Hood legend, starring Keven Costner as Robin, Morgan Freeman as the Moorish warrior Azeem, and Alan Rickman as the Sheriff of Nottingham.

Le Pacte des Loups (Brotherhood of the Wolf)
Christophe Gans, 2001

Although it wasn't filmed in Languedoc-Roussillon, this fantasy film staring Samuel Le Bihan, Vincent Cassel, Emile Dequenne and Monica Bellucci was inspired by the true story of the Bête du Gévaudan in the Lozère.

French Odyssey
Rick Stein, 2007

A BBC series rather than a film, but Rick Stein's culinary adventures on the Canal du Midi will set your mouth watering for the good things of Languedoc.

Many of the books about Languedoc-Roussillon are about the Cathars; for a list, see page 201.

Fiction

The Accursed Treasure of Rennes-le-Château
Gérard de Sède (English translation 2001
Published in 1967 as *L'Or de Rennes* or *Le Trésor Maudit*, this influential novel changed the way the world looked at Rennes-le-Château.

Labyrinth
Kate Mosse, 2006
An adventure story that links heroine Dr Alice Tanner, discoverer of a mysterious but evil tomb, with Alaïs, a herbalist living in Carcassonne at the time of the Albigensian Crusade.

Non-fiction

Travels with a Donkey in the Cévennes
Robert Louis Stevenson, 1879
One of the first modern travel books, and one of the most charming, Stevenson's youthful account still inspires hundreds of readers to follow in his footsteps.

The Holy Blood and the Holy Grail
Michael Baigent, Richard Leigh, Henry Lincoln, 1983
After De Sède's novel, came a BBC2 documentary and this bestseller. It's a gripping account of ancient and Merovingian conspiracies, all centred around Rennes-le-Château.

Ermengard of Narbonne and the World of the Troubadours
Frederic L Cheyette, 2001
A scholarly history of the Viscomtesse who held a court of love in Narbonne, but also one of the best evocations in English of Occitan civilization.

Medieval Carcassonne.

Virgile's Vineyard
Patrick Moon, 2003
A London lawyer inherits a house in Languedoc and writes about his neighbours' winemaking – young Vergile representing the new exciting Languedoc wines, Manu the old plonk.

Notes from the Languedoc
Rupert Wright, 2005
Times' journalist Rupert Wright delves into the fascinating history of Languedoc while rhapsodizing on the joys of living there

Languedoc-Roussillon: the Wines & Winemakers
Paul Strang, 2006
This is wine expert Paul Strang's excellent introduction to the history, politics, traditions and terroir of France's most dynamic wine region, complete with photos and maps.

Hot Sun, Cool Shadow: Savouring the Food, History and Mystery of the Languedoc
Angela Murrills, 2007
An award-winning food writer's account of Languedoc, with illustrations by her partner Peter Matthews, who like many fell in love with the region and bought the dream house.

Contents

Fête de Saint Louis, Sète.

About the region

History

Prehistory & pre-Roman

Although it's not widely known, since most of the discoveries were made in the last 20 years, Languedoc-Roussillon was a major stomping ground for dinosaurs 65 million years ago. Two key places are Espéraza in the Aude, where digs have revealed the fossils and eggs of some 35 species (including some of the most complete dinosaur skeletons found in France), and Mèze, near the Bassin de Thau, where large clutches of dinosaur eggs were uncovered in the 1990s.

Not only dinosaurs, but a very early edition of humanity made its mark in Languedoc-Roussillon. Traces of *Homo erectus* go back one million years, but the most important finds were discovered in a vast shelter in Tautavel in Roussillon (450,000 BC), where palaeontologists found a huge cache of fossils, enough to reconstruct the physique of one of the first Europeans, or Tautavel Man.

Evidence as to what happened afterwards is slight. Signs of Neanderthals were found near Ganges (60,000 BC), and traces of Cro-Magnons have been found in the Gard (30,000 BC), although if any of them decorated caves – as elsewhere in southwest France – they have yet to be found.

Leap ahead to around 6500 BC, when the Ice Age glaciers had retreated, and the reindeer, woolly mammoths and other big game the earliest humans depended on had disappeared. New technologies made their way out of the Middle East to herald a new age – the Neolithic. Animals were domesticated and the first shepherds tramped transhumance routes still used today. They built dry stone-vaulted shelters which go by many names in the south of France: in Languedoc they're called *capitelles* and you can still spot them on the highlands of the *causses* and *garrigue*, rebuilt over thousands of years. Down in the valleys and plains, the Neolithic revolution introduced agriculture. This society of shepherds and farmers began erecting megalithic menhirs and dolmens in 3500 BC; some 700 survive in Languedoc-Roussillon today, concentrated in the Minervois and north of Montpellier, especially around Lodève and the Pic de St Loup. Nîmes' archaeology museum (see page 217) contains several statue-menhirs, carved with rudimentary faces, similar to ones found elsewhere in Liguria, Tuscany and Corsica.

Where to see...

Prehistory & pre-Roman

Cham des Bondons Mont Lozère, page 128
Dinosauria Espéraza, page 205
Dolmen Coste-Rouge St-Michel-de-Grandmont, page 162
Musée de l'Ephèbe Le Cap d'Agde, page 170
Musée de Préhistoire Tautavel, page 242
Musée Parc des Dinosaures Mèze, page 169
Oppidum d'Ensérune, page 174
Oppidum de Nages, page 89

Excavations of dinosaur fossils, Espéraza.

Copper was mined in the Corbières by around 2500 BC, and in the ninth century BC, towards the end of the subsequent Bronze Age, the local residents ('Iberians' according to ancient writers, or Celto-Iberians) were founding walled hilltop settlements (*oppida*) not far from the coast, and trading with the Phoenicians, Etruscan and Greek merchants who sailed along these shores. The well-preserved oppidum of Ensérune was one of the most important and richest of these settlements, judging by the finds in its museum. Others, at Nîmes, Béziers and Carcassonne, now lie buried deep under modern cities.

The Greeks, with their founding of a new colony, Masallia (Marseille) around 600 BC, soon became the most important presence along France's Mediterranean coast. In Languedoc their main settlement was Agde at the mouth of the Hérault, which had the best natural harbour. The Greeks introduced olives, and taught the locals how to make wine from the native vines that grew so well. Languedoc-Roussillon would never be the same again.

In the fifth century new tribes, the Volques (or Volcae) and Sardones, moved in; one of their surviving settlements was the oppidum at Nages. In those early days, the Greek colonists in France were allied with a small but feisty city called Rome, united against both the Etruscans – who fought the Greeks for commercial dominance in the Western Mediterranean – and the Carthaginians – who had colonized much of Spain. As Rome slowly conquered the Etruscans, tensions mounted until 218 BC, when Hannibal decided on a showdown in Italy, marching his elephants across the south of France, having through diplomacy assured the friendship of Languedoc's tribes. The Volcae, however, were loyal to Rome and unsuccessfully challenged Hannibal at the Battle of Rhône Crossing; no one is quite sure how he managed to get his elephants across the big river.

After Rome's conquest of Spain (206 BC), old Greek-Celt tensions and rivalries reached such a point that Marseille appealed to Rome for aid. Rome was more than happy to come in 125 BC – and stay.

About the region

Les Arènes, Nîmes.

Romans & the Dark Ages

Initially the Romans called the entire south of France 'Provence' or simply 'province' - it was Rome's first, and offered plenty of new lands to settle and reward to the veterans of the legions. Being Romans, building a good road was their first concern. The trail had already been blazed in myth by Hercules on his way to Gibraltar (the Pillars of Hercules) and trod by Hannibal's armies and, as it was begun in 118 BC under the pro-consul Cneius Domitius Ahenobarbus, it became known as the Via Domitia, crossing Languedoc-Roussillon from Beaucaire to the Pyrenees pass of Le Perthus.

Today, the A9 autoroute covers much of the Via Domitia (but you can see a stretch near the Mas des Tourelles in Beaucaire). Along the road, the Romans provided mansiones, inns that offered shelter, food and fresh horses for officials – a word that would survive in the south of France and Catalonia as a mas, or farmhouse. The Via Domitia met the Via Aquitania to Toulouse and Bordeaux at Narbo Martius (Narbonne), which at the time was a bustling port near the mouth of the then navigable

Where to see...

Romans & Dark Ages

Aude. This port and crossroads were so strategic that Narbonne became the capital of Provence.

After the Greeks at Marseille were defeated by Julius Caesar in 49 BC (they had made the fatal mistake of backing Pompey at the end of the Gallic Wars), the newer, Romanized towns in Languedoc (notably Nîmes and Narbonne) took on more importance – so much so that what is now Provence, Languedoc-Roussillon and the Dauphine were renamed Gallia Narbonensis by the time of Augustus.

The peace that followed brought Gallia Narbonensis a golden age of prosperity. Temples, aqueducts, theatres and amphitheatres went up, and life was very good for some: villas were decorated with mosaics and paintings and had heated swimming pools. Yet at the edges of the empire, Rome's wars dragged on and taxes rose; by the second century AD, people were selling themselves into serfdom to survive.

The first of many invasions of Languedoc-Roussillon by Germanic tribes happened in the 250s, but most were merely passing through on their way to the richer spoils of Spain. The Visigoths, or Western Goths, who captured Narbonne in 413, were different; they meant to stay. In 476, with the fall of Rome, they took control and made Toulouse their capital.

The Visigoths were Christian, but they subscribed to the Arianism, regarded as a heresy. Their territories west of the Rhône became known as Septimania, from the seven cities – Narbonne, Agde, Béziers, Elne, Nîmes, Maguelonne and Lodève. Their presence and Arianism made them a target for another tribe of *foederati* – the orthodox Catholic Franks of the north. In a practice run for the Albigensian Crusade, Clovis I, King of the Franks, used religion as a pretext for attacking and defeating the tolerant King Alaric II and the Visigoths in 507, taking over Toulouse and all their lands north of Septimania and Spain.

Two hundred years later (in 719), Spain and Septimania in turn were overrun, this time by the Moors in their great push out of North Africa. The Visigoths often sided with them, but in the end it was the Franks again under Pippin (father of Charlemagne) who prevailed by 759 with the reconquest of Narbonne. He granted a number of fiefs to the local Visigothic lords (who had by then converted to Catholicism) – so many, in fact, that the Franks gave Septimania a new name; Gothia. In 792, the Moors of al-Andalus attacked again, but Charlemagne and his cousin Guilhem de Gellone, the Count of Toulouse, stopped them at Carcassonne and Narbonne; Guilhem was the first to take the title of Prince of Gothia, beginning Toulouse's traditional role as the capital of Languedoc.

But Carolingian influences would be short-lived in Languedoc. The south of France was different, and it sounded different. Two main Latin dialects were spoken in what is now France at the end of the Roman Empire. They differed most conspicuously on how each pronounced *Hoc ille* (It is so), a word that became *oui* in the north, and *oc* in the south. The latter, because it was the closest Romance language to Latin, became known as 'the plain Roman tongue', or Occitan.

In the mid-10th century, the powerful counts of Toulouse and Barcelona became increasingly independent. They especially felt the lingering loyalty they owed the Carolingians was extinguished with the rise of a new Frankish dynasty in Paris called the Capets.

Maison-Carrée, Nimes.

About the region

Middle Ages

This was a golden age for southwest France, for Aquitaine under its powerful dukes and for Languedoc and Roussillon under their equally powerful cousins, the counts of Toulouse and Barcelona. Trade was booming (iron mines in the Pyrenees gave the Catalans their head start, evidenced today by the numerous very early frescoed chapels), rich abbeys were founded, pilgrims were on the move, fairs were established and local seigneurs built themselves remarkable castles. Both Languedoc and Roussillon had a sizeable local Jewish population, including many scholars and translators, and contacts increased with the literate, sophisticated civilization of al-Andalus just to the south, where mystical Sufi poets wrote of ideal love; others described the rather more sensuous delights of nights of wine and romance.

The elite of the South were captivated by the beauty of al-Andalus, and even as the Christians set

> **66** It was among the poets and song-smiths of her own lands that Ermengard was best known, among the troubadours… The forms they invented continue to inspire the poetic imagination 800 years later. From Hollywood to blues singers, their themes are still with us. **99**
>
> *Ermengard of Narbonne and the World of the Troubadours*, Fredric L Cheyette

about demolishing it in their holy war of the Reconquista, the south of France and Catalonia used it as inspiration to create the most sophisticated culture in Christian Europe, and were the first to express themselves in a vernacular tongue. Eleanor of Aquitaine's grandfather, Count William (d 1127) – who had Spanish-Moorish blood – was one of the first troubadours (a word probably derived from the Arabic for lute) and one of the bawdiest.

Ideal love was Christianized into love for the Virgin Mary, but it also trickled down into a new respect for women. Noble women held courts of love, promoting poetry, music and chivalry. One of the best known was the Viscomtesse Ermengard of Narbonne, a widow who held her own among the great lords of the land in the last half of the 12th century, and played a leading role in its culture – a dazzling hybrid that had little to do with typical feudal relationships of lords and vassals in Northern France.

New ideas were tolerated, including religious ones and, as the Catholic Church became ever wealthier and more corrupt, many people were attracted or at least sympathetic to the dualist philosophy of the Cathars (see page 200). Alarmed by the popularity of the heresy (and the decline in tithes), Innocent III sent papal legate Pierre de Castelnau to Beaucaire in 1208 to demand that Count Raymond VI of Toulouse persecute the Cathars. He refused, and one of his hot-headed squires assassinated Castelnau. Furious, Innocent

Saint-Gilles Abbey.

Cathédrale St-Just, Narbonne.

preached the Crusade, known to history as the Albigensian, offering Crusaders not only rewards in the afterlife, but also the Cathars' lands and titles in this one. The ruthlessly efficient Simon de Montfort and the nobility of Northern France swooped down on Languedoc. Even so, the war swung back and forth until Louis VIII took over in person. By the end, an estimated one million Cathars and Catholics were killed. Languedoc's independence was officially extinguished when the forced marriage of Raymond VI of Toulouse's daughter to Alphonse, younger brother of Louis IX, ended without issue.

Louis IX confiscated and re-fortified Carcassonne and the Cathar castles to defend them from their dispossessed lords, the *faydits*. If his barons coveted other properties owned by southerners or Jews, the Inquisition, founded in 1229, could always find a reason to have the owners evicted. Languedoc languished, especially under his successor Philip the Fair, who replenished his coffers by expelling the Jews in 1306 and decimating the Knights Templar in 1307; in 1309 he brought his pawn, the French Pope Clement, to Avignon on the former lands of the Counts of Toulouse, bequeathed by Alphonse to the Church. At last the towns along the Rhône prospered; Villeneuve-lès-Avignon became a bedroom suburb for cardinals.

Roussillon and Montpellier met a different fate when the count-kings of Barcelona set them up as part of the Kingdom of Mallorca in 1262, with Perpignan as capital. While the rest of Languedoc struggled, Montpellier began its rise to fame under the Catalans, thanks in large part to its famous medical school (see page 152). It continued to prosper even after Barcelona sold the city to the French in 1349, after the Black Death killed off a third of Languedoc's population.

About the region

Renaissance & the Wars of Religion

Meanwhile, the Treaty of Corbeil (1258) drew the border between France's new possessions and Aragon. The Château de Puilarens (then the southernmost in France) and the other former Cather castles, or 'Five Sons of Carcassonne' became outworks to impregnable Carcasonne itself. Whenever France and Aragon disagreed (which was often) troops would pile to and fro over the border.

As the Pyrenees would be easier to defend, Paris, as part of its long campaign to 'perfect' France's borders, coveted Roussillon. The union of Aragon and Castile, however, created a newly powerful and wealthy Spain. To keep the French out, Ferdinand and Isabella built a masterpiece of 1490s engineering, the Forteresse de Salses north of Perpignan (see page 242), but at the same time undermined their support in Roussillon by sending in the Spanish Inquisition and wrecking Perpignan's commerce by their single-minded concentration on the new Atlantic trade.

Even after the end of the Thirty Years' War (1648), France and Spain were still going at it, hammer and tongs. The French invasion and occupation of Catalonia led to Spain's ceding of Roussillon to France with the Treaty of the Pyrenees in 1659. Not everyone was happy: Louis XIV's military genius Vauban built Mont Louis and fortified the medieval town Villefranche-de-

Where to see...

Renaissance & the Wars of Religion

Arc de Triomphe Montpellier, page 150
Canal du Midi, page 178
Forteresse de Salses, page 242
Mont-Louis, page 255
Pézenas, page 158
Uzès, page 97
Villefranche-de-Conflent, page 253

Conflent to guard the new frontier and crush local dissidents. But it would be other dissidents who would fill the prisons here – Protestants.

After Arianism and the Cathars, this would be the third religious controversy to consume Languedoc in blood and fire. After the Hundred Years' War – Languedoc was spared this one, which devastated much of Aquitaine – it was ruled by a royal governor and the States General (*états généraux*), who met in Pézenas. The Catholic Church in France was closely identified with the Crown (which had the right to tax clerics, and appoint abbots and bishops), so when the new heresy arrived down the Rhône from Geneva, it was welcomed with open arms by the many in Languedoc (mostly peasants and merchants) disaffected with King and Church. Most were in eastern Languedoc, in the Gard, the Lozère and Hérault, where half of the population converted. By the 1540s it was open warfare; cathedrals, churches and abbeys, reliquaries and works of art were set alight or demolished stone by stone.

The first War of Religion ended in 1593, when the Protestant leader Henri of Navarre inherited the throne after converting to Catholicism ("Paris is worth a Mass", as he famously put it). He refused to indulge in the bigotry of the day, and in 1598 issued his Edict of Nantes, bringing an end to the wars by re-establishing the Huguenots' civil rights and setting up safe havens for them, mainly in the south.

The privileges of his far-sighted act, however, were slowly eroded under Louis XIII. The age of absolute monarchy was on its way. The governor of Languedoc, Henri II, Duc de Montmorency, led a siege against the restive Protestants in Montpellier and was appointed Marshal of France but couldn't countenance Louis XIII's minister, Cardinal Richelieu, who was systematically stripping France's provinces of their remaining rights. Montmorency joined forces with the king's brother, Gaston, Duke d'Orléans, and rebelled, only to be defeated by Richelieu and beheaded in Toulouse in 1632. Richelieu squashed any future dissent by demolishing castles (such as Beaucaire) and walls (Montpellier) across Languedoc.

Despite these setbacks, Protestant Nîmes became a major textile centre. One of the greatest engineering feats of the century, the Canal du Midi was completed in 1680. But what should have been a tremendous boost for Languedoc soured five years later when Louis XIV revoked the Edict of Nantes. Many Huguenots had already emigrated to the more tolerant climes of London and Berlin to escape the king's brutal policy of *dragonnades* (quartering violent soldiers with Protestant families to force them to convert). Now their temples were burned; preachers were given two weeks to abjure their faith or leave France, and those who refused were tortured and killed; entire congregations were exiled to Canada. It was an economic disaster for France, as 200,000 of her brightest and most industrious citizens fled abroad or ended up in prison or the galleys.

Above: Le Pont de Montvert.
Left: Arc de Triomphe, Montpellier.

Camisards, Revolution & wine

Languedoc's 18th century started with yet another war. Too poor or stubborn to emigrate, independent-minded Protestant shepherds and villagers took refuge in the wilds of the Cévennes. Many of their preachers were extremists or mystics who saw themselves as Old Testament 'prophets in the Desert'. They and their followers, once a new round in the Wars of Religion broke out in 1702, were known as the Camisards (from the Occitan *camisa*, (shirt) because of the white shirts they wore at night when most of the attacks against their persecutors took place. The War of the

Where to see...

Camisards, Revolution & wine

Ecusson Montpellier, page 150
Musée de la Soie St-Hippolyte-du-Fort, page 103
Musée des Vallées Cévenoles St-Jean-du-Gard, page 103
Musée du Désert Mialet, page 103

About the region

Camisards stands out as a precursor of modern guerrilla warfare: Louis XIV sent 25,000 troops to the Cévennes, and they were held at bay by some 3000 Camisards, who knew the mountains and forests and their hiding places like the backs of their hands. Atrocities mounted on both sides. The war reached its peak in 1704, and carried on until Louis' death in 1715; even afterwards, Protestants were still subject to persecution until a law in 1787 reinstated their civil rights.

Louis XIV had moved the capital of Languedoc from Pézenas to Montpellier, which erected an Arc de Triomphe in his honour. Once he was safely dead and buried, even the uneasy truce that followed was good enough to allow the Canal du Midi to reach its potential. The surviving Protestants restarted their textile industries in Nîmes, along with a new one – silk. Although mulberry trees and silk worms had been introduced in the Cévennes as early as the 1200s, it was only in the 18th century that the region enjoyed enough peace (and good enough transport) for it to prosper. Demand was high: silk stockings were the rage in Paris.

Silk worms on a mulberry leaf.

One great event of the period branded local dreams and imagination, even into the present: a slew of killings by a man or a wolf, or perhaps another creature altogether, known as the Bête du Gévaudan (the old name for the Lozère); see box, page 124. The terror it wrought was like an omen for yet another upheaval: the French Revolution.

The Revolution actually had little direct impact on Languedoc, which after all its many calamities was relatively low on aristocrats to guillotine. Roussillon saw more battles, as Catholic Spain declared war against the God-denying French republicans. The Protestants took another whack at the church façades and cloisters, and the great monasteries (the Chartreuse du Val de Bénédiction, St-Michel-de-Cuxa, Valmagne and Fontfroide) were abandoned.

What the Revolution did inherit from the series of Louis XIII-XVI was the urge to centralize all power in Paris and undermine any lingering regional identity once and for all. The age-old provinces and duchies of France were abolished and replaced by uniform administrative *départements*, named after rivers and mountains and each governed by a *préfet* sent down from Paris. After the Revolution, a certain Abbé Grégoire led a national campaign to further homogenize France by eliminating all 'patois' such as Occitan, Basque, Breton and Catalan: from now on, Paris declared, everyone would write and speak French. Occitan, Europe's first literary language, had already been reduced to an oral language. Now children caught speaking it at school were punished.

Although the 19th-century Industrial Revolution in the UK would dampen Languedoc's nascent textile business, a new source of income was found to replace it: wine. Languedoc-Roussillon had produced fine wines since the fifth century BC, but the rapid industrialization of Northern Europe changed everything, as millions abandoned their farms for the slums of the great cities to work in the factories, creating a huge demand for cheap red wine or *gros rouge*. Best of all, there was the Canal du Midi and, by the mid-19th century, the railroad to get it to market.

Remembering the Revolution.

The landowners of Languedoc-Roussillon responded by covering every arable patch of land with vines, only to have their livelihood completely wiped out in 1875 by tiny vine-eating lice called phylloxera, accidently introduced in wooden packages from America. The large estates were quickly able to replant with phylloxera-immune American rootstock, initiating a second wine boom in the 1880s. The new wines were so thin that they had to be fortified with strong stuff from Algeria, which along with Italy began to seriously compete with Languedoc in the cheap wine trade, especially when the laws were changed to allow the sale of cheap *la piquette* (eau de vie mixed with water and sugar).

The 20th century to the present

The new century found Languedoc-Roussillon and its grape monoculture in desperate straits. The cheap wines from Italy and Algeria flooded the market and led to a collapse in price and a complete economic meltdown, which left thousands of people close to starvation.

The winegrowers found their hero in Marcelin Albert, a *vigneron* from the Minervois, who in 1907 led the first great agricultural revolt in France, demanding an end to the sale of *la piquette* and other adulterated wines. Albert gathered ever-larger crowds wherever he went, reaching 600,000 during a rally in Montpellier. Prime Minister Clemenceau, in one his most ignoble moments, decided to crush the movement by force, and sent in troops who opened fire and killed five during a demonstration in Narbonne. The next day the troops, who were mostly from Languedoc, mutinied, and Albert was on the verge of calling for a general strike. Clemenceau, however, tricked him into coming to Paris and convinced him to calm the situation, loaning him a 100 franc note so he could return to Languedoc – only to announce to journalists that Albert had accepted the money as a bribe. Albert's associates in Languedoc turned on him, and his movement fell apart. Many an impoverished winemaker abandoned the land to work in the factories, and then died on the battlefields during the First World War. With no able-bodied young men to work in the fields,

Marina of La Grande Motte.

rural populations were decimated. There was, however, one lasting legacy of the Revolt of the Vignerons: the strength of the wine cooperatives in Languedoc-Roussillon, which today account for 70% of the region's production.

There was an influx of new blood, however, during the Spanish Civil war (1936-1939); Republican refugees poured into Languedoc-Roussillon, contributing their DNA, surnames and culture to Languedoc's mix. Many of them would join the Resistance, notably at the end of 1942 after the Americans landed in North Africa, and even more after the Americans liberated Provence, two months after D-Day in Normandy.

In 1962, Languedoc-Roussillon absorbed some 100,000 Pied Noirs from Algeria, followed by immigrants from across North Africa to fill the many positions that opened up as the French economy began to boom. In the mid-1960s, De Gaulle's government, dismayed that so many of these new and old workers were taking their holidays in

Franco's new cheap mass tourism paradise of the Costa Brava, started a campaign to keep their money at home. Not keen to have them all turn up on the elite's Côte d'Azur, however, Paris decided that Languedoc-Roussillon would be the new 'Florida of France', subsidizing the creation of resorts along the long sandy beaches – after thoroughly dousing the surrounding wetlands in DDT.

Although rules regarding wine sales were tightened (adulterated wines and *la piquette* are now strictly forbidden), Languedoc-Roussillon continued to supply much of France and the world's plonk into the 1980s. Then, a few savvy *vignerons* decided that the only way to survive in the new global marketplace was to produce better wines. Applying the latest techniques to this rugged, rocky land made for wine (and little else) brought improvements that have earned the wines accolades from connoisseurs around the world. Even so, the strength of the euro, the competition, and the fact that even the French are drinking less wine (the new drink-driving laws have put paid to the old boozy lunches) has meant hard times for many; a new group of Languedoc 'wine terrorists', the CRAV (*comité régional d'action viticole*) have attacked various supermarkets and importers.

The population decline has not only been reversed, but in recent years Languedoc-Roussillon has taken pride in being the fastest-growing region in France; some 400,000 new residents are expected by 2015. The growth of tourism and the lure of a relatively unspoiled Mediterranean region for newcomers (both French and foreign) are two reasons, but much of the credit for the new gung-ho Languedoc has to go to the controversial, sometimes politically incorrect but irrepressible dynamo Georges Frêche, the visionary mayor who changed the face of Montpellier from 1997-2004. Since 2006 he has been President of the Region of Languedoc-Roussillon, a position created in 1981 when François Mitterand reversed centuries of centralization to create the modern French regions. Devolution is in, so far at a snail's pace, but with Georges Frêche at the helm (one of his first acts was to open up Maisons de Languedoc-Roussillon to promote the region in London, Milan, New York and Shanghai), stay tuned.

Where to see...

The 20th century to the present

Odysseum, Montpellier.

Art & architecture

Cathédrale de Maguelone.

Romanesque & Gothic Languedoc-Roussillon

Before the 13th century, Languedoc and neighbouring Roussillon were one of the wealthiest corners of Europe, and they built accordingly. What has survived the depredations of the Albigensian Crusaders, the Protestants in the Wars of Religion (they were the worst) and the Revolution is a mere fraction of the art and architecture created here during the medieval heyday. But it's a fraction with verve and imagination, and is well worth seeking out.

As its name implies, Romanesque grew out of the Roman styles, and architects and artists in the south of France had some exceptional models close at hand to study: Arles, just over the Rhône, was an important art centre. Not surprisingly, the most classicizing Romanesque work in Languedoc-Roussillon proper is the façade of the abbey church of St-Gilles-du-Gard just on the other side of the big river. St Gilles' three doorways resemble Roman triumphal arches, sculpted lavishly with New Testament themes. Beyond this masterpiece, vivid bits of friezes and fragments stuck like collages into the walls of the much-rebuilt churches at nearby

Beaucaire and Nîmes offer enticing clues of former splendours left shattered by Protestant hammers. Uzès has a superb 12th-century round bell tower, the Tour Fenestrelle, resembling a French tower of Pisa, which managed to survive because the Protestants found it useful as a watchtower.

Further west, handsome churches have survived intact, if stripped of much of their original decoration: the striking abbey churches at St-Guilhem-le-Désert and Fontfroide, Maguelone (the Cathedral of the Sands), and the world's only seven-sided church at Rieux-Minervois. Yet, what Languedoc may lack in Romanesque churches, it more than makes up for with some of Europe's top military masterpieces built (or rebuilt) by the kings of France. These include Carcassonne, the Cathar castles and Aigues-Mortes.

Because Protestantism didn't make many inroads in Catalan Roussillon, it was spared the art attacks, and has the richest collection of surviving Romanesque art. The region's only 'named' sculptor, the Master of Cabestany, was actually only identified in the 1930s, through the rediscovery of a tympanum at Cabestany. He had such a unique personal style that art historians have been able to identify his handiwork from Navarre to Tuscany, as well as in the Abbaye de St-Hilaire near Limoux, Rieux-Minervois and Le Boulou.

Another masterpiece outside Perpignan, the Cathedral of Elne, has one of the finest and best-preserved Romanesque cloisters in France. This, and the 12th-century rose-coloured marble capitals in the cloisters of St-Michel-de-Cuxa (partly now in the Cloisters Museum in New York) and the Prieuré de Serrabone up in the Conflet valley are among the masterpieces of early Catalan art – more fanciful, floral and arabesque than the classicizing work in the Gard. It doesn't have the sculptural ornaments, but for sheer beauty in a stunning setting, isolated 11th-century St-Martin-du-Canigou further up the Conflet is hard to beat. Roussillon also has some rare Romanesque frescoes, primitive and naive but brimming with life, at the Hospici d'Illa and St-Martin-de-Fenollar.

Narbonne has one of the first Gothic churches ever built in the south, St-Paul-Serge, begun in 1229. The other great Gothic cathedrals built after the Albigensian Crusade, in Narbonne, Béziers, Mende and Valmagne, are all by Northern architects, as if to put their orthodox stamp firmly on the conquest of the South. Their breathtaking Northern verticality stands in sharp contrast to Perpignan's immensely wide, single-nave Catalan Gothic cathedral of St-Jean by master builder Guilhem de Sagrera. It has the only enclosed Gothic cemetery (Campo Santo) in France, although its best-known work of art is pure Northern Gothic – the harrowing, realistic statue of the *Dévot Christ* (1307). The city's ornate 13th-century Palais des Rois de Majorque, Loge and Hôtel de Ville are among the best surviving secular works of the age. For the greatest Gothic painting in Languedoc-Roussillon, however, you'll need to go to Villeneuve-lès-Avignon, where the *Couronnement de la Vierge* by Enguerrand Quarton, inspired by the Italian International Gothic masters working for the Pope across the river, graces the Musée St Pierre de Luxembourg.

Mende's Gothic-style cathedral.

Grand Siècle & the Age of Enlightenment

The 17th century in France was the *Grand Siècle*. Although it wasn't as grand in Languedoc-Roussillon, the region at least enjoyed a few decades of relative peace after the Wars of Religion and began to slowly rebuild, beginning with its churches that had been demolished by the Protestants. The Cathedral of Mende was rebuilt in its original Gothic style, although minus its once-famous bell, which the Protestants had melted down for canons. In Nîmes, Montpellier and elsewhere, the results were more of a mixture of styles and not terribly interesting. The building of the Canal du Midi and annexation of Roussillon brought money for a fresh blast of art and architecture into the region, even if it wasn't good for all the castles, which no longer had a purpose and were left to rot or were cannibalized for their stone.

There was enough general prosperity, in fact, to make it worth young Molière's trouble to bring a theatre troop down to Pézenas, then the capital of Languedoc. It was a town filled with aristocrats, where governors and other members of the States General lived in elegant pale stone mansions (*hôtels particuliers*). These elegant ashlar townhouses, often boasting massive doorways, luminous interior courtyards and grand exterior or interior stairways with stone or forged-iron balustrades, have an austere beauty that make them one of the glories of Languedoc. You'll find streets lined with them in ducal Uzès, Nîmes, Montpellier and Beaucaire (where buckets of money flowed thanks to the huge annual Fair of St Madeleine, see box, page 92). When Montpellier was made the capital of Languedoc, its *hôtels particuliers* were renovated and became ever grander and more ornate. Some have since been converted into hotels and museums, whilst a handful of others are accessible on guided tours.

Along with the *hôtels particuliers,* every lord and lady in Montpellier had to have a country château or 'folly'. Some of these, too, have been converted into luxury hotels; two, the Château de la Mogère and Château Flaugergues, now engulfed by greater Montpellier, are open for visits. Another, the

Carcassonne's iconic architecture.

Château de Villevieille just outside Sommières (a charming town that had to be completely rebuilt in the 17th century), is also open for visits, and is exceptionally rare in that its pre-Revolution interiors have survived intact.

One of the greatest French artists of the age haled from Perpignan: Hyacinthe Rigaud was court painter to Louis XIV in Versailles and a master of the psychologically penetrating portrait. Perpignan's Musée des Beaux Arts has a room dedicated to him, with an excellent collection of his works (including one of his masterpieces, the *Portrait of Cardinal Bouillon* of 1709). You can also get a feel for the age, at least a feel for the age's clerical potentates, in the lavish 17th- and 18th-century apartments and galleries of the archbishops of Narbonne.

Local sensibilities, perhaps because of the strong Protestant ethos, didn't care much for the baroque frills and curlicues (outside of a weakness for outrageously ornate church organs in sculpted cases – prime examples are in Narbonne, Uzès and Béziers). In totally Catholic Roussillon, however, you can get a baroque fix in the towering, hypnotically detailed wooden polychrome retables (altarpieces) that adorn the walls of Perpignan's cathedral and church of St-Jacques. The churches of Collioure and Prades also have exceptional examples by one of the great Catalan masters of the genre, the sculptor Josep Sunyer.

The 18th century, France's Age of Enlightenment, shone as bright as a 30-watt bulb in Languedoc, which suffered a relapse in fortune with Louis XIV's Revocation of the Edict of Nantes (see History, page 32). Even so, it did see some enduring and impressive public works, including the Jardins de la Fontaine in Nîmes (one of the first public gardens in the country), the creation of Montpellier's Place de la Comédie, as well as the Sun King's proud Arc de Triomphe and statue in the Place de Peyrou. It was also the time of planting plane trees along the roads of France; in Languedoc, because of its essential poverty and lack of subsequent road-widening, they've survived better than anywhere else.

About the region

Modern & contemporary art & architecture

The lion's share of modern and contemporary art in the south of France may be just over the Rhône in Provence and the Côte d'Azur, but Languedoc-Roussillon has had its moments of glory, too. Like much in the region, these moments have been fitful and eclectic rather than the result of a great native movement.

One of these bright spots happened in the mid-19th century, when Montpellier's wealthy Alfred Bruyas, who inherited a large fortune, decided single-handedly to make the city's Musée Fabre a centre for the art of the day (it was a fairly unusual idea back then, when museums concentrated on Old Masters). He became the patron of the revolutionary realist painter Gustav Courbet, inviting him to Montpellier and then hanging his works along with Delacroix, Millet and the other rising stars. There was one native son among them – Frédéric Bazille, a proto-Impressionist who tragically died young. Elsewhere, at around the same time, another Languedoc native, Marie Petiet was painting luminous domestic visions in Limoux.

The light and beauty of Roussillon's Côte Vermeille attracted some other art revolutionaries at the turn of the 20th century. In 1905 Henri Matisse and André Derain followed Paul Signac to the bijou fishing town of Collioure and made art history by liberating colour from reality – an effort that saw the shocked critics back in Paris label them 'Fauves' (Wild Beasts). Although Matisse ended up on the other end of France's Mediterranean in Nice, others followed the trail they blazed to Collioure; among them Picasso, Braque, Gris, Soutine, Chagall, Masson, Manolo and Pignon, followed later by Miró, Tàpies, Viallat, Toni Grand, etc. The second wave of artists, many of them Cubists, preferred to set up their easels inland in the pretty town of Céret, which unlike Collioure has a museum of modern art, with notable donations from Picasso and Matisse.

If few of these modern art lions were natives of Languedoc-Roussillon, one of France's best-known

Henri Matisse and André Derain followed Paul Signac to the bijou fishing town of Collioure and made art history by liberating colour from reality.

20th-century sculptors, Aristide Maillol, certainly was. A proud Catalan nationalist from Banyuls-sur-Mer, he spent his last years on a farm just outside town, which today houses a collection of some 40 of his works. Nearby Port-Vendres had its moment of celebrity too – in the 1920s, the great Charles Rennie Mackintosh gave up his career in architecture and design to paint beautiful watercolours here; recently a walk around his favourite views has been set up in his honour. Painter François Desnoyer (d 1972), a master of colourful and jaunty landscapes, is another who set up his easel in Roussillon, in this case at St-Cyprien Plage. It is now home to the Collection François Desnoyer, featuring the artist's works along with his own private collection.

Among living artists, perhaps the best represented is the 'painter of black' Pierre Soulages,

Carré d'Art, Nîmes.

whose donation of 20 paintings (1951-2006) is now one of the highlights of the Musée Fabre. On the opposite end of the aesthete scale, there are brothers Richard and Hervé Di Rosa of Sète, Pop artists whose joyful Musée International des Arts Modestes in their hometown may well make you laugh out loud.

In the early 20th century, Languedoc-Roussillon was among France's poorest regions, so no one had much money to build anything until the 1960s when President Charles De Gaulle ordered six new resorts be planted on the sands. The challenge of a blank slate was most enthusiastically taken up at La Grande Motte, which went for a futuristic look with giant ziggurats and mod buildings, which after a patina of several decades have a curious time-capsule charm.

Soon after, another blank canvas opened up, this time between the old centre of Montpellier and the River Lez. This presented a once-in-a-lifetime opportunity for mayor Georges Frêche to make a statement about the city's ambitions, which he did in spades. He hired Barcelona architect Ricardo Bofill to create a monumental, neoclassical quarter called Antigone with housing, shops, cafés and restaurants for 10,000 people along an axis (reminiscent of Paris' 'Grande Axe' from the Louvre to La Défense). Lambasted as a folly when building began in 1983, it has since come into its own, and is currently being expanded along the river as Montpellier marches towards the sea.

Nîmes briefly tried to compete by commissioning the elegant, minimalist Carré d'Art, a contemporary art museum designed by Sir Norman Foster. But it's another of Sir Norman's works that has everyone talking – the Viaduc de Millau, taking one of the main *autoroutes* to the South over the vast valley of the Tarn between the Lozère and Hérault. It was completed in 2004 and is pure breathtaking magic.

Languedoc-Roussillon today

Regionalism

Ever since the gut-wrenching blow of the Albigensian Crusade, Paris's campaign to absorb the heart and soul of Languedoc-Roussillon has been methodical and highly successful. Little has been left to chance. Even in 1981, when François Mitterand created France's administrative regions, he carefully divided the historic county of Toulouse in two, making the western half into the Midi-Pyrénées. In 1992 the constitution made French the only language of the state, although as a sop to the country's many minorities, the teaching of Catalan and Occitan was officially permitted in schools for the first time. Recently, Languedoc-Roussillon's new regional symbol, a cluster of white and yellow snowflakes on a red background, replaced the old one bearing stripes and the 12-pointed cross of Toulouse.

So what do you see today? There's nothing like the independence or autonomy movements that exist in the Basque country and Corsica, but there's certainly a growing sense of regional nostalgia. Bilingual street signs combine French with Occitan or Catalan. Cars and shops are decorated with Occitania stickers bearing the 12-pointed cross. Festivals revive traditional songs and dances. The 800th anniversary of the massacre of Béziers was marked in 2009 by a year of conferences and talks. In the interesting times we live in, even the Gnostic dualist beliefs of the Cathars are making a comeback, as people begin to wonder whether a Good Creator could have got it so wrong.

After 40 years of suppression by Franco, the Catalan language is having such a revival in Catalonia that enthusiasm to speak and learn is wafting over the now-open border into Roussillon or 'Catalunya Nord' – a name first officially used by the *département*'s Conseil Général in 2007. Even after 300 plus years of French dominance, there are over 200,000 Catalan speakers in Roussillon, half of whom consider themselves fluent (including many descendants of Catalan refugees from the Spanish Civil War).

In comparison, Occitan, Europe's very first vernacular literary language, admired by Dante and Petrarch, has become more of a specialist interest. A century ago there were still 10 million speakers spread across southern France, the western valleys of Piedmont and the isolated Vall d'Aran in the Pyrenees. In the 21st century, only an estimated 2½ million people can speak or at least understand Occitan, and they're mostly a rural aging population; you hardly ever hear it spoken outside of homes.

Still, some of the young are taking it up – currently 10% of students attend Occitan language schools or classes. They can take the *Baccalauréat* in Occitan, hear it spoken daily on radio and TV Occitània, read the week's news in Occitan in the

At the bullfight, Nîmes.

newspaper or read novels in Occitan by such writers as Jean Bodon del Rouergue and Max Roqueta. There's a centre for the study of troubadour songs, CREMM Trobar, outside Carcassonne in Pennautier, and new Occitan-language groups such as the Aude's polyphonic La Mal Coifée. Websites such as viaoccitanacatalana.org promote cultural and linguistic unity.

Georges Frêche, President of the Regional Council, recently raised eyebrows when he proposed renaming Languedoc-Roussillon Septimania, a name historically more accurate for the current borders (Frêche, after all, was a professor of Classics before going into politics). The proposal was scoffed at; it's not Roman-Visigoth *Septimania* that the people daydream of in their atavistic moments, but the reunification of the County of Toulouse, joining Languedoc with its lost westerly half, the Midi-Pyrénées. As power slowly devolves to the regions in the European Union, they may even get their wish.

Bullfights

If one thing truly sets Languedoc-Roussillon apart from the rest of France, it's a passion for bullfighting (*tauromachie*). It could well be the result of pure atavism; Nîmes held its first bullfight (1853) as soon as the slums were cleared out of the Arènes, where the last animal fights had taken place some 1500 years before. Spanish-style corridas and encierros have been extremely popular ever since.

Languedoc also has its own bull games, the bloodless *Courses Camarguaises*, which Beaucaire claims to have invented in the 19th century. The bulls come from the nearby Camargue, chosen when young for their cleverness, and then trained for the ring. Facing them are the *razeteurs,* teams of agile and daring young men in white who have 15 minutes to pluck a *cocade* (ribbon) and cut the *attributs* (threads) placed between, and wrapped around, the bull's horns. Whenever the annoyed bull charges, they leap over barriers – all to the lively strains of Bizet's *Carmen.* The sportiest bulls make a pile of money for their *manadiers* and earn a happy retirement on the ranch; in Beaucaire the greatest are remembered with statues.

Nature & environment

Extending from the River Rhône to the Spanish border, Languedoc-Roussillon's five *départements* have been compared to a giant amphitheatre overlooking the Mediterranean: a majestic curve of mountains from the Cévennes in the east through the Black Mountains of Haut Languedoc, down to the Corbières and culminating in the Pyrenees. Below these mountains lie the hills of the *garrigue*, and below the garrigue, the coastal plains. This mix encompasses an extraordinary diversity of landscapes, from rice paddies and lagoons to lush valleys of orchards and rolling hills of vineyards, from limestone plateaux to schist and granite mountains snow-capped into June.

Over the next 140 million years, tiny shellfish fossilized on the seabed to form a thick limestone crust, which was heaved upwards in a third cataclysmic shudder, creating the high *causses* or *plateaux* of the Lozère and the rugged *garrigue* that characterize much of the northern Languedoc. The Lozère's magnificently austere Causse de Méjean and Causse de Sauveterre are striking examples of the former, where sheep herding is one of the few viable ways of making a living. In the old days, the shepherds had to keep a close eye to guard their flocks from the wolves, but the last ones were hunted down and killed in the early 20th century. Today, you can see some wolves in semi-liberty in the Parc des Loups du Gévaudan (see page 124),

Grands causses & the garrigue

It took hundreds of millions of years, spiked by cataclysmic upheavals, to achieve this state of affairs. Iberia smashed into France 450 million years ago, forming the Pyrenees and jagged Côte Vermeille. Round two, 200 million years later, saw much of Languedoc-Roussillon sink into the sea, leaving only the Pyrenees and the Cévennes, and the rest of the Massif Central above water.

Above: Brown bear, Les Angles.
Opposite: Dragonfly, Camargue.

What makes all the limestone of the *causses* and *garrigue* especially fascinating is t he tireless work of water. Over the last 60 million years, rain formed fissures and rivers found their way down the cracks, creating dramatic ravines deep enough to have their own microclimates – the Gorges du Tarn and Gorges de la Jonte are the most famous of a dozen spectacular canyons in the region. There are tremendous cirques (the astonishing Cirque de Navacelles), as well as a dozen caves worthy of a troll king's mountain hall (Grottes de Demoiselles and Clamouse), swallow holes (the Aven Armand) and resurgent rivers (Abîme de Bramabiau). Among the creatures here are the recently reintroduced vultures, easiest to spot from the Belvédère des Vautaurs, soaring on the thermals high above the Gorges de la Jonte.

The Cévennes

part of an effort to rehabilitate them after the trauma of the 18th-century nightmare of the Bête du Gévaudan (see History, page 34).

The *garrigue*, on the other hand, is in many ways a man-made landscape. Once covered with oak forests, it was deforested over the centuries for charcoal burning and iron working, then replanted with olives, vines and grain. In other places, where the soil was poorer, it was used as pasture for sheep and goats, whose voraciousness left much of the land exposed to weathering. Today, a shrubby, fragrant mix of stunted holm and kermes oaks, Aleppo pine, arbutus, juniper, laurel, thyme, rosemary and cistus – not unlike Corsica's famous maquis – carpet much of the *garrigue*, along with a fair number of vines. The landscapes around Le Pic St-Loup and northern Hérault are typical. The *garrigue*'s diversity, exposures and various microclimates are the joy of Languedoc's master winemakers, and some places, like Roquebrun on the River Orb, have climates similar to the Côte d'Azur.

Shared by the Lozère and the Gard, the Cévennes have been listed as one of UNESCO's World Biosphere Reserves since 1985 and are now further protected in the Parc National des Cévennes, one of France's largest national parks. For the south of France, the Cévennes are surprisingly moist: in autumn, the cold air from the Atlantic meets the warm winds off the Mediterranean, causing torrential downpours known as *épisodes cévenoles*. One of the tallest mountains, Mont Aigouul (1567 m), literally 'the watery one', is the wettest spot in France. Its summit is host to the last manned weather station. In October 1963 it recorded a record of 607 mm (nearly 2 ft) of rain in a 24-hour period.

When it's not being ridiculously extreme, the climate in the Cévennes ranges from subtropical to alpine. The Cévennes support over 2000 species of flora, including mulberry trees which were once the source of a thriving silk industry; 40,000 ha of chestnut groves, the main source of food for the human population (and the pigs and wild boar) for a thousand years; and mushrooms – some 90% of European species have been found here. Over the years, 2420 reported animal species have been sighted, including *mouflons*, otters and black woodpeckers. Recently, capercaillies and beavers have been reintroduced. The national park's headquarters in Florac is a mine of information (see page 127).

Corbières & Pyrenees

Stretching below the Black Mountains of Haut Languedoc, the wide vale of the River Aude from Carcassonne to Narbonne offers some respite from the surrounding mountains (as well as offering an age-old invasion route up to Toulouse and Bordeaux from the Mediterranean). *Garrigue*-type landscapes continue in the Corbières south of Carcassonne, only wilder and steeper, a prelude to the Pyrenees, sliced with narrow gorges and patched with vineyards and tufts of sweet broom. High above a lonely gorge you may spot a Bonelli's eagle among the more common buzzards, kites and falcons.

In Roussillon, the Pyrenees have a splendid landmark in the Pic du Canigou (2784 m), a mountain so prominent it was long thought to be the highest summit in the range. Further west, Capcir is a favourite destination for nature lovers, a retreat far away from the hurly-burly, complete with a lovely bevy of little glacial lakes at the Lac des Bouillouses. Izards and marmottes are usually easy to spot; at Les Angles there's a park dedicated to the wildlife of the Pyrenees, home to brown bears, bison, wolves, stags, etc. Open daily all year, one of its two trails can be used in the winter, with snowshoes (T04 68 04 32 76).

The volcanoes in the Pyrenees are dormant or extinct, but they have left a legacy of hot springs – Moltig-les-Bains, Vernet-les-Bains and Alet-les-Bains are famed for their curative properties, while the Bains de St-Thomas and Dorres and Llô in the majestic plateau of the Cerdagne have naturally heated outdoor pools for the whole family. This is also the place to come for meadows full of wild flowers in June. It's one of the sunniest spots in France, with the clearest skies – the reason it hosts the world's largest solar oven.

Plains & coast

Most of the population of Languedoc-Roussillon lives in the cities on the temperate coastal plains, where you'll also find most of the vines, olive groves, sunflowers and lavender; in short, everything to remind you that this is the hot and sunny Mediterranean. None of it, however, is as fertile as the rich plain around Perpignan, which provides France with many of its earliest fruits and vegetables (no place in the country produces more parsley or cherries), as well as some of its best natural sweet wines and aperitifs. Roussillon's southernmost stretch of shore is the Côte Vermeille, the region's prettiest, a tumble of red-tinted rocks and coves. The waters are exceptionally rich in anchovies, and part of it is a marine reserve. The entire coastal area generally stays much warmer than inland Languedoc – warm enough to support the Sigean African Reserve, a giant safari park near Narbonne, and a tortoise breeding centre in Roussillon.

Along with the Rhône, Languedoc-Roussillon's big rivers – the Hérault, Aude, Orb and Têt – all end in a network of great salt marshes or *étangs* (the largest, the Bassin de Thau, is one of France's great shellfish nurseries). Vast sandy beaches extend for miles, dotted with resorts. Yet even today, some 60% of the region's coast has remained undeveloped – as it's a bit flat and a bit dreary, you can see why. Waders and other birds think it's a paradise; the best bit, the Camargue or Rhône delta, is a natural park where black bulls and white horses roam in semi-liberty. Pink flamingos, which number in their tens of thousands, are one of the region's symbols, but over 200 other different bird species have been spotted here, especially during migration periods in the spring and autumn.

Roussillon's southernmost stretch of shore is the Côte Vermeille, the region's prettiest, a tumble of red-tinted rocks and coves.

Festivals & events

Languedoc-Roussillon loves a party and puts on a full calendar of festivities and events. A select few are listed below, but to include them all would take up all the pages of this book.

Prestigious ballet, music, theatre and film festivals take place in the cities year round, especially in Montpellier. Elsewhere, age-old traditions (among them, the bear festival in Arles-sur-Tech and the Good Friday procession of La Sanch in Perpignan) have survived more or less intact, and where they haven't, the locals love to put on jousts, troubadour singsongs and other events dedicated to evoking the good old pre-Simon de Montfort days. In summer, juices flow at outdoor music festivals and in two major events that in France are unique to the region: the summer ferias, with their bulls (see bullfighting, page 45), music, bodegas and general merriment, and the nautical jousts or *joutes nautiques* (see page 168). Do check the websites or tourist offices for exact dates and times; increasingly you can also buy tickets online before you go.

National holidays

1 January
March/April Easter Sunday
March/April Easter Monday
1 May (Fête du Travail)
8 May (VE Day)
May/June Ascension
May/June Pentecost
May/June Pentecost Monday
14 July (Bastille Day)
15 August (Assumption)
1 November (All Saints')
11 November (Armistice Day)
25 December (Christmas)

Above: Nautical jousts, Sète.
Opposite: Pau Casals festival banner.

Carnival: Los Fecos
Limoux, T04 68 31 35 09, limoux.fr.
Los Fecos goes back four centuries and features 24 town guilds, each with their own costumes, who take turns parading at weekends in Place de la République from mid-January to mid-March (it's the longest running festival in France). There's music, joking and satirizing in Occitan – and drinking of Blanquette.

Festival de Flamenco
Théâtre de Nîmes, 1 place de la Calade, T04 66 36 65 10, theatredenimes.com.
Attracts some of the finest performers from Spain and southern France.

Journée de la Truffe
Uzès, T04 66 22 68 88, uzes-tourisme.com.
The third Sunday in January, when truffles are for sale and every restaurant serves a truffle menu.

Fête de l'Ours
Arles-sur-Tech, T04 68 39 11 99, ville-arles-sur-tech. fr; Prats-du-Mollo-la-Preste, T04 68 39 70 83, pratsdemollolapreste.com.
The Vallespir's two festivals of the bear date back to prehistoric times. There's a morning procession, followed in the afternoon by the 'hunting' and 'shaving' of the 'bear' (people in sheepskins and blackened faces) and dances: all good rowdy fun

Festo di Poutoun
Roquemaure, saintvalentin.org.
The Festival of the Kiss takes place on Valentine's Day weekend, when the relics of St Valentine, brought to Roquemaure's collegiate church in 1868 to protect the vines from phylloxera, are taken around the town followed by 800 people in 19th-century costume. There's plenty of smooching along the way.

About the region

Fête du Cochon
St-Pons-de-Thomières, T04 67 97 39 39, saint-pons-tourisme.com.
Feast on freshly roasted pork, *saucisse* and other pork produce.

Fête du Mimosa
Roquebrun, T04 67 89 79 97, roquebrun.org.
Carnival of flowers, with floats and crafts.

Le Poulain
Pézenas, T04 67 98 36 40, ot-pezenas-valdherault. com.
Traditional carnival and procession, featuring a parade with a giant mock colt. It has been the town's totem beast since 1226, when a foal was born here to the favourite mare of Louis VIII.

March

Feria de la Primavera
Nîmes, T04 66 58 38 00, ot-nimes.fr.
Early March or late February (four weeks before Easter), the first bullfights of the year.

April

Procession de la Sanch
Perpignan.
Haunting, solemn Good Friday procession of the medieval Brotherhood of the Holy Blood, who were founded by St Vincent Ferrer.

Médiévales
Sommières, T04 66 80 99 30, ot-sommieres.fr.
Lively celebrations with parades, music, troubadours, a medieval market, etc.

May

Cavalcade
Pézenas, T04 67 98 36 40, ot-pezenas-valdherault. com.
Celebration of the town's glory days, with a procession in historic costumes, a handicraft market and more.

June

Feria de Pentecôte
Nîmes, T04 66 58 38 00, ot-nimes.fr.
Founded in 1952, this feria attracts nearly a million people over five days (Thu-Mon) around Pentecost (Whitsun). There are a range of bullfights, but also bodegas, wine, floats, bands, fireworks, music and dancing in the streets.

Fête du Drac
Beaucaire, T04 66 59 26 57, ot-beaucaire.fr.
Traditional festival honouring the town's emblematic dragon.

Festival de Maguelone
Cathédrale de Maguelone, Palavas, T04 67 60 69 92, musiqueancienneamaguelone.com.
Two weeks of medieval, Renaissance and baroque music.

Festa Major
Perpignan and throughout Roussillon.
St John's Day, when torches are relayed down from the Pic du Canigou to light a thousand bonfires all across northern and southern Catalonia.

Uzès Danse
2 place aux Herbes, T04 66 03 15 39, uzesdanse.fr.
Festival of contemporary and experimental dance and workshops, held for a week in mid-June at locations throughout Uzès.

Procession de la Sanch, Perpignan.

Festival de Radio France
Montpellier, T04 67 02 02 01,
festivalradiofrancemontpellier.com.
Classical, jazz, chamber music, electronic, reggae, etc. Concerts, including many free events, mostly take place in the Corum.

Nuits Musicales
Uzès, T04 66 62 20 00, nuitsmusicalesuzes.org.
Founded in 1971, this mid-July music festival is one of the most prestigious in France. It features some of the world's top ensembles playing from the baroque, Renaissance and classical repertoire. Book well in advance (tickets go on sale mid-Apr).

Festival des 2 Cités
Carcassonne, T04 68 11 59 15,
festivaldecarcassonne.com.
The two Carcassonnes (upper and lower) celebrate with pop, opera, jazz and orchestral concerts of all kinds. There's a spectacular fireworks display on 14 July.

Le Printemps des Comédiens
Montpellier, T04 67 63 66 67,
printempsdescomediens.com.
The venue is the Château d'O, for the biggest theatre and performing arts festival in France after Avignon.

Montpellier Danse
Montpellier, T08 00 60 07 40, montpellierdanse.com.
Performances by over 20 ballet companies, from mid-June to early July.

Estivals
Tickets at the Palmarium (by the tourist office),
Perpignan, T08 92 70 53 05, estivales.com.
Highly eclectic music festival in the Campo Santo and other prime locations, from June to mid-September.

Bastille Day
Narbonne, festivalnarbonne.org.
Four days of celebrations and fireworks.

Festival Jazz à Sète
Théâtre de la Mer, T08 92 68 36 22, jazzasete.com.
Not only jazz, but flamenco, blues and soul, this festival attracts headline performers such as Jeff Beck to Sète's seaside theatre during the second week of July.

Festival de la Sardane
Foment de la Sardane, Céret, T04 68 87 46 49, ceret.fr.
A massive mid-July celebration of all things Catalan, with costumes and much dancing of the *sardane*, the national circle dance, to the lilting music of the top *coblas* from across Catalonia.

Medieval festivals, Carcassonne.

takes place for six weeks in July and August in the spa's bijou theatre dating from 1878. See also December.

Fêtes de la Madeleine
Beaucaire, T04 66 59 26 57, ot-beaucaire.fr.
Huge celebration during the last 10 days of July, which commemorates the town's historic fair. Corridas and *courses*, a wine fair, bodegas, and much more.

Festival Pau Casals
Prades, T04 68 96 33 07, prades-festival-casals.com.
Founded in 1950 by exiled cellist Pau Casals, this is one of the top chamber music festivals in Europe, featuring performances in St-Michel-de-Cuxa and elsewhere in late July to mid-August.

August

Course du Canigou
Vernet-les-Bains, courseducanigou.com.
This strenuous 34-km mountain marathon from Vernet-les-Bains to the top of the Pic du Canigou and back takes place in early August and attracts over 800 participants.

Fiest'a Sète
Sète, T04 67 74 48 44, fiestasete.com.
Some of the greatest musicians from Cuba, Africa, Brazil and the Caribbean perform in Sète during the first week of August.

Feria de Béziers
Arènes de Béziers, T04 67 76 13 45, arenes-de-beziers.com.
Taking place over four days around 15 August, Bézier's feria is the single biggest event in Languedoc-Roussillon, drawing over one million people. *Corridas* in the Arènes, concerts, bodegas, street festivals and parties.

Medieval Festival
Arles-sur-Tech, T04 68 39 11 99, ville-arles-sur-tech.fr.
Knights, troubadours and ladies fair recapture the spirit of the Middle Ages, culminating in a big medieval banquet.

Festival de Thau
Mèze, Frontigan and Gigeac, T04 67 43 93 08, festivaldethau.com.
World and alternative music festival that keeps the baby oysters up late for three weeks in July.

Festival de Lamalou
Théâtre du Casino, Lamalou-les-Bains, T04 67 95 67 35, festivaldelamalou.com.
Summer festival of operettas and music theatre (mostly French, but also *Hello Dolly!* and *Carmen*)

Fêtes de la St-Vincent

Collioure, book with the tourist office T04 68 82 15 47.
The biggest celebration on the Côte Vermeille, with bullfights, music, etc. There's also a magical firework display over the port.

September

Feria des Vendanges

Nîmes, T04 66 58 38 00, ot-nimes.fr.
The Harvest Feria, similar to the Feria de Pentecôte but smaller, generally takes place the third weekend in September.

Visa pour l'Image

Perpignan, T04 68 62 38 00, visapourlimage.com.
A city-wide celebration of historic and contemporary photojournalism from around the world.

Jazzèbre

Perpignan, T04 68 35 37 46, jazzebre.com.
Jazz and world music in Perpignan and surrounding towns, from late September to October.

Gypsy show, Nîmes.

October

Fête de la Châtaigne

St-Pons-de-Thomières, T04 67 97 39 39, saint-pons-tourisme.com.
Late October fête dedicated to chestnuts in all their glory.

Festival International du Cinéma Méditerranéen

Montpellier, T04 67 58 43 47, cinemed.tm.fr.
Takes place the last week in October and is dedicated to documentaries, shorts and independent films from around the Mediterranean.

Festival de la soupe

Florac, T04 66 45 01 14, mescevennes.com/sortir/festival-soupe.
Markets, music and soup tasting and judging, from 31 October to 1 November.

November

Fête du Marron d'Olargues et du Vin Nouveau

Orlargues, T04 67 97 71 76, olargues.org.
Festival of chestnuts and *vin primeur.*

December

Festival de Lamalou

Théâtre du Casino, Lamalou-les-Bains, T04 67 95 67 35, festivaldelamalou.com.
Winter festival of operettas and music theatre.

Marchés de Noël

Christmas markets throughout the region, notably in Pézenas, Carcassonne and Montpellier.

Sleeping

When it comes to accommodation, Languedoc-Roussillon has a bit of everything, from sleek city hotels, designer B&Bs and converted castles to basic campsites in river gorges, shelters along Grande Randonnée (GR) long-distance paths and mountain huts on the Pic du Canigou. Gîtes, too, range across the spectrum, from simple studio apartments to luxurious historical conversions with all the frills, sleeping a dozen people or more.

While prices in Languedoc-Roussillon are generally in line with the rest of France, in recent years the strict EU fire safety and health regulations have led to the closure of many of the old-fashioned hotels in small towns and rural areas. Prices in the

survivors have inched up along with the new rules, and if you're touring, hotels for a night, especially in the country, can be hard to find on spec, especially if you come in summer (when hotels are often full) or winter (when many close).

Stepping up to fill the gap, however, are a burgeoning number of people opening *chambres d'hôtes* (bed and breakfasts), where a typical double room is priced roughly the same as a one-star hotel (€50-70). Breakfast isn't always included in the price; if it's not, the average rate seems to be €10. Some top-range hotels charge as much as €30. Most of the hotels in the region have restaurants and offer good-value breakfast/dinner packages, even for one night (*soirée étape*). Nearly all have at least one family room, and offer discounts or free stays for children. The strong euro has made owners more flexible, and out of high season it never hurts to ask for their best offer.

Prices also depend very much on where and when you go, whether your room has a view or a balcony, if it's situated at the back (usually quieter) or front of the hotel, what plumbing is on offer (en suite or not) and the newness of the fittings – many hotels and B&Bs charge a different price for every room. The Lozère on the whole offers the best value for money, while prices in popular destinations such as Carcassonne, Montpellier, Nîmes and Collioure will be considerably more. That said, unless you go in peak season (July and August), you can often find special online offers on their websites. Outside of the ski areas, the cheapest times to visit are around November-March, although be aware that many hotels and B & Bs outside the cities close down completely.

Hôtel de Région, Montpellier.

Hotels

Hotels in France are graded from one to five stars according to their amenities. There are several umbrella organizations for hotels that guarantee certain standards – two of the best known are the middle-of-the-road Logis de France (generally two to three stars) and the very posh Relais & Châteaux (four or five stars, always connected to fine restaurants). The old one-star classic hotels with 20-second *minuteries* light timers on the stairs and in the halls, rock-hard sausage pillows, flowered wallpaper and toilets down the hall that made travelling in Languedoc a bit of an adventure are now becoming quite hard to find. That said, the sausage pillows still preside over many a rural hotel bed. Most rooms now have individual air conditioning, which can be essential in the summer months, and the majority offer free Wi-Fi, or at least internet that guests are welcome to use. Hotel parking garage fees start at €10 a night.

The main hotel discount websites such as lastminute.com, kayak.com or venere.com mostly concentrate on the chains. There are plenty of these (Kyriad, Campanile, Ibis, Mercure, Formule1) in Languedoc-Roussillon, especially by the beaches, or in and around the cities or major *autoroute* junctions – all pleasant, and all pretty much the same, so we haven't included them in the text.

Most hotels have check-out times between 1100 and 1200. Most websites show pictures of the rooms, so you generally have an idea of what you're getting before you arrive. If you're arriving on spec, you may like to have a look at the room before committing.

Chambres d'hôtes (B&Bs)

If you like boutique hotels, Languedoc-Roussillon has a few, but there are far more boutique guesthouses and B&Bs. Many are located in old stone farmhouses (*mas*), *hôtels particuliers* or châteaux. Being close to posh Provence, the Gard has the most, but you'll find some lovely ones in the Cévennes of the Lozère, outside Béziers in the

Minervois, Pézenas, and in or around the cities. Many are owned by good cooks who prepare convivial *table d'hôte* meals; some owners have impressive wine cellars and offer tastings; others have mini spas and offer courses and tours. Some will also collect you from the train station or nearest airport. Many (because of French laws limiting B&Bs to five rooms) have self-catering apartments or a mix of rooms, suites, apartments and gîtes.

Because there's no reception or permanent staff, do make sure the owners know when to expect you. Also, don't hesitate to print out the maps on the websites – some are quite hard to find in the countryside (but are all the more peaceful and relaxing for it). Not all take credit cards, so be sure to ask when you book.

Farm stays

While not as well established as Italy's *agriturismo* industry, staying on farms is growing in popularity in Languedoc-Roussillon. Farms offer inexpensive accommodation and the chance to get back to nature at the same time. Some offer camping, others *chambres d'hôtes* and gîtes. Do check to see if they accept credit cards.

Camping

A large percentage of visitors, especially in July and August, camp or stay in mobile homes by the sea. The big sands are well equipped with campsites, and the highest concentration is at Argèles Plage in Roussillon; if you want to shed all by the sea, Le Cap d'Agde has the largest naturist campsite in the world. Other popular (and decidedly more tranquil) campsites are along the rivers, set in the trees usually near swimming holes. Free camping (*camping sauvage*) is generally discouraged, and illegal in the national parks.

Campsites are graded like hotels from one to five stars, depending on the facilities on offer. Some have their own water parks, while others, sometimes municipally owned, are fairly basic. If you haven't brought your own, most will rent you a motorhome, caravan, bungalow or tent.

Gîtes d'étapes & refuges

Gîtes d'étapes are communal shelters set up along the GR long-distance paths, usually equipped with bunk beds in dorm rooms (bring your own sleeping bag) and basic kitchen facilities; you can pinpoint them at gite-etape.com. The mountain *refuges* in the Pyrenees are similar, but often serve meals; local tourist offices have phone numbers, as it's best to ring ahead to make sure there's space.

Self-catering

Outside of camping, this is often the cheapest option for a holiday, especially if you're travelling *en famille*. An increasingly popular option is the self-catering gîte as a part of a larger holiday complex (a hotel or swish B&B), which offers the best of both worlds – privacy and cooking facilities, but also the chance to enjoy all the added amenities, such as the spa, pool, restaurant, tennis courts, etc. The Jardins de St Benoît (see page 222) inland from Sigean in the Aude takes this to a whole new level in the region. Most rentals start on Saturday and in high season they are by the week; however, you can also find weekend rents or even cheaper weekday rentals, often with a minimum stay of two or three days.

For only slightly more than you'd typically pay to stay in a gîte, you can see a good swathe of Languedoc from a barge on the Canal du Midi or Canal Rhône-Sète (see page 191).

Booking

If you're coming to Languedoc-Roussillon in July and August, it's absolutely essential to book ahead, but it's a very good idea to do so at other times, too. You

Useful websites

B&Bs
chambresdhotes.org
fleursdesoleil.fr
frenchentree.com/languedoc-bed-breakfast

Camping & mobile homes
campingfrance.com
camping.hpaguide.com
campings-languedoc-roussillon.com
eurocamp.co.uk
keycamp.co.uk

Farm stays
accueil-paysan.com
bienvenue-a-la-ferme.com/languedoc-roussillon.

Self-catering
cheznous.com
clevacances.com
creme-de-languedoc.com
frenchconnections.co.uk
gites-de-france.com
golanguedoc.com
holiday-rentals.co.uk
ownersdirect.co.uk
vfbholidays.co.uk
vrbo.com

can book a wide range of accommodation and holiday packages (hotels, campsites, gîtes, farm holidays, B&Bs) directly through the official regional tourist board website en.sunfrance.com. They also have an impressive list of accommodation options for people with disabilities – Languedoc-Roussillon is proud to have more than any other region.

Otherwise, it's easiest to book directly through your accommodation's website. Many offer online or early-bird discounts, or packages combining meals, spa sessions and so on. Be sure to print out the confirmation in case there's any problem (they are usually very well run, but just in case), and then re-confirm by email or phone a day or two before to let them know your estimated time of arrival, especially if you're arriving at night. You'll usually be asked to give a credit card number for the first night to hold the booking.

Eating & drinking

Centuries of poverty have kept Languedoc-Roussillon from developing into one of France's culinary regions, but today's chefs are well on track to change all that. It isn't surprising, as at their fingertips they have a palette of fresh ingredients to work with that few other regions in France can match – seafood and shellfish, bouquets of fragrant herbs, wild honeys, beef and lamb from the *causses*, flavour-packed fruit and vegetables ripened in the Mediterranean sun, goat cheeses from the Cévennes, wild mushrooms and truffles, duck and olives. Generalizations, though, are hard to make; because of the region's wildly varied geography and climates, each local area has its own specialities.

Ameri K Club Bar, Cap de Sète.

Regional specialities

In the **Gard**, the bulls raised in the petit Camargue are prized for their beef, which is served in a dozen ways, including as a *daube* or stew called *taureau à la gardiane*, made with olives, garlic and red wine and served on the Camargue's own rice. Nîmes is famous for its *brandade*, a hearty purée of salt cod with olive oil and garlic, and *tapenades*, a classic nibble made from ground olives, olive oil and garlic, ready to be spread on bread or used for dips. Uzès is the one place in Languedoc-Roussillon with a black truffle market, while the Cévennes are celebrated for their fabulous array of autumn mushrooms. They also produce Languedoc's best-known cheese, *pélardons* – discs of goat cheese.

Flavour-packed lamb and Aubrac beef grazed on the *causses*, delicious charcuterie from the

The €10 picnic

Pick up crusty bread at the *boulangerie*, then hit the nearest market for charcuterie from the Cévennes, olives, fresh cheeses and fruit. Don't miss the *tielles* in the Halles at Sète; Nîmes does great tapenade to spread on bread; on the Côte Vermeille, spread it with *anchoïade* (ground anchovies with garlic, onions and olive oil).

Above: Cookery lesson, Barjac B&B, Gard.
Left: Cassoulet. Below: Picnic essential.

Cévennes, and trout hold pride of place on the rustic table of the **Lozère**, although restaurants rarely serve traditional soul food dishes such as *pouteille* (beef, trotter and potato stew) or *le sac d'os* (like a haggis, but with a pig stomach). You will, however, find the classic warm and hearty shepherd's dish (puréed potatoes mixed with milk, cream, the local *tomme fraîche* cheese, lard and butter), or a *potée cévenole* (made with pork, bacon and cabbage) and rich chestnut soups and honeys.

In the **Hérault**, with its Bassin de Thau and fishing ports, seafood holds pride of place, with a variety of fish soups and stews, including Languedoc's version of *bouillabaisse* with ham and leeks, or Sète's *bourride*, a fish soup made from monkfish, anglerfish and/or cuttlefish. Sète is also famous for its *tielles* (pies filled with cuttlefish and onion) and mussels and baby octopus served on a spit. In Pézenas look for *petits pâtés de Pézenas* – little curried mutton pastries, said to have been introduced by the chef of the Viceroy of India.

Olives are grown at the western end of the Hérault and in the Aude – the tiny *picholine* but also the larger, crescent-shaped green *lucques*, generally acclaimed as France's finest table olives.

The signature dish of the **Aude** is cassoulet: a meltingly rich and flavoursome mélange of duck confits, pork, garlic, sausage (and sometimes lamb and even partridge) and Tarbais beans, baked in a clay pot for four to six hours in the oven. Castelnaudary, west of Carcassonne, claims to be the world capital of the dish.

Lying within the greatest southwestern France kingdom of duck, the Aude produces its own fine range of terrines, pâtés, maigrets, foie gras, and the ideal fat for making sautée potatoes. Limoux is known for its duck fricassée and some restaurants even have all-duck menus. There are truffles in winter too, at Villeneuve-Minervois.

In **Roussillon**, don't expect to find much of the new wave of razzle dazzle Catalan cuisine invented just over the border at El Bulli, although you will find more traditional Catalan influences in the

About the region

fancier restaurants, featuring recipes that combine often unexpected sea and mountain ingredients (*mar i muntanya*), or sweet and savoury. Snails are extremely popular and here they serve them barbecued as a *cargolade* during the wine harvest. In autumn, one of the specialities is a *roussillonnade* – grilled cèpes with sausage. The charcuterie and free-range meats from the Cerdagne are justly renowned, as are the anchovies (and anchovy by-products, such as anchovy-stuffed olives) on the Côte Vermeille – Côte d'Anchois (Anchovy Coast) as the locals sometimes call it. The all-time classic dessert is *crème catalane*, lightly flavoured with cinnamon and anise under a caramel coating.

Practicalities

Languedoc-Roussillon shuts down for lunch between 1200 and 1400, or even 1500 in many places. It's wise to get to your restaurant as soon as you can after 1200; to arrive much later, especially in rural areas, is to miss out on the *plat du jour* (dish of the day), or even risk being turned away. The dinner witching hour is from 1930 to 2030; if you're going to arrive later, be sure to tell the restaurant when you book. Throughout the guide, the days that restaurants are open for lunch and dinner have been indicated, and opening hours have been included when hours vary significantly from those listed above. In the cities, brasseries serve food throughout the day, at least in theory, although choices may well be limited outside classic French eating hours.

A bit confusingly, the French for menu is *carte*; the French use the word *menu* for a fixed priced meal, usually with several choices for the *entrée* (starter), *plat* (main course) and dessert. Generally a *menu* works out cheaper than ordering *à la carte*, and a lunch *menu* is nearly always better value than the dinner *menu*. A three-course lunch *formule* means little or no choice, but is cheapest of all. Some are under €10 and may even include a glass of wine (*vin compris*). Most restaurants offer at least one dinner menu under €25-30, although beware of the sometimes scandalous wine mark-ups.

A good many restaurants, including some of the best in Languedoc-Roussillon, are attached to hotels. In rural areas look for *ferme-auberges*, which are farms that prepare meals using their own meats and produce; some also offer packed lunches or snacks. In the bigger towns, bistrots and wine bars offer light evening meals or tapas.

Lunch with a view, Nîmes.

Grape harvest for Domaine de la Casa Blanca wine, Banyuls.

Wine

Wine is the lifeblood of Languedoc-Roussillon. The region, an enormous patchwork of different types of rocky soils, exposures and microclimates – all the things that make up the French word *terroir* – is divided unevenly into 24 AOC (*Appellation d'Origine Contrôlée*) growing regions. Combine these AOC wines with the *Vins de Pays d'Oc* and *vins de table*, and it produces more wine than anywhere else in France. If you want to point a finger at the region responsible for Europe's wine lake, point here with both hands. In the past couple of decades, however, the wine has improved by leaps and bounds.

Some wines have been well known for years. Minervois, elegant structured AOC wines named after the beautiful village of Minerve, was planted by Roman veterans and much appreciated back in Rome by Cicero. Powerful deep red Fitou, grown near Narbonne in the southern Corbières, was one of Louis XIV's favourites and is the region's oldest AOC (since 1948). The classic quaffable Côtes du Rhône, made on both the Gard and Provence sides of the big river, were one of France's first AOC regions, and encompass light, dry AOC Tavel, the original rosé, and neighbouring AOC Lirac. Costières de Nîmes is a rather unusual wine, made from grapes grown in the Petite Camargue.

Most of the big wine excitement in recent years has been concentrated in the *appellation* Côteaux du Languedoc, which extends from the Upper Hérault to Narbonne and Carcassonne. It's so vast that it has been subdivided into smaller zones such as Pic-St-Loup, Le Clape, Grès de Montpellier and the newest AOC area, Cabières. Coteaux du Languedoc also encompasses the well-established St-Chinian and its powerful neighbour Faugères, the most tannic of Languedoc's wines, grown since the early Middle Ages on sea-facing hills north of Béziers.

The rocky, arid Corbières, another vast region, has had its AOC credentials only since 1985 but has come on strong ever since. Subdivided into 11 *terroirs*, such as Boutenac, Lagrasse, Lézignan and Sigean, and producing full-bodied and spicy red wines (80%), they have also considerably improved in recent years, with an emphasis on bringing out the individual flavours and character of each area.

Although best known for red wines, most AOC areas also produce a percentage of whites. One of the classics is Picpoul de Pinet, literally 'lip stinger', an indigenous grape grown around Mèze and the Bassin de Thau, which goes well with seafood. AOC Côtes de Roussillon produce good whites made from Macabeu and local Malvoisie, as well as spicy medium-bodied reds. Limoux produces the world's oldest bubbly – the Blanquette de Limoux.

The sunny coastal areas of Roussillon produce natural sweet red and white wines under the name AOC Grand Roussillon, as well as others with their own AOC designations (Banyuls, Collioure, Rivesaltes and Maury), which make ideal aperitifs. Marseillan is the home of Noilly Prat, a white vermouth aged in barrels left in the sun (see page 169).

Most of all, quantity-wise, Languedoc produces *Vins de Pays d'Oc* (50% of all wine). These have less strict rules about the varieties of grapes that have to be used, and so have allowed some winemakers to experiment and create genuine marvels. One of the best ways to learn more (short of drinking your way through every label) is to attend a regional wine-tasting class – something that has become increasingly popular in recent years (see page 76).

Menu reader

General

à point/ bien cuit/saignant/ bleu
medium/well/done/rare/very rare (eg steak)

aigre-doux sweet and sour

à la jardinière with garden vegetables

au feu de bois cooked over a wood fire

au four baked

beignets fritters

brochette on a spit

chaud hot

cru raw

cuit cooked

émincé thinly sliced

en croûte in a pastry crust

en papillote baked in parchment (or foil)

epicé spicy

farci stuffed

feuilleté puff pastry

fourré stuffed

fort strong

frais, fraîche fresh

frit fried

froid cold

fumé smoked

galette flaky pastry case or pancake

garni with vegetables

(au) gratin topped with breadcrumbs

haché minced

médaillon round piece

mousse mousse or foam

pané breaded

paupiette rolled thin slices

pavé slab

piquant spicy hot

salé salted, spicy

sucré sweet

tranche slice

vapeur steamed

velouté thick smooth sauce or soup

Useful phrases

I'd like to reserve a table
Je voudrais réserver une table
What do you recommend?
Qu'est-ce que vous me conseillez?
What's the dish of the day?
Qu'est-ce c'est le plat du jour?
I'd like the set menu
Je vais prendre le menu/la formule
Does it come with salad?
Est-ce que c'est servi avec de la salade?
I'd like something to drink
Je voudrais quelque chose à boire
I'm a vegetarian   *Je suis végétarien/végétarienne*
I don't eat...   *Je ne mange pas de...*
Where are the toilets?   *Où sont les toilettes?*
The bill, please   *L'addition, s'il vous plaît*

Drinks (*boissons*)

eau naturelle/gazeuse still/sparkling water

apéritif pre-dinner drink

bière/pression beer/draught beer

bouteille bottle

un café coffee

un crème coffee with hot milk

jus de fruit fruit juice

un thé tea

une tisane herbal tea

verre glass

vin blanc/rosé/rouge white/rosé/red wine

Fruit & vegetables (*fruits & légumes*)

abricot apricot

ananas pineapple

artichaut artichoke

asperges asparagus

aubergine aubergine (eggplant)

avocat avocado

banane banana

betterave beetroot

blette chard

cassis blackcurrant

céleri (-rave) celery (celeriac)

cèpes boletus mushrooms

cerise cherry

Red or white?

citron lemon
champignons mushrooms
chanterelles wild yellow mushrooms
chou cabbage
choufleur cauliflower
ciboulette chives
citron vert lime
citrouille pumpkin
coco (noix de) coconut
concombre cucumber
cornichons gherkins
courgettes courgettes (zucchini)
cresson watercress
échalote shallot
endive chicory (endive)
épinards spinach
fenouil fennel
fèves broad (fava)beans
fraises (des bois) strawberries (wild)
framboises raspberries
groseilles redcurrants
haricots beans
haricots verts green (French) beans
laitue lettuce
lentilles lentils
maïs (épis de) sweetcorn (on the cob)
morilles morel mushrooms

navet turnip
mangue mango
mûre (sauvage) mulberry, blackberry
myrtilles bilberries
oignons onions
pamplemousse grapefruit
pastèque watermelon
pêche peach
petits pois peas
poire pear
poireaux leeks
pois chiches chickpeas
poivron sweet pepper
pomme apple
pomme de terre potato
potiron pumpkin
prune/pruneau plum/prune
radis radishes
raisins (secs) grapes (raisins)
reine-claude greengage plums
roquette rocket (arugula)

Meat (*viande*)
agneau lamb
ailerons wings
bifteck beefsteak
blanc breast or white meat
bœuf beef
boudin blanc/noir white/black pudding
caille quail
canard, caneton duck, duckling
capre kid
cassoulet beans baked with sausage and duck
cervelle brain
chair flesh, meat
chapon capon
charcuterie mixed cold meats, salami, etc
cheval horsemeat
civet meat (usually game) stewed in wine and blood sauce
cœur heart
confit meat cooked and preserved in its own fat
côte, côtelette chop, cutlet
cuisse thigh or leg
dinde, dindon turkey

Menu reader

entrecôte ribsteak
épaule shoulder
faux-filet sirloin
foie liver
gésier gizzard
gibier game
gigot leg of lamb
gras/graisse fat
grillade grilled meat
jambon ham
jarret knuckle
lapin rabbit
lardons diced bacon
lièvre hare
maigret breast of duck
marcassin young wild boar
noix de veau (agneau) topside of veal (lamb)
oie goose
os bone
petit salé salt pork
pintade guinea fowl
porc pork
pot au feu meat and vegetables cooked in stock
poulet chicken
poussin young chicken
queue de bœuf oxtail
ris (de veau) sweetbreads (veal)
rognons kidneys
rôti roast
sanglier wild boar
saucisses sausages
saucisson dry sausage
selle (d'agneau) saddle (of lamb)
tournedos thick round slices of beef fillet
travers de porc spare ribs
veau veal
venaison venison

Fish, seafood & shellfish (poissons, fruits de mer & coquillages)

anchois anchovies
anguille eel
bar sea bass
barbue brill
bourride Languedoc's bouillabaisse

brandade salt cod with mashed potatoes and olive oil
bulot whelk
cabillaud cod
calmar squid
colin hake
congre conger eel
coques cockles
coquillages shellfish
coquilles St-Jacques scallops
crabe crab
crevettes prawns
darne slice or steak of fish
daurade sea bream
écrevisse crayfish
espadon swordfish
flétan halibut
gambas giant prawns
grondin red gurnard
homard Atlantic lobster
huîtres oysters
langouste spiny lobster
langoustines Dublin Bay prawns
limande lemon sole
lotte monkfish
loup sea bass
merlan whiting
mérou grouper
morue salt cod
moules mussels
palourdes clams
poulpe octopus
praires small clams
raie skate
rascasse scorpion fish
rouget red mullet
sar silver bream
saumon salmon
saint-pierre John Dory
seiche cuttlefish
telline tiny clam
thon tuna
truite trout

Desserts

bavarois mousse or custard in a mould
charlotte sponge fingers and custard cream dessert
chantilly sweet whipped cream
clafoutis batter fruit cake
coulis thick fruit sauce
coupe ice cream; a scoop or in a dish
crème anglaise custard
crème brûlée cold custard dessert topped with caramelized sugar
gâteau cake
glace ice cream
parfait frozen mousse
profiteroles choux pastry balls, often filled with chocolate or ice cream
sablé shortbread
savarin a filled cake, shaped like a ring

Other

addition bill
ail garlic

Local honey.

aïoli garlic mayonnaise
amandes almonds
amuse-gueule appetizers
aneth dill
beurre butter
bouquet garni mixed herbs
brebis (fromage de) sheep's cheese
cacahouètes peanuts
cannelle cinnamon
chèvre goat's cheese
crème fraîche light sour cream
confiture jam
crudités raw vegetable platter
escargots snails
frites chips (French fries)
fromage cheese
genièvre juniper
gingembre ginger
huile (d'olive) oil (olive)
lait milk
marrons chestnuts
miel honey
menthe mint
moutarde mustard
noisette hazelnut
noix walnuts
nouilles noodles
œufs eggs
oseille sorrel
pain bread
pâte pastry, crust
pâtes pasta
pélardon goat's cheese from the Cévennes
persil parsley
pignons pinenuts
piment chili
poivre pepper
potage soup
riz rice
sarrasin buckwheat
sel salt
sucre sugar
truffes truffles
vinaigre vinegar
yaourt yoghurt

Entertainment

La Ola Beach Bar, Plage du Lido, Sète.

Languedoc-Roussillon has its fair share of entertainment, and it's as eclectic as everything else in the region, serving up a mix of old and new, traditional and alternative. Much of it is obviously centred in the cities, especially Montpellier, where the huge student population guarantees that you'll always find something to do. During the summer there are hundreds of outdoor concerts of all kinds, festivals going full throttle, and discos – especially near the coastal resorts – are thronged with clubbers.

Bars & clubs

Bars in Languedoc tend to double as cafés, and fill up particularly in the early evening from 1800-2000 as people stop for an aperitif before going home or out in the evening. Some have live music at weekends (which often constitutes the sole winter entertainment in villages) and stay open until the wee hours. Clubs, with a few exceptions, are outside the city centres, often in industrial zones or by the sea and here the action doesn't usually get

Music

Languedoc-Roussillon, birthplace of *chansonniers* Georges Brassens and Charles Trenet, is fairly besotted with music. Harking back to its medieval roots, the region has given birth to new troubadours and New Occitan song groups, and groups such as the clarinettist Laurent Audemard's brass and wind Une Anche Passe dedicated to European (and particularly Mediterranean) roots music. In Roussillon you'll find traditional Catalan bands (*coblas*), such as the Cobla Mil-Lenaria, that play lilting songs to accompany the traditional circle dance or *sardane*. Local popular music tends to have a strong south-of-the-border slant – from the omnipresent brass *bandas* that cheer on local rugby sides, to followers of the Gypsy Kings. In Nîmes they love flamenco (including 'New Flamenco' by such bands as Rumba Is Compas).

With all its money and huge student population, Montpellier has Languedoc's most vibrant music scene. Rock, blues and jazz are especially popular, and you can hear all kinds at Le Jam, Le Rockstore (see page 187) and other venues. One of the more unusual local groups is Rinôçérôse, which plays a mix of rock and electronic dance music, and was founded by Jean-Philippe Freu and Patrice Carrié who have day jobs as psychologists.

The departmental capitals, even little Mende up in the Lozère, all have theatres with classical music and opera programmes, as does Béziers and Narbonne. Ballet is very popular in Montpellier, where the Centre Chorégraphique National de Montpellier under the direction of Mathilde Monnier has, since its foundation in 2001, quickly emerged as one of France's most creative and exciting dance centres, hosting top choreographers from around the world.

underway until 0100. In Perpignan and Montpellier special late-night buses make the rounds of the clubs from the city centre at weekends, so you (or your offspring) don't have to worry about driving home after having a good time. Keep an eye peeled for posters and leaflets of coming events.

Children

As French regions go, Languedoc-Roussillon is one of the best for keeping the kids entertained, whether they're toddlers or teenagers. Children love Carcassonne and the realistic summer jousts of Le Chevalier de la Foi (see page 226) or the Parc Historique de Beaucaire (see page 117), where they can watch swords being made and gladiators and medieval knights using them. There are huge sandy beaches, aquariums along the coast (and a brand new state-of-the-art one, the Mare Nostrum in Montpellier, see page 155), water parks, at least a dozen forest adventure parks where they can play Tarzan in the treetops, and the unique and wonderful Vallon de Villaret (see page 123) in the Lozère. Kids who like dinosaurs will adore Espéraza's Dinosauria (see page 205) and the full-scale models at the Musée-Parc des Dinosaures

in Mèze (see page 169). Other kid pleasers are the animal parks, such as Sigean African Reserve (see page 221) and Lunaret Zoo and Serre Amazonienne (see page 155) both in Montpellier. There are wolves in the Parc des Loups du Gévaudan (see page 124), and tortoises in La Vallée des Tortues (see page 268). For little kids, the farm animals at Ferme de Découverte in Roussillon (see page 267) will be a hit.

Gay & lesbian

Montpellier is the gay capital of the south of France, host since 1994 of a Gay Pride March every June. It is the place where you'll find the most gay and lesbian bars and clubs, including the very first, the Café de la Mer (see page 187) – a good place to make new friends and find out what's happening. Exclusivity is rare, but most popular nightspots such as La Villa Rouge club are very gay friendly (or hetero-friendly, depending on how you want to look at it). There's a gay beach at Villeneuve-les-Maguelones-Plage, and the naturist gay Plage d'Espiguette, isolated in the regional nature reserve of the Camargue.

Shopping

Languedoc-Roussillon's most popular destinations have their share of tourist-oriented boutiques, and at Aigues-Mortes, Villefranche-de-Conflent and especially in the Cité of Carcassonne you can fulfil all your plastic armour, tea towel or T-shirt needs in one fell swoop. For serious purchases, make a beeline for Montpellier, the undisputed shopping capital of Languedoc-Rousssillon: the entire Ecusson is full of glittering boutiques where you can find the latest Paris fashions, all kinds of gourmet treats, music and gift items from around the world, antiques and Pomme de Reinette, one of the best toy shops in France (see page 189). That said, every historic centre will turn up a surprise or two, often in shops that have been owned by the same families for generations. One of the best is the Maison Quinta in Perpignan (see page 266), a fascinating all-Catalan department store.

Antiques

Pézenas has a fair number of antique shops, although not too many bargains – these await the early birds at the *vide greniers* (literally, 'attic-emptiers'); every town and village seems to hold one or two a year, and the more remote and rural, the more likely you are to find a gem. Béziers is another good place to look, with a regular programme of antiques fairs in its Parc des Expositions.

Arts & crafts

Pézenas, now that it's retired from hosting the governors of Languedoc, has made a concerted effort to attract artists and craftspeople, and is probably the best place for made-on-the-spot creations from the most traditional to the avant garde. Other happy hunting grounds for original, handmade items from the area are Carcasonne's Le Vieux Lavoir/Coopérative Artisanale de la Cité (see page 227) and Les Confidences du Terroir (see page 140) in Ste-Enimie in the Gorges du Tarn.

Books

There are enough Anglophones in Languedoc-Roussillon to support English bookshops, or at least English sections in bookshops; you may even find an English bookstand at the local market. There are specialist bookshops as well, such as the Librairie Ancienne du Somail (see page 189), a vast multilingual book heaven that relocated from Paris to the Canal du Midi.

Ceramics

Montpellier was an important ceramics centre in the 18th century, but these days you're more likely to find pieces in museums or the better antique shops. St-Quentin-la-Poterie near Uzès, and Anduze

Place Dampmartin, Uzès.

in the Cévennes still manufacture ceramics, and both have good shops. Anduze is best known for its massive Renaissance-style garden pots, the sort used by the Medici to plant orange trees; come in a van if you want to take one home.

Clothing

In spite of Nîmes' proud textile history, hardly anything is made here now. However, for something different visit Les Indiennes de Nîmes (see page 115) for the block prints (*indiennes*) of the Midi, but also warm shepherds' cloaks and traditional *gardian* (French cowboy) hats and fashions. The old silk industry of the Cévennes has recently been revived in Grefeuilhe, north of St-Hippolyte-du-Fort, and wealthy Uzès has some gorgeous (and expensive) dress shops.

Food & wine

Languedoc-Roussillon's *halles* (covered markets) and outdoor markets are an endless source of inspiration, filled with good things for picnics or to prepare back at the gîte. Some of these make great gifts: olives (especially *lucques*, which only grow in western Languedoc), olive oils and tubs of tapenade; jars of anchovies from Collioure; jarred truffles from Uzès; honey and dried mushrooms from the Cévennes; hams from the Cerdagne; bouquets of dried herbs from the *garrigue*; or macaroons and crunchy almond biscuits (*croquants*). If you're driving and have a cold box, add cheeses and charcuterie to the list.

Languedoc, above all, makes wine. Even if you're flying home, you can squeeze a couple of special bottles carefully wrapped in towels and bags in your check-in luggage. If you don't know what to get, visit a *caviste* (wine merchant) and ask advice. French post offices sell special ready-to-send bottle boxes for sending wine home, although with the postage and customs duties for outside Europe this can be a rather pricey option.

Jewellery

Uzès is the headquarters of Bénédikt Aïchelé, one of France's top contemporary jewellery designers. In Roussillon, jewellers in Perpignan and Prades make beautiful necklaces, bracelets, brooches and more out of gold and garnets (the colours of Catalonia, of course) according to a special patented technique; some invite visitors back into their workshops to show how it's done.

Activities & tours

With its natural beauty and sunny climate, mountains, beaches, rivers and canals, Languedoc is a year-round destination for activities and sports. It's a cliché, but there really is something for everyone. In the mountains, you'll find all-round adventure companies such as Languedoc Nature (languedoc-nature.com), Cévennes Evasion (cevennes-evasion.com) and a good dozen or so in Roussillon's Pyrenees (see Activities & tours, page 269), which organize everything from maps and accommodation for long-distance walks or mountain-bike tours to some of the more extreme sports (canyoning, rock climbing, Via Ferrata and whitewater rafting). They supply qualified guides and instruction, but also all the necessary equipment and transport.

Canoeing & kayaking

Languedoc is one of the best places in France to paddle down a lazy river for a few hours, with spectacular gorges providing scenery along the way. The journey down the Gorges du Tarn (see page 132) is the best known, but in July and August it can seem a bit crowded. Other companies operate on the Hérault, Cèze, Gardon, Orb or Aude. For a complete list check out canoe-france.com.

Canyoning

Sliding, jumping and dangling on ropes down rivers and waterfalls, climbing and caving are all the manifold arts of canyoning. It is especially popular around the Pic du Canigou, the Cévennes and the gorges around Mont Lozère and Mont Aigoual.

Cycling

Languedoc-Roussillon has plenty to offer the cyclist, whether you want do the Tour de Lozère in eight days, follow the Tour de France routes up into the Pyrenees (the Les Angles route, for instance, is rated for experts only), or just do some gentle peddling along the 240 km of towpaths of the Canal du Midi. National airlines will usually transport a boxed bike; Eurostar will transport bagged bicycles, and you can take them for free on most French trains. Local tourist offices can direct you to bike hire shops and suggest the best routes.

Mountain bike (*vélo tout terrain*, or VTT in French) fans are well catered for, with 10 trails in the region set up by the *Fédération Française de Cyclisme*. The biggest one, Centre Aude en Pyrénées based in Quillan, has 780 km of trails at all levels of difficulty; one of the most challenging is the 18-stage Grande Traversée de l'Hérault or

Lozère.

Réseau Vert across the Hérault. Many of the all-round adventure companies offer guided rides.

Several companies organize cycling tours in the region, among them Belle France (bellefrance. co.uk) who offer a leisurely seven-night self-guided pedal down the Canal du Midi to the coast. French Cycling Holidays (frenchcyclingholidays.com) organize a rather more challenging six-night journey from Uzès, past the Gorges de la Vis and Cirque de Navacelles, ending up in Murviel-les-Béziers. Discover France (discoverfrance.com) run special Tour de France visits during the big race and week-long cycle tours around Carcassonne and the back-country villages around Montpellier.

Diving

The lagoons and sands that dominate Languedoc-Roussillon's coast mean it's not particularly interesting as a diving destination, with the great exception of the Côte Vermeille's marine reserve. The other good place to scuba is among the volcanic rocks off Le Cap d'Agde, where you'll find several outfitters.

Food & wine

Cookery courses in Languedoc-Roussillon are a fairly recent phenomenon. For serious wannabe chefs, there's the total-immersion Gastronicom (gastronomicom.fr) in Le Cap d'Agde, which offers one- to three-month certificate courses in all aspects of French cuisine and wine, along with French language classes.

Most courses are linked to stays in luxury B&Bs. Some of these include Petra Carter's classes in Mirepeisset (petracarter.com), outside Narbonne; the week-long cooking course in Uzès with New Zealand chef Peta Mathias; or a choice of courses at the Château de Lignan just outside Béziers (for both, see activegourmetholidays.com). In Fitou, chef Marc Bienne offers one- to seven-day courses concentrating on French Mediterranean and Catalan cuisine (bleu-cuisine.com). Miam-Miam up in the Cévennes at Le Vigan (stage-cuisine.com, see page 117) will teach you how to cook a wide range of dishes with herbs and spices. For wine touring, see page 76.

Golf

Golf is a status sport in France, and perhaps more than anything the 20 beautiful courses in Languedoc-Roussillon suggest that this once-impoverished region has truly arrived. Serious golfers may want to pick up a Languedoc-Roussillon Golf Pass (sudfrancegolf.com), which can be used at 13 participating courses. In low season (Oct-Apr) it costs €120 for three courses played in seven days; in high season it's €250 for five courses over 21 days.

Horse riding

Gallop on sturdy white horses in the Camargue and splash merrily along the beaches, or ride long distance through stunning mountain scenery: Languedoc-Roussillon offers it all. The Sentier Cathare, a beautiful and extremely varied walk, is a 250-km trail from the Mediterranean's Port-La-

Novelle past most of the Cathar castles to Foix in the Ariège, and it is one of the most popular riding trails in France. Alternatively, there's the Circuit des Traboucayres in the high Pyrenees, partly in Roussillon and partly in Spain. For a complete list of riding trails and stables in the region, see the *Comité Régional du Tourisme Equestre du Languedoc*'s website (in French) telr.net/tourisme-equestre.asp.

Walking

Beautiful, majestic, dramatic, unspoilt – the region offers splendid walking however fit you are. Walks range from gentle strolls to long-distance treks on a cross-country *Grande Randonnée* (GR), to trails up the Pic du Canigou or Mont Lozère. Because of the summer heat, however, the best times to go are spring and autumn.

Hiking for pleasure was practically invented in Languedoc, when Robert Louis Stevenson made his trek across the Cévennes, and today the Stevenson Trail (GR70) down through the Lozère to St-Jean-le-Gard attracts hundreds of walkers, with or without donkeys (see page 141). Other famous trails in the area are the ancient Régordane across the Cévennes down to the medieval pilgrimage site of St-Gilles-du-Gard (see page 105), old ways to Compostela, or the Sentier Cathare (see Horse riding, left), which takes 12 days to walk. Longest of all is the E4, the European footpath that crosses all of Languedoc-Roussillon from the Pyrenees, the Black Mountains, the Cévennes and then across the Rhône River.

Besides the GRs (waymarked in white and red) you'll also find *Sentiers de Grande Randonnée de Pays* (GRPs), waymarked in yellow and red, that will take you around a particular region over several days. *Sentiers de Promenade* (PRs) (waymarked in yellow) are short circuits, lasting several hours. The paths are maintained by the *Fédération Française de la Randonnée Pédestre* (ffrandonnee.fr), which also publishes maps and guides (topo-guides) to the trails.

Water sports

The long sandy beaches skirting the Mediterranean have their fair share of jet ski and windsurf rentals, as well as all the other seaside sports you might expect. One of the best-kept secrets of Languedoc-Roussillon, however, is the idyllic swimming in the many crystal-clear rivers and lakes, often in stunning settings. They are far less crowded, and far more relaxing, although the sandcastle builders in your family may not approve. Out of season, you'll find a number of indoor/outdoor pool complexes in and around cities.

Wellbeing

Endowed with 13 natural therapeutic springs, people have been coming to Languedoc-Roussillon since Roman times to take water cures. Most of these age-old watering holes have adapted to modern tastes and now offer a range of wellbeing and beauty treatments alongside their traditional cures for what ails you, including Bagnols-les-Bains in the Lozère, Rennes-les-Bains in the Aude, or Lamalou-les-Bains in the Hérault. Roussillon, however, has the most, beginning with Amélie-les-Bains, Moltig-les-Bains and the Bains de St-Thomas (see page 269) in the Pyrenees, where even in the depths of snowy winter you can bathe outside at natural hot springs.

Along the coast, you'll find thalassotherapy spas ready to employ their sea water treatments to make you thin, de-stressed and beautiful. You'll find them at La Grande Motte, Banyuls-sur-Mer, Port Barcares and Agde, the latter home to the new, très chic Balnéocap (see page 191).

Walking tour operators

Walking tour operators (guided and self-guided) can do much of the hard work for you on long-distance routes. They get you to the trail head, transport your baggage and organize your accommodation and meals. Some suggested ones are:

Agly Rando Tours, *aglyrando.com*. Roussillon and the southern Corbières, and around the Canal du Midi.

Sentiers de France, *sentiersdefrance.com*. The Côte Vermeille and Sentier Cathare.

Silver Green, *silvergreen.co.uk*. Cévennes, Gorges du Tarn, Gorges de la Jonte and the Garrigue.

Walking Languedoc, *walking-languedoc.com*. The Petite Camargue, the Régordane, the Stevenson Trail, the Garrigue and many more.

World Walks, *worldwalks.com*. The Sentier Cathare.

Wine courses in Languedoc-Roussillon

This, naturally, is a subject very dear to local hearts. What good is making better wines if people don't know how to appreciate them? The eager wine lover reads that the best wines coming out of Languedoc-Roussillon rival a good Bordeaux and cost half as much. But which ones? Just reading the statistics (see box, opposite) is daunting; even 70% of the French confess to being bewildered by the intricacies of 24 AOC regions and countless Vins de Pays. If they're confused, what chance do the rest of us have? A new wave of wine schools in Languedoc-Roussillon is determined to change all that.

Twenty years ago the idea of wine classes here would have made people smile. This, in spite of the fact that the region's natural advantages in climate and *terroir* made good winemaking relatively easy; vines need to 'suffer' to produce better wines, and on the region's dry tumble of hills and rocky *garrigue*, suffer they did. Unfortunately, much of the wine in the 20th century wasn't very good, but local *vignerons* could still make a decent living by selling quantity over quality. That is, until the rest of the world began to compete and sell better wines for less. See History, page 34, for more information.

Since the 1980s, Languedoc-Roussillon's winemakers have fought back, and both the AOC wines and *Vins de Pays d'Oc* have steadily, remarkably, astonishingly improved through state-of-the-art techniques, garnering critical acclaim far and wide. But with Languedoc's often rotten luck, the wines have improved just as the strong euro has upended the export market.

To compete, some *vignerons* have decided to go *mano a mano* with the world wines. They've planted international favourites like Pinot Noir, Cabernet Sauvignon and Merlot, going for the easy homogenous quaffable fruity taste, and concentrating on establishing a brand (one of the most successful is a French-British concern called FAT Bastard). Recently too, the French government has relented and allowed winemakers to follow international trends and put the name of the grapes on the wine label to better market them – although

this has been less of a big deal in Languedoc-Roussillon, where most wines are blended.

The wine classes (and the experts) are far more interested in the *vignerons* who have stuck to their *terroir*, and produce complex, highly individual wines, full of the earthy, sun-soaked herbal scent of the *garrigue*. They are wines of consummate character, and the more you learn about them and how they're made, the more fun they become.

One of the newest schools is the Vinécole (vinecole.com) at the Domaine Gayda near Limoux (see page 229), run by Master of Wine Matthew Stubbs and Emma Kershaw. They offer everything from 30-minute speed tastings to courses for would-be wine professionals. The day workshop (€175), where pleasure and the enjoyment of the wines is key, is an excellent beginner's course. It offers a tour of the vineyards and explanations on planting, pruning, yields and organic wines, followed by an explanation of winemaking – the sorting, maturation and fine points of oak, fining and filtration. Lunch is

followed by a hands-on workshop on the fine art of wine blending, followed by a tasting of Languedoc-Roussillon's most distrinctive wines. You can make a whole holiday of it at the Domaine, which also has gîtes, a pool, an excellent restaurant, and can arrange golf packages as well.

Wine touring around the region and meeting the *vignerons* themselves is fun, too. Montpellier-based English-speaking Dominique George runs Languedoc Wine Tours (languedoc-wine-tours.com), which offers a variety of tours, including one to the Bassin de Thau for Picpoul de Pinet and oysters, followed by lunch and a trip to Pic St-Loup and Faugères. The English-owned Domaine du Puits es Pratx, located in Ginestas in the Minervois offers two-day tours of surrounding vineyards (gowinedirect.com). Several different tours in the same Minvervois-Corbières area are offered by wine teacher Wendy Gedney's Vin en Vacances (thewinewisecompany.com), and Roussillon is covered by Suzanne and Karen O'Reilly with their French Tour Co (thefrenchtourco.com) full-day tours.

Contents

The Gard

Cévennes National Park.

Introduction

Bordering on Provence, the Gard shares its neighbour's sun-soaked landscapes, olive groves, vines and parasol pines; it shares the Rhône (the *Malabar* or 'strong man'), the Mistral wind and the Camargue, the Rhône's huge delta of sandy beaches, white horses, black bulls and pink flamingos. It also shares a rich Roman heritage – the Pont du Gard is the Eiffel Tower of Languedoc, and Nîmes boasts the Maison Carrée, the best-preserved ancient temple anywhere, and its amphitheatre is in better nick than the Colosseum.

Yet at the same time the Gard could only be in Languedoc. Having fought in the front lines of the Wars of Religion, the *département* still has the highest density of Protestants in France, many still living in the Cévennes region that it shares with the Lozère. They made short work of the churches so, apart from the sublime façade of St-Gilles-du-Gard, you won't have many on your must-see list. But elsewhere the Gard shines bright: among its highlights are St Louis' great walled town of Aigues-Mortes, the medieval market town of Beaucaire, the art town of Villeneuve-lès-Avignon and irresistible Uzès, the most beautiful town in all Languedoc.

What to see in...

...one day
A classic (literally) tour would start with a morning visiting the great Roman monuments of Nîmes and the Jardins de la Fontaine before moving on to the engineering marvel of the Pont du Gard, with a late afternoon and dinner in the classically beautiful little town of Uzès.

...a weekend or more
Carry on after Uzès, working your way down the banks of the Rhône to the Petite Camargue and its beaches. Stop en route to see the vineyards at Tavel, the Musée St Pierre de Luxembourg and the Carthusian monastery at Villeneuve-lès-Avignon (including a day trip over the river to Avignon, if you want), Beaucaire, the abbey of St-Gilles-du-Gard and medieval Aigues-Mortes.

Fortified town of Aigues-Mortes.

Nîmes

Founded on seven hills, Nîmes is the 'Rome of France' and proud of its splendid monuments: the Arènes, the Maison Carrée and the Tour Magne. A famous textile centre, it went furiously Protestant in the 16th century and took some hard knocks during the Wars of Religion. Today, its handsome warren of 18th-century townhouses is urbane and exceptionally lively, in no little part due to an infatuation with ferias, bullfights, tapas and flamenco – enough to earn it a new nickname: the 'Spain of France'.

Les Arènes

Place des Arènes, T04 66 21 82 56, arenes-nimes.com.
Jan-Feb, Nov-Dec 0930-1700, Mar and Oct
0900-1800; Apr-May and Sep 0900-1830;
Jun-Aug 0900-1900, closed during ferias and
concerts. €7.70, €5.90 student/child (7-17),
under 7s free. Free multilingual audio guide.
Map: Nîmes, p84.

Built during the city's heyday (around AD 100), this
majestic elliptical arena is the best-preserved
Roman amphitheatre in the world. At 133 m by
101 m, it ranks as the 20th largest of the 70
surviving arenas, and was built just after the Pont
du Gard, probably by the same engineers, and
probably by the grunt work of the same slaves. But
its preservation isn't entirely due to its impressively
solid construction: with the decline of Rome, this
stadium erected for the joy of killing was converted
into a castle by the Visigoths and the Franks, before
reverting into a slum, housing 2000 people. One of
the few things Napoleon did in Languedoc was
order the slum to be cleared in 1809. The first
bullfights took place here in 1853, and have been a
passion ever since. The city's three big annual ferias
are hosted here and the Arènes also comes in
handy for big rock concerts.

If neither are on the programme, you can take a
self-guided audio tour, complete with sound
effects, through the terraces where 23,000
spectators once thronged to cheer on their
favourite gladiators, to the arena itself (from the
Latin word for 'sand', which was spread to soak up
the blood) and into the interior galleries, which
house a fascinating exhibition on the gladiators.

Tip...

Save money on admission to the Arènes, the Maison
Carrée and the Tour Magne with a Nîmes Romaine
ticket (€9.80, €7.50 child 7-17) available at the three
sites. A similar ticket, good for all the city's museums,
is €9.40, €7 child (7-17).

Essentials

❶ Getting around The sights of Nîmes are easily
accessible on foot, and parking is generally available
on the boulevards around the historic centre. Taxi
T04 66 29 40 11, taxinimes.fr.

❷ Bus station The bus station is on boulevard
Varsovie; service to some towns is provided by
Kéolis, 2 boulevard Paul Sabatier, T04 68 25 13 74 and
Tessier, Le Pont Rouge, T04 68 25 85 45. For regional
bus travel, see page 275.

❸ Train station Nîmes' train station at boulevard
Sergent-Triaire is a 10-minute walk southwest of the
Arènes. For regional train travel, see page 274.

❹ ATM Banque Populaire, 10 place Salamandre;
BNP-Paribas, 15 boulevard Victor Hugo.

❺ Hospital CHU, Place du Pr R Debré, T04 66 68
68 68.

❻ Pharmacy Barbacane, 110 rue Barbacane; Roux
Barnet, 10 rue Courtejaire.

❼ Post office 19 boulevard Gambetta.

❽ Tourist information office 6 rue August, T04 66
58 38 00, ot-nimes.fr. October-March Monday-Friday
0830-1830, Saturday 0900-1830, Sunday and national
holidays 1000-1700; April-September Monday-Friday
0830-1900, Saturday 0900-1900, Sunday and national
holidays 1000-1800; July-August Monday-Friday
0830-2000, Saturday 0900-1900, Sunday and national
holidays 1000-1800.

Opposite: Place des Arènes. Below: The symbol of Nîmes.

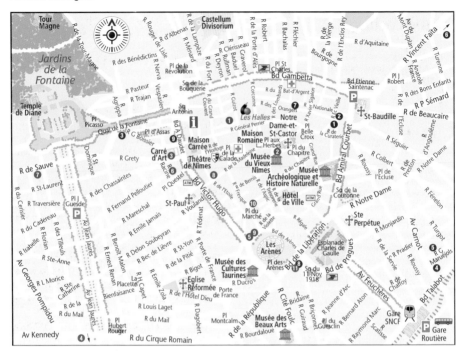

Maison Carrée

Place de la Maison Carrée, T04 66 21 82 56.
Jan-Feb, Nov-Dec 1000-1300 and 1400-1700, Mar
1000-1830, Apr-May and Sep 1000-1900; Oct
1000-1300 and 1400-1830; Jun-Aug 1000-1930.
€4.50, €3.70 student/child (7-17), under 7s free.
Map: Nîmes, above.

This charming bagatelle of a temple, known as the
'square house' for its sharp right angles, was built in
the first century BC by General Agrippa and
dedicated to cult of Augustus' deified grandsons. It
can, like the Arènes, lay fair claim to being the best
preserved of its kind in the world and again, this is
because the city always found some use for it that
precluded the locals from using it as a stone quarry
– at one point it served as a stable.

Maison Carrée.

Nîmes listings

The florid Corinthian columns and *cella* (inner sanctuary) are perfectly intact and the latter is now used for showing a 22-minute 3D gladiator film of rather dubious merit. Long blackened by time and fumes, restorers finished cleaning the temple in 2009 and their work was so thorough that locals are now grumbling it's so white it looks fake.

Carré d'Art (Musée d'Art Contemporain)

16 place de la Maison Carrée, T04 66 76 35 70,
carreartmusee.nimes.fr.
Tue-Sun 1000-1800. €5, €3.70 student.
Map: Nîmes, p84.

The simple, elegant beauty of the Maison Carrée has long posed a challenge to architects who wish to replicate similar virtues in their own buildings. Inaugurated in 1993, the sleek glass, cement and steel Carré d'Art is Sir Norman Foster's response, a building that echoes the famous temple in its five slender columns and light-filled interior. It holds a library of modern art, a bookshop, a café and a

museum of post-1960 works by such names as Warhol, Whiteread, Polke, Frize and Boltanski.

Cathédrale Notre Dame-et-St-Castor & around

Place aux Herbes.
Map: Nîmes, p84.

Rampaging Protestants made sure that Nîmes' **Cathedral**, consecrated in 1096, would not be a major attraction: they destroyed it, twice, in 1597 and 1622, leaving only the bell tower and a curious patchwork façade, featuring a dynamic Romanesque frieze depicting Old Testament scenes along with reliefs of Samson and the lion, and Alexander the Great being pulled to heaven by winged griffons. Just opposite the cathedral on the corner of Rue de la Madeleine, another Romanesque frieze decorates the 12th-century **Maison Romaine**, a rare medieval house.

From here Rue de l'Aspic leads to the **Place du Marché**, graced by a handsome **crocodile fountain** by Martial Raysse, and a palm tree. As you may have already noticed on the sewer lids, a crocodile chained to a palm is the city's symbol, as decreed by François I in 1535. The king had been delighted by the motif, which had appeared on an ancient coin minted in the city to commemorate Augustus' defeat of Anthony and Cleopatra in 31 BC (many of Nîmes' original colonists had fought as veterans of Caesar's legions in Egypt). Over the centuries, various benefactors donated stuffed crocodiles to the city, four of which are now suspended rather startlingly over the stair in the newly remodelled 18th-century **Hôtel de Ville**.

De Nîmes to denim

After the 16th-century Wars of Religion, many of Nîmes' Protestant merchants ended up in London where they sold the city's heavy serge cloth as 'de Nîmes', shortened after 1659 to 'denim'. In 1848, Levi Strauss took rolls dyed with bleu de Gênes (Genoa blue) to California, intending to make tents for the gold prospectors. He soon saw an even greater need for sturdy trousers. The rest is fashion history.

One-offs in the Gard

❶ The **Pont du Gard**, the highest Roman aqueduct ever built.

❷ The **Maison Carrée**, the best-preserved ancient temple in the world.

❸ **Aigues-Mortes**, the walled Crusader port, founded by St Louis.

❹ **Cave of the 100,000 soldiers** formation at the Grotte de Trabuc.

❺ The **only city hall with four stuffed crocodiles**, Nîmes.

From the Castellum Divisorium to the Jardins de la Fontaine

Map: Nîmes, p84.

Fussy mineral water drinkers would feel at home among the ancient Romans, who built the spectacular Pont du Gard just to bring top-quality spring water to Nîmes. The five million gallons that flowed down the aqueduct daily spilled into the round basin of the **Castellum Divisorium** on Rue de la Lampèze, before being distributed around the city through 10 lead pipes. It was rediscovered in the 19th century; the only other Castellum Divisorium to survive is in Pompeii.

From here, carry on south to the **Square Antonin**, where traffic spins around a statue of

Grotte de Trabuc.

La Tour Magne.

Antonius Pius (AD 86-161), one of the 'Five Good Emperors' of Rome, whose family came from Nîmes (the locals joke that he's holding out his hand to see if it's raining). Follow the leafy **Quai de la Fontaine** along the 18th-century canal dug to supply Nîmes' textile industry, and take a quick detour to the left to see the **Place d'Assas**, where Martial Raysse's esoteric fountain honours the Celtic water god Nemausus who gave his name to Rome's Colonia Nemausensis.

The spring Nemausus or **Fontaine** is the focus of the formal **Jardins de la Fontaine**, at the end of the quay. This lovely set piece of pools, grand balustrades and statues was laid out in 1735 and is the oldest example of civic gardens in France. Set back from the pools, its stone vaulting lost amid the parasol pines, stands the so-called **Temple of Diana** (it may have originally been a library), which served for many years as a convent church.

La Tour Magne

Mont Cavalier, T04 66 21 82 56.
Jan-Feb, Nov-Dec 1000-1300 and1400-1700, Mar 1000-1830, Apr-May and Sep 1000-1900, Oct 1000-1300 and 1400-1830, Jun-Aug 1000-1930. €2.70, €2.30 student/child (7-17).
Map: Nîmes, p84.

From the Jardins de la Fontaine, a path leads up to the site of the Celtic oppidum that pre-dated the Roman colony, now marked by the ruined but still impressive 32-m Tour Magne. Originally, the tower stood twice as high, and may have been used for

signals before it was incorporated into the city walls built by Augustus. The views on a clear day stretch to Mont Ventoux in Provence.

Musée des Beaux Arts

Rue de la Cité-Foulc, T04 66 67 38 21.
Sep-Jun Tue-Sun 1000-1800, 2nd Thu of the month 1000-2100, Jul-Aug Tue-Wed, Fri-Sun 1000-1800, Thu 1000-2100. €5, €3.70 student.
Map: Nîmes, p84.

Founded in 1824, Nîmes' eclectic trove of art includes an array of gems and curiosities, such as the biggest and most beautiful Roman mosaic found in the city, the *Marriage of Admetus*; the ceramic *Foulc Tondo* by Andrea della Robbia; paintings by Jacopo Bassano and Giambono; earthy Dutch and Flemish paintings and the striking if bizarre *Cromwell looking to the Coffin of Charles I*, by Paul Delaroche.

Musée du Vieux Nîmes

Place aux Herbes, T04 66 76 73 70.
Map: Nîmes, p84.

This little museum in the former bishop's palace has panelled rooms dedicated to Old Nîmes, including a small but choice collection of paintings and furnishings dating back to the Middle Ages. There are displays on the city's once all-important textile industry, and a new exhibition dedicated to the history of the colour blue, from the wild indigo of Africa and China and the woad (pastel) that made Toulouse's fortune, to the city's most famous product, denim (see page 85).

Musée Archéologique et Musée d'Histoire Naturelle

13 bd Amiral Courbet, T04 66 76 73 45.
Tue-Sun 1000-1800. Free.
Map: Nîmes, p84.

Housed in the former Jesuit College, Nîmes' archaeological collection was founded in 1762,

What the locals say

I live in the heart of Nîmes and for me nothing beats shopping for food in **Les Halles** (see page 115), the covered market, because of the sheer wealth, scent and variety of the produce, or visiting the market along the **Avenue Jean Jaurès** on a Friday morning, where you'll find a rich tapestry of the city's inhabitants.

For good value and an authentic old-fashioned French feel, **Restaurant Nicolas** (1 rue Poise) is not just a family-run restaurant but an institution. I first took my family there nearly 20 years ago. The food is simple and plentiful and perfect for those who shy from nouvelle cuisine. Walk off your meal in the **Jardins de la Fontaine** (see page 87), a combination of classical French and romantic English-garden design, or drive out to the **Centre du Scamandre** on the road to Stes-Maries-de-la-Mer. This is a lesser-known bird reserve, rich in wildlife, and a wonderful place to walk.

Laura Chanter is Editor of the Languedoc Sun

Les Halles.

Musée des Cultures Taurines

6 rue Alexandre Ducros, T04 66 36 83 77. Sep-Jun Tue-Sun 1000-1800, 2nd Thu of the month 1000-2100; Jul-Aug Tue-Wed, Fri-Sun 1000-1800, Thu 1000-2100. €5, €3.70 student Map: Nîmes, p84.

Not far from the Arènes, this museum has exhibits on the history of bullfighting in the South of France, matadors' 'suit of lights' and more.

and grows every time someone digs a hole in the city or along the Via Domitia: most items relate to daily life. The great prize is a Celtic lintel of galloping horses and heads.

The natural history museum is in the same building and has a special quaintness. The exhibits originated as a cabinet of curiosities collected in the 18th century by local Jean-François Séguier. There are statue-menhirs, Languedoc's oldest sculptures (4500-2000 BC), and an ethnographic section arranged in the 1930s, during the heyday of French colonialism.

Sommières & around

West of Nîmes, charming Sommières is the essence of Languedoc. It's a languid pétanque-playing under the plane trees kind of town that has defied change, mainly because its river, the Vidourie, frequently floods (in 2002 the waters came up to the village's second floors). In AD 31, Emperor Tiberius built Sommières' landmark, a splendid **Roman bridge** that even after 2000 years of duty looks as good as new. It was even more impressive at first, extending for 17 arches, but medieval Sommières built embankments and a tangle of streets over 10 of them. The **clock tower gate** at the bridge, like much of the town, dates from the 17th century, when all had to be rebuilt after the Wars of Religion.

Since 1183, Sommières has held a lively Saturday market; it's so old that it still has a stone in the market place called the Pierre d'Inquant where slaves once stood, waiting to be sold. For lovely views, walk up to the **Tour Bermond**, a last remnant of Sommières' castle (Jul-Aug Sun-Fri 1600-1900, €2, under 12s free). The pretty village's lazy ways suited novelist Lawrence Durrell, who lived here from 1966 until his death in 1990. **The Espace Lawrence Durrell** has a permanent exhibition on his life at 90 Impasse de Camp-Chéri (T04 66 80 96 74, asso. larrydurrell.free.fr, open by appointment).

Château de Villevieille

1 km from Sommières on the D40, direction Nîmes, T06 70 61 81 49, chateau-de-villevieille.fr.
Apr-Jun and Oct Sat-Sun and national holidays 1400-1900, Jul-Sep daily 1400-2000. €8, €5 student/child, under 10s free.

Overlooking the Vidourle valley, the Château de Villevieille started off in the 11th century as a rectangular tower built by Bermond d'Anduze. His descendant became a Cathar, so St Louis confiscated his lands in 1240, which he later exchanged for Aigues-Mortes. The castle went through various owners and transformations until reaching its current aspect in the 16th century: three wings around a rectangular courtyard behind a graceful Renaissance façade.

And so it has stayed. Villevieille was never one of France's grandest châteaux, but what is rare is that both it and its 17th- to 18th-century furnishings survived all of Languedoc's vicissitudes intact, because even the *sans culottes* of the Revolution respected its owner, the marquis

Philippe de Pavée, as a friend of Voltaire. The visit includes a dozen rooms with ornate panelling, woodwork and plasterwork ceilings, mirrors, furniture, the original kitchen and a large china collection.

Oppidum de Nages

Nages et Solorgues, T04 66 35 05 26.
The Mairie has a museum of finds (Tue and Fri 0830-1145, Mon and Wed 0830-1145, 1400-1800, Thu 0830-1245 and 1700-1900).

East of Sommières, this hilltop oppidum with a walled grid of streets and towers was occupied by a Celtic tribe called the Volques Arécomiques from the third to first century BC.

Oppidum de Nages.

Tip...

Look in local shops for 'Terre de Sommières' (or *sépiolite*, a carbonate of magnesium) mined in nearby Salinelles. Discovered in the 20th century, it's just the thing for removing nasty oil stains, and it's 100% natural, too.

East of Nîmes

After the Albigensian Crusade, the lands east of the Rhône were inherited by Rome, making the big river into a frontier between king and pope, and creating an opportunity for two fascinating towns to play about in history's headlines.

Le Port, Beaucaire.

With nearby Nîmes, Avignon, Arles and the Pont du Gard hogging the limelight, the delightful old town of Beaucaire tends to get slightly overlooked. Set under the Massif de l'Aiguille on the Via Domitia, at the junction of the Rhône and the Canal du Rhône à Sète, Beaucaire has a proud Roman past, a castle that defied Simon de Montfort, a mania for bulls and sumptuous *hôtels particuliers* from the glory days when it held the queen of Mediterranean fairs. Another relic of past riches is the large 18th-century neoclassical church, **Notre Dame des Pommiers**, with its convex façade and a fine frieze of the Last Supper from its Romanesque predecessor.

Château de Beaucaire & Musée Auguste Jacquet

T04 66 59 90 07.
Apr-Oct Wed-Mon 1000-1230 and 1415-1800; Nov-Mar Wed-Mon 1000-1200 and 1400-1715. €4.70, €1.35 child.

Set on a 35-m rock, Beaucaire's castle had a serious workout after 1208, when a local squire assassinated the papal legate Pierre de Castelnau – the spark that led Innocent III to declare the Albigensian Crusade. The Crusaders occupied the town, but Count Raymond VII of Toulouse, who was born here, boldly recaptured it in 1216 – except for the castle, where the Crusaders took refuge. Simon de Montfort came to rescue them, but Beaucaire, besieged from both sides – from the Crusaders inside and Montfort outside – held out for 13 weeks until Montfort gave up. In gratitude, Count Raymond granted Beaucaire the right to

Tip...

The Office de Tourisme (24 cours Gambetta, T04 66 59 26 57, ot-beaucaire.fr) offers guided visits (€4.30) of the interiors of the otherwise inaccessible *hôtels particuliers*.

The Drac of Beaucaire

Beaucaire's prettiest square, Place de la République, contains something rather unexpected: a statue of a large green dragon. This is the Drac, who in the Middle Ages lived in the Rhône but often took the form of a handsome young man, walking the streets of Beaucaire. He had a son, a baby Drac, and he kidnapped a young washerwoman to nurse it. One of her tasks was to rub it down with a special 'dragon grease' that would make it invisible, which she accidentally rubbed in her eye, allowing her to see him as a dragon. After seven years of service, the Drac let her return to Beaucaire. One day, however, as he was strolling, she recognized him and called out. He was so miffed that he tore out her eye and vanished, and was never seen again.

hold a duty-free fair, the ancestor of the one that for centuries made the town a household name.

Beaucaire eventually became a royal town, and was besieged again in 1632 by Louis XIV's rebellious brother Gaston d'Orléans; Beaucaire sent him packing and Richelieu, to prevent further such nonsense, gutted the castle. Shady gardens now fill the walls, along with Beaucaire's archaeology and history museum. Its finds go back 40,000 years, including impressive Gallo-Roman items, rare alchemist's equipment found at the Abbaye de St-Roman, and lithographs and more on the Foire de la Madeleine.

Le Mas Gallo-Romain des Tourelles

4294 rte de St-Gilles, T04 66 59 19 72, tourelles.com.
Apr-Oct daily 1400-1800, Jul-Aug Mon-Sat 1000-1200 and daily 1400-1900, Nov, Feb and Mar Sat 1400-1800, Dec-Jan 1400-1700. €4.90, €1.50 child.

A vineyard with a difference, this Mas occupies the ruins of a Gallo-Roman amphora factory and recreates the winemaking techniques of the period with a mighty tree trunk wine press. Visits include a walk in the Roman garden with its vines and ruins and a 10-minute film showing how the Romans made wine (come on the second Sunday in

Around the region

September to see the staff dressed as serfs, harvesting and pressing the grapes). You can also taste wines made to ancient recipes such as *turriculae* (a white wine flavoured with sea water) and *mulsum* (a white wine flavoured with honey).

L'Abbaye de St-Roman

Mas des Tourelles, 4294 rte de Bellegarde, T04 66 59 19 72, abbaye-saint-roman.com.
Jul-Aug daily 1000-1300 and1400-1900, Apr-Jun and Sep Tue-Sun 1000-1300 and 1400-1800, Mar and Oct Tue-Sun 1400-1700, Nov-Feb Sun, school holidays 1400-1700. €5.50, under 18s free. Note that it's a 15-min walk uphill from the car park, and not suitable for anyone with walking difficulties.

In the fifth century, when life was precarious, a group of hermit followers of St Roman (d 460) began to excavate this refuge in the limestone high above Beaucaire in imitation of the lives of the Desert Fathers. It later became a Benedictine abbey and carried on until the 15th century; today you can visit the chapel, the abbot's seat, monkish cells dug out of the rock and 250 graves cut out of the stone, open to the sky.

Villeneuve-lès-Avignon

The 'New Town near Avignon' faces its far bigger famous namesake across the Rhône, and if you've never been, you should pop over to see the Palais des Papes and the excellent Musée du Petit Palais. The papacy's 1309-1378 stint in Avignon, or 'Babylonian Captivity' as Petrarch called it, was in fact so luxurious, wanton and squalid that some of the more pious cardinals were given permission to live on the French side of the river. The 15 palaces, known as *livrées cardinalices* (on land 'freed' from the original owner) were hardly monastic, however, as the typical cardinal employed a staff of 100. Once the popes returned to Rome, the *livrées* were abandoned and fell into ruin.

Chartreuse du Val de Bénédiction

58 rue de la République, T04 90 15 24 24, chartreuse.org.
Oct-Mar Mon-Fri 0930-1700, Sat-Sun 1000-1700, Apr-Sep daily 0930-1800. €6.50, €4.50 concession, under 18s free. Last tickets sold 30 mins before closing.

In 1356, when Cardinal Etienne Aubert was elected pope and became Innocent VI, he donated his *livrée* to the Carthusians. For over four centuries, the Carthusians made it into the biggest and richest charterhouse in France, until it was abandoned during the Revolution, sold off in lots, and became a dangerous slum.

Now restored, grand and austere, a self-guided tour starts in the cavernous church, with the alabaster effigy and tomb of Innocent VI and views straight through to the Fort St-André. There are three huge cloisters, and a dining room (*tinel*), with some of the best acoustics in France, designed so the monk in charge of reading could be heard by all – important as the brethren were limited to one

The Foire de la Madeleine

The original fair founded by the Count of Toulouse didn't survive the French victory over Languedoc, but in 1464 Louis IX revived the notion, instituting the Foire de la Madeleine to take place in Beaucaire during the last week of July. For Beaucaire it was like hitting the jackpot. For years it was the biggest fair in the Mediterranean, attracting 300,000 traders who famously exchanged more money in six days than the port of Marseilles saw in a year. It lost its duty free privileges after Waterloo and dwindled away by the mid-19th century. Today, Beaucaire remembers it with a wonderfully atmospheric fête, featuring a historic parade, *gardiens* (cowboys) from the Camargue, bodegas, concerts, bulls in the streets – about 100 or so charging through – and Courses Camarguaises, which the locals claim to have invented, and excel at, erecting statues of the bulls who provided the most sport. For more information on Courses Camarguaises, see 45.

hour of conversation per week. The *tinel*'s chapel has charming but damaged 14th-century frescoes by Matteo Giovannetti.

Since 1991, the Chartreuse has taken on a new life as the Centre National des Ecritures du Spectacle. Playwrights, composers and scriptwriters receive grants to come here and present their work during the Avignon Festival, the biggest performance shindig in France.

Musée St Pierre de Luxembourg

3 rue de la République, T04 90 27 49 66.
Oct-Mar Tue-Sun 1000-1200 and 1400-1730;
Apr-Sep daily 1000-1230 and 1500-1900. €3.

Housed in a former *livrée*, this museum brings together works of art that once belonged to the area's monasteries, churches and cardinals, along with two masterpieces: downstairs is a beautiful, intricate 14th-century Virgin and Child carved from an elephant's tusk, and upstairs is the exquisite *Couronnement de la Vierge* by painter-illuminator Enguerrand Quarton (c 1410-1466), famous as the first distinctly French painter of the Renaissance.

Fort Saint-André

Puy Andeon, T04 90 25 45 35.
Mid-Sep to mid-May 1000-1300 and 1400-1700;
mid-May to mid-Sep 1000-1300 and 1400-1800.
€5 to visit the 2 round towers.

In the sixth century, a saintly Visigothic princess died in her hermitage on the mighty rock of Puy Andeon, and in the 10th century Benedictine monks built the abbey of St-André to shelter her relics. The fort was begun by Philip the Fair, the same king who in 1305 had bribed the Cardinals to elect a French pope, Clement V, then suggested the move to Avignon. The castle, however, emphasized who was boss on this side of the

Villeneuve-lès-Avignon.

Around the region

Rhône. There are superb views as far as the Alpilles and Mont Ventoux from the towers; legend has it the Man in the Iron Mask was imprisoned here for one night.

Jardins de l'Ancienne Abbaye de St-André

Puy Andeon, T04 90 25 55 95.
Oct-Mar Tue-Sun 1000-1200 and 1400-1700, Apr-Sep Tue-Sun 1000-1230 and 1400-1800. €5.

The once-splendid abbey of St-André is now private property, but you can visit the enchanting Italianate gardens. From May to early June, masses of irises and roses are in full sumptuous bloom.

Tour Philippe Le Bel

Av Gabriel Péri, T04 32 70 08 57.
Oct-Mar Tue-Sun 1000-1200 and 1400-1700, Apr-Sep Tue-Sat 1000-1230 and 1400-1830. €1.80.

Tour Philippe Le Bel.

It looks like new, this shimmering white tower built to guard the bridge of St-Bénézet, the now-half-bridge famous in the song *Sur le pont d'Avignon*. Walk up the spiral stairway to the top terrace for a splendid view of the bridge, Avignon and Villeneuve.

Collégiale Notre Dame

Oct-Mar 1000-1200 and 1400-1730, Apr-Sep 1000-1230 and 1500-1900.

Cardinal Arnaud de Via, nephew of Pope John XXII, built Villeneuve's church in the 14th century. It has a copy of *Pietà*, attributed to Enguerrand Quarton (the original was carted off to the Louvre in 1901), and an ornate marble altar dating back to 1745, inherited from the Chartreuse.

Tavel

The pebbly domains of Châteauneuf-du-Pâpe, promoted by the medieval popes, lie just north of Avignon, while just opposite on the Languedoc side is the sleepy little village of Tavel. This is where France's original rosé wine is made, a favourite of kings Philip IV and Louis XIV and one of the few that improve with aging. Another famous Côte du Rhône area, Lirac, is right next door, and produces reds and whites as well as rosés.

L'Académie du Vin et du Goût

Château de Clary, Roquemaure, follow the signs from the Roquemare exit (No 22) off the A9, T04 66 33 04 86, academie-du-vin.fr.
Sep-Jun daily 0900-1800, Jul-Aug daily 0900-1900. €4.

Set in a large forest midway between the Tavel and Lirac AOC growing areas, this handsome 18th-century château is devoted to Côtes du Rhône wines, olive oils and herbs; they also offer wine classes.

Right: Tavel's wine cellars.

Nîmes to Bagnols-sur-Cèze

This route takes you past two of the crown jewels of the Gard, Uzès and the Pont du Gard, before ending up at Bagnols-sur-Cèze and its fine art museum.

The most beautiful and aristocratic town in Languedoc, Uzès is charming and knows it. Imagine little squares with splashing fountains shaded by plane trees, elegant hôtels particuliers under sun-soaked tile roofs, lovely boutiques, a sumptuous market on Wednesday mornings and all day Saturday with black truffles in winter, and a prestigious summer music festival.

Place du Duché

Place du Duché , T04 66 22 18 96, uzes.com. Sep-Jun 1000-1200 and 1400-1800, Jul-Aug 1000-1230, 1400-1830. Guided tour of the apartments, caves and donjon. €15, €11 young person (12-16), €5 child (7-11), under 7s free. Tour Bermond only, €10.

The only château in France permitted to call itself a 'Duché', and residence of Jacques de Crussol (b 1957) and his duchess, this pile in the middle of Uzès occupies the site of the Gallo-Roman castle of Ucetia. In the 11th century, the lords of Uzès installed themselves here in the **Tour Bermond**, which dominates the town's skyline. If you tramp up the 135 steps, it offers great views over the old tiled roofs of the town. The elegant Renaissance façade of the residence, commissioned after the family's elevation to the ducal title, features an unusual combination of all three classical orders (Doric, Ionic and Corinthian), attributed to the artist Philibert Delorme. The guided tour includes the 15th-century Gothic **chapel**, the formal **apartments** decorated in the style of Louis XV and XVI and filled with family portraits and memorabilia, and the cellar, originally designed to stockpile food in case of siege, and now housing abundant evidence of the family's current concern – winemaking.

Left: View from the Tour Bermond du Duché, Uzès.

Cathédrale St-Théodorit

Promenade des Marronniers.

The seat of a bishop since the fifth century, the cathedral of Uzès occupies the spot of a first-century AD temple to Augustus, on a chestnut-lined promenade. Three saints (Firmin, Ferréol and Théodorit) served as bishops here, and the church was famous as the most ornate in the south of France. The Protestants destroyed it (this was a period when even the Bishop of Uzès converted to Protestantism) leaving only the wonderful round 12th-century bell tower, the Tour Fenestrelle (tower of windows) to recall its former glory. The current church dates from the 17th century, but it was stripped bare during the Revolution, sparing only the magnificent 17th-century organ, gilded and set in painted shutters unique in France.

Musée Georges Borias & around

Place de l'Evêché, T04 66 22 40 23, uzesmusee. blogspot.com. Nov-Dec and Feb Tue-Sun 1400-1700, Mar-Jun, Sep-Oct Tue-Sun 1500-1800, Jul-Aug Tue-Sun 1000-1200 and 1500-1800. €3, €1.20 child.

This is Uzès' attic, located in the right wing of the neoclassical Palais Episcopal by the cathedral. It has eclectic relics from the city's history, an ethnographic collection from Africa, Venezuela, Cambodia and Oceania gathered by Uzétian travellers, locally made ceramics and a room dedicated to the Nobel prize-winning author André Gide, whose family came from Uzès.

He wasn't the only member of the French literati to sojourn here: a plaque on the surrounding promenade commemorates Racine, who came to finish his studies here in 1661, aged 22. His uncle, the cathedral's Vicar-General, hoped he would forget his love of poetry; instead, Racine was ravished by the beauty of the South (and the girls). "Even our nights are more beautiful than your days …" he wrote back to Paris.

Just below the cathedral, facing the little square where traffic is funnelled around the centre, the

Around the region

Hôtel du Baron de Castille is the grandest of the town's *hôtels particuliers*. In the 19th century, the Baron fell so in love with Rome and its colonnades that he stuck some on the façade.

Le Jardin Médiéval

Impasse Port-Royal, T04 66 22 38 21.
Apr-Jun and Sep Mon-Fri 1400-1800, Sat-Sun 1030-1230, Jul-Aug daily 1030-1230 and1400-1800, Oct daily 1400-1700. €4.

Within the walls of Uzès' 'other château', the Château Raynon, these medieval gardens were established in 1995 to showcase the medicinal and culinary herbs, flowers and vegetables grown in these parts in the Middle Ages. The visit ends with a nice cup of herbal tea.

Musée des Bonbons.

Musée des Bonbons

Pont des Charrettes, T04 66 22 74 39, haribo.fr.
Sep-Jun Tue-Sun 1000-1300 and 1400-1800 (last entry 1715), Jul-Aug Tue-Sun 1000-1900 (last entry 1815). €6, €3 young person/child (5-15).

In 1996, the Haribo factory on the edge of Uzès opened up a museum designed to please almost everyone. Exhibits cover the history of sweets and their manufacture, with a natural emphasis on Haribo's gummy bears, liquorice, etc, with lots of tastings and interactive fun.

Musée de la Céramique Méditerranéenne

14 rue de la Fontaine, St-Quentin-la-Poterie (5 km north of Uzès), T04 66 03 65 86, musee-poterie-mediterranee.com.
Feb-May and Oct Wed-Sun 1400-1800, Jun Wed-Sun 1000-1300 and 1500-1900, Jul-Aug daily 1000-1300 and 1500-1900, Sep Wed-Sun 1000-1200 and 1400-1800, Nov-Jan by appointment only. €3, €2.30 under 18s.

St-Quentin-la-Poterie made beautiful tiles for the popes in Avignon and for centuries supplied all local ceramic needs. Located in a former olive oil mill, St-Quentin's museum offers a look at everyday pots in use across the Mediterranean region from the 18th century to the present.

Le Musée 1900

*Moulin de Chalier, Arpaillargues (3 km west of Uzès), T04 66 22 58 64, moulin-de-chalier.fr.*Feb-Jun and Sep Tue-Sun 1000-1200 and 1400-1900, Jul-Aug daily 1000-1900, Oct Tue-Sun 1400-1830, Nov-Dec school holidays daily 1000-1200 and 1400-1800; closed Jan. €7, €6 young person (13-16), €5 child (3-12), special family deals available.

This is a fascinating accumulation of late 19th- and early 20th-century relics, gathered and restored by Gaston Baron and his family. There are unusual tools, trains, tractors and thousands of toys, especially French teddy bears.

The Dukes of Uzès

In 1565 the Viscount of Uzès, who managed to broker peace between the Protestants and Catholics in Languedoc, was made a duke by Charles IX, and ever since the Duc de Montmorency lost his title and head in 1632 (see page 33), the Crussol family has been number one among the peers of France, with a distinguished history in France's wars: *Ferro non Auro* (iron, not gold) is their motto. When Louis XVIII once asked the incumbent duke why his family never managed to produce a maréchal, he famously replied: "Because we all get killed first." He wasn't exaggerating – some 21 dukes have been wounded or killed in battle. One of their tasks was to proclaim at royal funerals "The king is dead. Long live the King!" But they weren't all gruff military men – one, for instance, corresponded with Voltaire.

They've had a knack for wedding women of character, including the Duchess Anne de Rochechouart de Mortemart (1847-1933), the great granddaughter of the Veuve Clicquot, a writer, sculptress and feminist who rode and hunted into her 80s, killing over 2000 deer in her lifetime. She was the first woman in France to get a driving licence (and speeding ticket, in 1889, for going 15 kph), and used her immense champagne fortune to finance General Boulanger's attempt to overthrow la République in the 1880s; at the same time she was a good friend of the famous anarchist Louise Michel. Her daughter-in-law convinced culture minister André Malraux to make Uzès one of the first French towns covered by a preservation order in 1964.

Tour Fenestrelle.

Vers Pont du Gard

Pont du Gard

Vers-Pont-du-Gard, near Remoulins, T08 20 90 33 30, pontdugard.fr.
The aqueduct is always open. The museum, film and high-tech exhibition at the Site du Pont du Gard is open 0930-1730, Jul-Aug 0930-2000, closed Mon morning and 17 Nov-21 Dec and 5 Jan-15 Mar. €12, €9 young person/child (6-17), free 1st Sun of each month. Parking €5.

Paris has the Eiffel Tower, Normandy the Mont St-Michel and Languedoc has this sublime masterpiece of ancient engineering. Spanning the River Gardon, the Pont du Gard is the highest aqueduct ever built by Roman engineers, a triple-tiered chute carrying water from Uzès' Fontaines de l'Eure to Nîmes. It's only the most visible part of the nearly 50-km aqueduct (only 20 km as the crow flies, but to build it directly would have required digging an 8-km tunnel). About 90% of the aqueduct was underground, running at a nearly flat 0.4 gradient; the total fall from the source to the Castellum in Nîmes is only 17 m. In its prime it carried 35,000 cu m of water every day, but by the ninth century, after functioning for five centuries without maintenance, it became too encrusted with deposits to use.

Pont du Gard.

The stones of the Pont du Gard, some weighing six tons, were cut to fit perfectly, so the entire structure was built without a speck of mortar. On some stones, you can still see the builder's marks, as well as the holes and protruding stones that once supported the scaffolding. Estimates are that it took some thousand workers three years to build.

The lowest tier was widened in the 18th century to support a road that was used until 1998, when the Gardon flooded, causing serious damage to the surroundings, but not to the perfectly built aqueduct. Even so, it was the spark for a major renovation - stones were cut from the original quarries in Vers to replace some that had seriously eroded, and car parks and the current visitors' centre and exhibits were created. Book ahead for the guided tour of the water conduit on the aqueduct's top level, 49 m over the Gardon; or paddle down the river to see the aqueduct in its full glory.

Tip...

The Pont du Gard is a busy place. In season avoid the rush (and catch the best light) by arriving very early in the morning or late in the afternoon, around 1900.

Bagnols has grown an encrustation of suburbia since the construction of the nuclear plant nearby at Marcoule, but lovers of 20th-century art won't want to miss the museum in the heart of town.

Musée Albert-André

Hôtel de Ville, place Mallet, T04 66 50 50 56.
Jan, Mar-Jun, Sep-Dec Tue-Sun 1000-1200 and 1400-1800; Jul-Aug Tue-Sun 1500-1800; closed Feb. Free.

Bagnols' Hôtel de Ville is the most classic French Mairie imaginable, complete with a bust of Marianne over the door. A museum upstairs was founded in 1868, and in 1917 a local painter, Albert André, became curator and gathered together a fine collection of modern art, all of which burned in 1924 in a fire accidentally caused by local firemen. The despondent André appealed to his friends in the art world, and the lost works were replaced by paintings and sculptures by Renoir, Monet, Signac, Marquet (whose richly coloured *14 juillet au Havre*, of 1906 is the museum's pièce de résistance), Bonnard, Vollard, Matisse, Van Dongen, Berthe Morisot, Maillol, Picasso and Claudel.

The Southern Cévennes

The Lozère may have the most dramatic scenery, but the Gard's portion of the Cévennes National Park (see page 126) offers plenty to see and do. Start in Anduze, a delightful medieval town famous for its pottery, and in particular arty large garden pots.

Just north of Anduze in Mialet, the **Musée du Désert** (T04 66 85 02 72, museedudesert.com, Mar-Nov 0930-1200 and 1400-1800, Jul-Aug 0930-1900, €5) is dedicated to Protestantism and the War of the Camisards, and is full of insights into the lives and clandestine worship of the Huguenots in the Cévennes.

Just 2 km from here, the beautiful **Grotte de Trabuc** (T04 66 85 03 28, grottes-de-france.com/traacc, Apr-Jun and Sep 1030-1130 and 1430-1730, Jul-Aug 1015-1830, Mar and Oct 1430-1530, Feb and Nov Sun and school holidays 1430-1630, €8.40, €5.30 child 5-12) is filled with colourful crystals, subterranean rivers, lakes and waterfalls. Its nickname is the 'cave of the 100,000 soldiers' – not for any Camisards who hid here, but for the unique and mysterious formation of an army of stalagmites.

Another thing to do in Anduze is take the steam train, the **Train à vapeur des Cévennes** (T04 66 60 59 00, trainavapeur.com, Apr-Aug 3-4 trains daily, Sep Tue-Sun, Oct Tue-Thu and Sat-Sun, €13 return, €10 single, €8 child 4-12 return, €6.50 child single) which chugs and billows its way to St-Jean-du-Gard in 40 minutes, with a stop at **La Bambouseraie** (Générargues, T04 66 61 70 47, bambouseraie.com, Mar to mid-Nov 0930-1700, mid-Mar to mid-Sep 0930-1830, €7.50, €4.50 under 12s). This remarkable garden is famous for the bamboo and other exotic flora planted by a wealthy spice merchant in 1856 – an undertaking so ambitious, in fact, that it ruined him. The family of the current owners has lovingly tended the garden for decades.

At the end of the line is **St-Jean-du-Gard**, the centre of a web of walking paths. Its **Musée des Vallées Cévenoles** (95 Grand' Rue, T04 66 85 19 48, pagesperso-orange.fr/museedesvalleescevenoles, Nov-Mar Tue and Thu 0900-1200 and 1400-1800, Sun 1400-1800, Apr-Oct daily 1000-1230 and 1400-1900, Jul-Aug 1000-1900, €4.70, €3.70 student, under 12s free), in an 18th-century postal relay station, covers the artistic and cultural life in the Cévennes. It has exhibits and photos on the silk industry (*sériciculture*), chestnuts, and the life of the shepherd and muleteer, as well as old pewter, ceramics from Moustier, antique tiles, furniture and Huguenot jewels.

If you're intrigued by the silken side of the Cévennes, head southwest of Anduze to St-Hippolyte-du-Fort, where it's covered from raising cocoons to weaving at the **Musée de la Soie** (Place 8 Mai, T04 66 77 66 47, museedelasoie-cevennes.com, Apr-8 Nov Tue-Sun 1000-1230 and 1400-1800, Jul-Aug daily 1000-1230 and 1400-1800, €4.90, €2.90 young person/child 6-15). Silk-making, however, isn't all in the past: in Monoblet (15-minutes north) a company called Grefeuilhe has brought the old Cévenole silk industry back to life.

Further west, **Le Vigan** was a major silk producer. In its centre the 12th-century Vieux Pont gracefully spans the Hérault. **The Musée Cévenol** (1 rue des Calquières, T04 67 81 06 86, Apr-Oct Wed-Mon 1000-1200 and 1400-1800, Nov-Mar Wed only 1000-1200 and 1400-1800, €4.50, €2.30 under 18), in an 18th-century silk mill, has excellent displays on the area's trades – basketry, pottery, glass-making, boules and, of course, the silk industry and its influence on Coco Chanel, who had family ties to the area.

Tip...

Check the Train à vapeur's website (trainavapeur. com) for times to make sure you get the steam engine; sometimes in peak season it's replaced with a more mundane diesel locomotive.

La Petite Camargue

The Rhône ends in the Camargue, the biggest delta in Western Europe, offering a wild wide-open breath of fresh air along France's built-up Mediterranean shore. A third is covered with wetlands and salt lagoons while the rest is pasture, rice paddies and dunes – a rich biodiversity protected since 1970 as a Regional Park.

The Languedoc slice of the triangle is the Petite Camargue or Camargue Gardoise, formed by the Rhône's main distributary, the Petit Rhône. It has two major landmarks: the magnificent Romanesque church at St-Gilles and St Louis' fortified port town of Aigues-Mortes.

Salins du Midi.

L'Abbatiale de St-Gilles

In the medieval centre, for information contact the tourist office, T04 66 87 33 75.
Free entry but tours of the crypt, Vis and ruins €4, €2 child (under 18).

Aegidos, or Gilles (650-710), was a gentle Greek hermit who settled here and made friends with a doe, who supplied him with milk. The king wounded her during a hunt and tracked her, only to meet Gilles, who scolded him for his cruelty towards a defenceless animal. The king was so moved by his goodness that he founded a monastery to house the other holy men who came to be near Gilles.

After his death, Gilles' reputation grew with his miracles, and his tomb became a pilgrimage site. A splendid new church and monastery were begun in 1116. The Chemin de St-Gilles (La Régordane) linked the abbey to Le Puy-en-Vélay through the Cévennes, and it became a clearing house for pilgrims continuing to either Compostela, Rome or Jerusalem. In the 12th and 13th centuries, iit was so busy that 134 moneychangers worked here.

Things began to go wrong when the channel connecting St-Gilles to the sea silted up (hence St Louis' need to build a new port, Aigues-Mortes). In 1622, they went really wrong when Protestants turned the monastery into a fort. After 1650 the church was partially rebuilt, salvaging much of the sculpture around the **three portals**, which are the crown jewel of Romanesque art in Languedoc. Inspired by Roman triumphal arches and carved by the school of nearby Arles in Provence, the sculptures recount the life of Jesus and his Apostles, the Three Marys and Mary Magdalene.

The re-built interior holds little interest, but if you take the guided tour you can visit the ruins of the much grander medieval church, the 11th-century **crypt**, containing the tombs of St Gilles and the ill-fated papal legate Pierre de Castelnau, and the famous **Vis de St-Gilles** a spiral staircase built in 1142. When viewed from beneath, the steps of the Vis de St-Gilles are invisible – a tour de force studied by stone masons ever since.

La Maison Romane

Place de la République, T04 66 87 40 42.
Jul-Aug and national holidays 0900-1200 and 1500-1900. Free.

Tradition has it that this 12th-century house opposite the abbey was the family home of Guy Foulques, the troubadour and judge elected pope (Clement IV) in 1265. It contains a beautiful 14th-century polychrome statue of St Gilles, a painting of Pope Clement and information on the various pilgrimages that passed through here. There's the 'stone of the Apostles', a beautifully preserved fragment of four Apostles from the abbey's tympanum discovered in a nearby house in 1950, and a room devoted to the ornithology of the Camargue.

The icons of the Camargue

The Camargue hosts over 400 bird species over the course of the year, but the most visible is its great symbol, the **pink flamingo**. Massive flocks live off the delta's plankton, and make raised nests of mud in briny ponds.

The Camargue's little **horses** are a sturdy breed that date back to prehistoric times; born black or brown, they turn white by the time they are four. They are ridden by **gardians** (cowboys), who wear black hats, carry tridents and traditionally live in thatched *cabanes*.

The *gardians* herd the Camargue's **black bulls**, who live on *manades* (ranches). Like the horses, these bulls are an ancient breed adapted to the delta, smaller and faster than Spanish *toros* but weighing up to 450 kg all the same. They are raised for their meat – prized by gourmets – and for the *Courses Camarguaises* (see page 45). In late spring, the round-up and branding (*ferrade*) of year-old bulls is a festive occasion, when guests are invited to join in.

Around the region

Aigues-Mortes 'Dead Waters' was founded by
Louis IX in 1241, back when this sliver of coast was
Paris' only toehold on the Mediterranean. He built
a castle and port and sailed to the Crusades from
here in 1248 and in 1270 (on the last journey he
died of plague in Tunis).

Philippe III added the mighty walls and
Aigues-Mortes carried on as a bustling
Mediterranean port until the dead waters lived up
to their name, silting over and leaving it high and
dry. Tourism and an ancient standby, salt, keep the
wolf away from the door. The big beach resort of
Le Grau de Roi is 8 km away.

Tours et remparts

*Logis du Gouverneur d'Aigues-Mortes, T04 66 53
61 55, aigues-mortes.monuments-nationaux.fr.*
May-Aug 1000-1900, Sep-Apr 1000-1730. Ticket
office closes from 1300-1400 and 45 mins
before closing time. €7, €4.50 student/
concession, free for under 18s and EU citizens
under 26. Audio guide in English.

From certain angles, Aigues-Mortes' 1.5 km of walls
and towers resemble a mirage rising out of the
coastal plain. The tour takes in the mighty
gatehouse and the cylindrical **Tour de Constance**,
the last remnant of St Louis' castle.

With its 20-ft-thick walls, it was later used as a
prison for Templars and Protestants. There are also
good views over the town, laid out in a grid like
many new medieval towns (*bastides*) in France;
note how here the plan is slightly irregular, to keep
the wind from racing through the streets.

Salins du Midi

Rte du Grau du Roi, T04 66 73 40 02, salins.com.
75-min tours available Mar 1430, Apr-May 1000,
1100, 1430, 1600 and 1700, Jun 1000, 1430 and
1530, Jul-Aug 1000-1750 (tours leave throughout
the day), Sep-Oct 1030, 1100, 1430, 1500 and
1600. €8.20, €6 child (under 13), family
discounts available.

Aigues-Mortes.

These red-tinted salt pans, first developed by the
Romans, are said to be the oldest still operating in
the Mediterranean and cover an area slightly larger
than Paris, producing 450,000 tonnes a year. The
visit takes 1½ hours and includes a train tour, film,
the museum of salt and a boutique where you can
buy *fleur de sel de Camargue* (the top unrefined
crystals, prized by gourmets).

Tip...

One less than loveable creature of the Camargue is the mosquito. If you plan to explore, come slathered with repellent, and bring some spare, too.

Seaquarium

Av du Palais de la Mer, Le Grau du Roi, T04 66 51 57 57, seaquarium.fr.
Apr-Jun and Sep 1000-1930, Jul-Aug 0930-2330, Oct-Mar 1000-1830. €11.30, €8.30 young person/child (5-15), under 5s free. Last tickets sold 1 hr before closing.

This big aquarium features a coral reef, an undersea tunnel, a wide selection of Mediterranean creatures, sea lions and a new giant *requinarium* (shark tank).

Aigues-Mortes' 1.5 km of walls and towers resemble a mirage rising out of the coastal plain.

Sleeping

Nîmes

Jardins Secrets €€€€

3 rue Gaston Maruéjols, T04 66 84 82 64, jardinssecrets.net.
Map: Nîmes, p84.

A perfect choice for couples, this intimate boutique hotel is set in a luxuriant garden. The seven rooms and seven suites come with old-fashioned bathrooms, hand-painted wallpaper, chandeliers, antiques and curios with a painterly eye to detail. The Roman bath-style spa offers a wide choice of massages and treatments, and there's a pretty outdoor pool.

New Hôtel La Baume €€€€

21 rue Nationale, T04 66 76 28 42, new-hotel.com/labaume/fr.
Map: Nîmes, p84.

Just north of the Maison Carrée, this pale stone, 17th-century residence has a charming open courtyard and offers 34 modern rooms in warm oranges and yellows (some have listed ceilings) with air conditioning and minibars. Breakfast is served in an attractive vaulted room.

Hôtel Imperator €€€

Quai de la Fontaine, T04 66 21 90 30, hotel-imperator.com.
Map: Nîmes, p84.

This classic hotel, vintage 1929, has recently had a major facelift.

Its 62 plush rooms are either modern or nostalgically provincial, but all are cosy and equipped with minibars and satellite TV. There's private parking, an antique lift, a shady garden, the Hemingway bar (of course he was here!) and a gourmet restaurant.

Hôtel La Maison de Sophie €€€

31 av Carnot, T04 66 70 96 10, hotel-lamaisondesophie.com.
Map: Nîmes, p84.

A short walk from the train station, the five spacious rooms in this art-deco charmer offer a peaceful oasis in the bustling city. The painted ceilings, marble

The kitchen of Jardins Secrets.

floors, Corinthian columns and woodwork have been lovingly restored and the furnishings match the period as well. Old-fashioned roses scent the garden, and there's an octagonal outdoor pool.

Royal Hotel €€
3 bd Alphonse Daudet, T04 66 58 28 27, royalhotel-nimes.com. Map: Nîmes, p84.
'Royal' is a tad grand, but these 22 rooms in this cult boho hotel are full of character, with wooden floors, eclectic furnishings and plasma TVs. Ask for a room overlooking quiet Place d'Assas; on the other side, the hotel's excellent tapas restaurant tends to be a bit noisy late at night. Note that Parking Vinci by the Maison Carrée is the closest car park.

Acanthe du Temple €
1 rue Charles Babut, T04 66 67 54 61, hotel-temple.com. Map: Nîmes, p84.
Centrally located and within easy walking distance of the sights, this family-run hotel named after the acanthus leaves on the capitals of the Maison Carrée has been a favourite of budget-minded visitors since 1960. Rooms can be a little small and fairly basic, but are very clean and tidy. There's free Wi-Fi and parking for €10 a day.

Hôtel Central €
2 place du Château, T04 66 67 27 75, hotel-central.org. Map: Nîmes, p84.

In the heart of the old city, the Central is a handsome two-star hotel in a late 18th-century building, with 15 basic blue and white en suites equipped with fans. Room 20 has the best view over the tile roofs.

Self-catering
Mas de Gasc
Ste Anastasie, T04 66 81 07 54, masdegasc.com. Map: Nîmes, p84.
Twelve kilometres from Nîmes towards Uzès, this utterly tranquil 18th-century Langodocien farmhouse set amid the pines sleeps four and offers a pool and Wi-Fi. High-season rentals are €790 per week.

Résidalys Le Cheval Blanc
1 place des Arènes, T04 66 76 05 22, odalys-vacation-rental.com/ vacation-rental-Nimes.html. Map: Nîmes, p84.
Next to the Arènes, this 18th-century textile factory has been converted into 32 airy modern apartments with beamed ceilings, air conditioning, TV, kitchenette and internet; larger ones, with mezzanine bedrooms, sleep up to six. Try to get a front room. Studios start at €95.

East of Nîmes

Les Maisons de Baumanière (Le Prieuré) €€€€
7 place du Chapitre, Villeneuve-lès-Avignon, T04 90 15 90 15, leprieure.com.

Sleep like a cardinal in this luxurious 14th-century palace built by the nephew of Pope John XXII. Converted into a monastery, and then a hotel in 1943, its 26 rooms have recently been re-done in sleek white, black and browns, combining antiques with state-of-the-art facilities. Wisteria perfumes the lovely garden and there's a pool, two tennis courts and a superb restaurant.

Maison Felisa €€€
6 rue des Barris, St-Laurent-des-Arbres, T04 66 39 99 84, maison-felisa.com.
Swiss owners Isa and Philippe run this chic guesthouse north of Villeneuve-lès-Avignon with the motto "make sense of your senses". Even the sheets in the five rooms are washed with flower-scented water. Along with designer rooms they offer yoga, wellness treatments and *table d'hôte* featuring Indian, Provençale, and Thai cuisine.

Les Jardins de la Livrée €€
4 bis Champ de Bataille, Villeneuve-lès-Avignon, T04 90 26 05 05, la-livree.oxatis.com.
Set in the medieval garden walls of a cardinal's palace, the four en suite rooms in this B&B are simple but comfortable and have extremely simpatico owners. There's a pretty pool, and in fine weather breakfast is served on the terrace. Prices go up during the Avignon Festival.

Listings

Comptoir de St Hilaire €€€€

Mas de la Rouquette, St-Hilaire-de-Brethmas, T04 66 30 82 65, comptoir-saint-hilaire.com.
Located near Alès, between Uzès and the Cévennes, this is perhaps the most romantic hideaway in all Languedoc. It's an 18th-century *mas*, where each of the three rooms and three suites is more enchanting than the next. There's a pool and tennis courts, all surrounded by 50 ha of woodland.

Hôtel du Général d'Entraigues €€€

Place de l'Evêché, Uzès, T04 66 22 32 68, hoteldentraigues.com.
This cosy 36-room hotel occupies a 15th- to 17th-century townhouse and offers a wide choice of rooms, suites and apartments in different styles and at different prices (including a few under €100), all with air conditioning. There's a panoramic walled terrace with a pool and garage and a fine restaurant, Les Jardins du Castille.

La Bégude Saint-Pierre €€€

Vers-Pont-du-Gard, T04 66 63 63 63, hotel-saintpierre.fr.
This hotel is an oasis in a 17th-century stone building near the Pont du Gard (a short walk away, or they'll loan you a bike). The 20 south-facing rooms come in sun-drenched Provençal colours, with oak beams and private terraces. There's also a charming restaurant.

Hôtel du Général d'Entraigues, Uzès.

Bize de la Tour €€

*2 place du Portail, Remoulins,
T04 66 22 39 33, bizedelatour.com.*
Just 3 km from the Pont du Gard,
this romantic B&B in a handsome
stone *maison de maître* has four
gorgeous bedrooms decorated
with antiques and rich colours.
The cosy public rooms with
fireplaces are perfect for relaxing
after a hard day's touring. The
price includes a filling gourmand
breakfast.

Demeure Monte Arena €€

*6 place de la Plaine, Montaren-
et-St-Médiers, Uzès, T04 66 03 12
49, monte-arena.com.*
Four kilometres from Uzès, this
chambre d'hôte set in a walled
garden is superb in every detail,
from the hosts who make you
feel at home straightaway to the
organic breakfasts and delicious
dinners on offer. Antiques and
contemporary pieces furnish
the rooms, each of which even
have their own specially
designed scent. No credit cards.

Hostellerie Provençale €€

*1-3 rue de la Grande Bourgade,
Uzès, T04 66 22 11 06,
hostellerieprovencale.com.*
Central and charming little
hotel in a 300-year-old
building, it has nine rooms,
some with exposed beams,
stone walls and queen-sized
beds. There is air conditioning,
luxurious bathrooms, flat-
screen TVs and Wi-Fi. Check
their website for details of
romantic or truffle weekends.

Hôtel Château du Rey €€

*Pont d'Hérault (near Le Vigan, on
the Ganges road), T04 67 82 40 06,
chateau-du-rey.com.* Apr-Sep.
This picturesque 13th-century
castle with two round towers
(restored by Viollet-le-Duc in
1848) is set in a large leafy park
with a pool. There are 12
contemporary-styled bedrooms
in soft colours, and a popular
restaurant, L'Abeuradou, with
tables on the romantic terrace or
in a 700-year old *bergerie*.

Hôtel Mas de la Prairie €

*Av du Sergent Triaire, Le Vigan, T04
67 81 80 80, masdelaprairie.com.*
Le Vigan is along one of the main
roads in the Cévennes and
northern Hérault, and this 25-room
hotel and restaurant with a covered
pool is fine for a night or two.

Villa Mazarin €€€

*35 bd Gambetta, Aigues-Mortes,
T04 66 73 90 48, villa-mazarin.
camargue.fr.*
Within the walls of Aigues-
Mortes, this romantic retreat
occupies a 15th-century villa that
once hosted kings. The 20
air-conditioned rooms are all
different, with high ceilings,
classic furnishings and big beds
and bathrooms. Be warned
though, you may find it hard
to pull yourself away from the
lovely pool, jacuzzi and sauna
to actually go out and see the
sights. Underground parking
€10 a night.

Hôtel du Canal €€

*440 rte de Nîmes, Aigues-Mortes,
T04 66 80 50 04, hotel-canal-
aigues-mortes.com.*
A popular choice for its warm
hospitality, this contemporary
boutique hotel (restructured from a
1950s building) sits on a duck-filled
canal, a five-minute walk from the
walled city. The rooms, equipped
with air conditioning, Wi-Fi and
flat-screen TVs, are functional but
stylish and soundproofed. There's
a pool and a pretty terrace, free
parking and an excellent breakfast.

Hôtel des Croisades €

*2 rue du Port, Aigues-Mortes,
T04 66 53 67 85, lescroisades.fr.*
It looks like a big house, but this
friendly, family-oriented hotel
(some of the rooms on the
ground floor sleep up to five)
offers the best value in Aigues-
Mortes. Some rooms face the port
towards the Tour de Constance,
whilst others overlook the garden,
where a buffet breakfast is served
in summer. Rooms come with air
conditioning and Wi-Fi.

Hôtel Le Cours €

*10 av François Griffeuille,
St-Gilles-du-Gard, T04 66 87 31
93, hotel-le-cours.com.*
A short stroll down from the
famous abbey, overlooking the
plane trees, this 32-room Logis
de France hotel is equipped with
air conditioning and Wi-Fi and
makes a good stopover. The
soirée étape at €61 per person for
dinner, bed and breakfast is a
good deal.

Eating & drinking

Nîmes

Le Darling €€€€
40 rue de la Madeleine, T04 66 67 04 99, ledarling.com.
Thu-Sat and Tue for dinner, Sun for lunch and dinner.
Map: Nîmes, p84.
Le Darling is fashionable, relaxed and refined, and scented with the delicious aromas wafting from the kitchen. Chef Vincent Croizard hails from New Caledonia, and does magical things with spices and colours, such as the lightly seared Bouzigues oysters, with cardamom and spinach in lemon grass oil. The menu changes with the seasons. Reservations recommended.

Le Lisita €€€€
2 bd des Arènes, T04 66 67 29 15, lelisita.com.
Tue-Sat for lunch and dinner.
Map: Nîmes, p84.
This luminous, contemporary restaurant is in an 18th-century stone building by the amphitheatre, where chef Olivier Douet lets top ingredients (foie gras, scallops, monkfish, veal sweetbreads, lamb) shine with a minimum of fuss. Sommelier Stéphane Debaille presides over an exceptionally rich cellar; you can even finish with a fancy cigar. Lunch menus start at €24.

Aux Plaisirs des Halles €€€
4 rue Littré, T04 66 36 01 02, auxplaisirsdeshalles.com.
Tue-Sat for lunch and dinner.
Map: Nîmes, p84.
Near the market, this contemporary bistro with a pretty patio serves inspired takes on the sunny cuisine of the south (seafood *a la plancha*, magret with taboulé and summer fruits, etc), beautiful desserts and home-baked bread. There's an excellent €21.50 *menu du jour*.

Ever In €€
1 place Séverine, av Jean Jaurès, T04 66 76 21 81, ever-in.fr.
Mon-Sat 0700-0100 (meals served 1130-1430 and 1930-2230).
Map: Nîmes, p84.
See and be seen in this trendy restaurant cocktail lounge/café/ tapas bar. The menu is limited but offers simple fresh cuisine, with a good selection of salads. Alternatively, just come to try one of the 33 cocktails.

Le Bouchon et l'Assiette €€
5 bis rue de Sauve, T04 66 62 02 93, resto-restaurant-gastronomique-nimes-gard. bouchon-assiette.fr.
Thu-Mon for lunch and dinner.
Map: Nîmes, p84.
Seasonal creative cuisine is the mainstay at this charming little restaurant near the Jardins de la Fontaine. The menu changes every two months and offers delights such as sea bream fillet and fennel confit in a sea urchin emulsion. Weekday lunch menu €17.

L'Ancien Théâtre €
4 rue Racine, T04 66 21 30 75.
Tue-Fri for lunch and dinner, Sat for dinner.
Map: Nîmes, p84.
Near the Maison Carrée, this little restaurant is perfect for a tête-à-tête while savouring the chef's excellent *brandade* (Nîmes' classic salt cod and potato purée). Affordable, well-prepared seafood features on a menu that changes every two months.

Wine Bar Le Cheval Blanc €
1 place des Arènes, T04 66 76 19 59, winebar-lechevalblanc.com.
Sun-Thu for lunch and 1900-2300, Fri-Sat for lunch and 1900-2400.
Map: Nîmes, p84.
The original 'White Horse' has been reborn as a cosy bar/ restaurant under the old stone vaults, with prestigious bottles crammed up to the ceiling. The wines are matched with tasty seafood and succulent *boeuf d'Aubrac* steaks.

Cafés & bars

Bar des Beaux Arts
17 place aux Herbes, T04 66 67 97 97.
Mon-Sat 0700-2000.
Map: Nîmes, p84.
A lovely place to sit and watch the world go by in one of Nîmes' prettiest squares.

Ciel de Nîmes
Place de la Maison Carrée, 3rd floor, T04 66 36 71 70.
Tue-Sun 1000-1800.
Map: Nîmes, p84.

Place de la République, Beaucaire.

Five of the best

Squares for an apéritif

❶ **Place aux Herbes**, Uzès

❷ **Place de la République**, Beaucaire

❸ **Place des Arènes**, Nîmes

❹ **Place des Docteurs Dax**, Sommières

❺ **Place du Marché**, Nîmes

On the top of the Carré d'Art, a peaceful haven for a pick-me-up and perhaps a gooey *fondant au chocolat*.

La Grande Bourse

2 bd des Arènes, T04 66 67 68 69, la-grande-bourse.com.
Open 0630-0100.
Map: Nîmes, p84.
With sidewalk tables offering strategic views of the Arènes, this traditional bar/brasserie is always busy. They also do brunch and food until late.

Pâtisserie Courtois

8 place du Marché, T04 66 67 20 09.
Open 0800-1900.
Map: Nîmes, p84.
Nîmes' oldest pastry shop (1882) and a wonderful place for a coffee, tea or cake.

East of Nîmes

L'Ail Heure €€€

43 rue Château, Beaucaire, T04 66 59 67 75.
Mon-Fri for lunch and dinner, Sat for dinner.
The most creative food in Beaucaire is prepared by Luc Andreu, who has worked in some of France's top restaurants. The menu constantly changes, but expect the unexpected – *cappuccino de caviare de champignons, pressé de foie gras* or *figues confites et caramel de Muscat* – served in a dining room with the patina of old France. Lunch menu €17.

La Guinguette du Vieux Moulin €€

5 rue du Vieux-Moulin, Villeneuve-lès-Avignon, T04 90 94 50 72, guinguettevieuxmoulin. com.
Mar-Oct Tue-Sun for lunch, Mon-Sat for dinner, Oct-Easter Tue-Sun for lunch, Fri-Sat for dinner.

This retro restaurant on the Rhône merrily evokes the 19th-century *guinguettes* in Renoir paintings. The food is uncomplicated but delicious, and there are frequent jazz and chanson soirées. From mid-June to August they do spit roast meats with music and dancers (€29), and a €25 *sardinade* for Sunday lunch – a buffet of starters, barbecued sardines, desserts and wines. Reservations essential.

La Table de Marguerite €€

Mas de la Cassole, rte de Fourques, Beaucaire, T04 66 59 17 00, latabledemarguerite.fr.
Feb-Dec Wed-Thu and Sun for lunch, Fri-Sat for lunch and 1730-2100.
Come here for country dining and generous servings of grandma Marguerite's Mediterranean recipes, made with fresh-picked ingredients. Friday's menu features *bouillabaisse* and other seafood. Good list of local, affordable wines. It's wise to book.

Nîmes to Bagnols-sur-Cèze

La Parenthèse €€€
1-3 rue de la Grande Bourgade,
Uzès, T04 66 22 11 06,
hostellerieprovencale.com.
Wed-Sun for lunch and dinner.
Fresh seasonal ingredients
(scallops roasted with sesame,
ravioli filled with sweetbreads
and morel mushrooms) are the
focus at this welcoming art-filled
hotel/restaurant. In January and
February plump for the truffles.
€34 menu.

La Taverne €€
9 rue Xavier Sigalon, Uzès, T04 66
22 13 10, lataverne-uzes.com.
Mon-Sun for lunch and dinner.
In the leafy courtyard in the town
centre, or in the cosy old-
fashioned dining room, this
restaurant serves southwest
French favourites – *brandade de*
Nîmes and scrambled eggs with
truffles, cassoulet and foie gras.

Gard truffles.

MilleZime €
6 bd Gambetta, Uzès, T04 66 22
27 82, restaurant-millezime.fr.
Sep-Jun Tue-Sat for lunch and
dinner, Sun for lunch, Jul-Aug
daily for lunch and dinner.
A romantic wine bar/restaurant
under stone vaults in the centre
that offers an array of tasty salads
and market-based cuisine. The
menu changes weekly and
there's a good list of Côtes
du Rhône.

La Petite Camargue

Le S €€€
38 rue de la République,
Aigues-Mortes, T04 66 53 74 60,
le-s.fr.
Tue, Wed and Fri-Sun for lunch
and dinner, Thu for dinner.
This little restaurant decorated
in chocolate and vanilla tones
serves up arty dishes filled with
the scents of herbs and spices –
you won't go wrong following
the advice of the friendly
waitress. The menu changes
every three months. Good
wine cellar.

Le Pont d'Artois €€
253 av du Pont de Provence,
T04 66 77 64 60.
Jul-Aug daily for lunch and
dinner, Sep-Jun Tue-Sun for
lunch and dinner.
A new restaurant on the canal
that's earned a big thumbs up
from the locals for its pretty
decor, relaxed atmosphere
and market cuisine.

Entertainment

Nîmes

Classical music & opera
Théâtre de Nîmes
1 place de la Calade, T04 66 36 65
10, theatredenimes.com.
The city's main venue for opera,
classical concerts and plays. In
January it livens things up with
a Festival de Flamenco.

Clubs
Lulu Club
10 Impasse de la Curaterie,
lulu-club.com.
Fri, Sat and nights before
national holidays from 2400.
Gay/straight disco with DJs and a
fun-loving crowd.

The Pelican
54 rte de Beaucaire, T04 66 29 63
28, thepelican.fr.
Tue-Sun 1800-0200.
Former warehouse decorated
in a Louisiana theme, this bar/
restaurant serves a huge
selection of beers and cocktails
with a great mix of music (jazz,
Cajun, soul, blues, Memphis,
Motown); live performances on
Thursday and Friday.

La Petite Camargue

Clubs
La Churascaïa
Mas Ste Anne, Montcalm,
Vauvert, T06 20 32 32 35.
Easter-Oct.
Massive gay-friendly summer
club (capacity 5000) going

strong since the 1960s, midway between Aigues-Mortes and Nîmes.

Le Riviera
856 rue Ampère, in the industrial zone of Vauvert, T04 66 80 49 79.
Tue-Sun 1800-0200.
Year-round club near, and similar to, La Churascaiä. Thursday and Friday.

Best picnic spots

Les Halles in Nîmes (see Shopping, opposite) or the delightful Saturday market in Uzès are the best places to shop for *tapenade*, *pélardons*, crusty bread and other goodies before heading out to the banks of Gardon at the base of the Pont du Gard (see page 100). You can picnic on the grass outside the mighty walls of Aigues-Mortes (see page 106), or find a shady spot (and go for a swim in the river Cèze) at Frigoulet, off the D901, near St-André-de-Roquepertuis.

Oliviers & Company.

Shopping

Nîmes

Clothing
Les Indiennes de Nîmes
2 bd des Arènes, T04 66 36 19 75.
Mon 1400-1900, Tue-Sat 1000-1230 and 1400-1900.
Authentic shepherd's capes, waistcoats, Camargue *gardian* vests, as well as items for the home in traditional wood-block prints (*indiennes*).

Crafts
Boutique Provençale
10 place de la Maison Carrée, T04 66 67 81 71.
Mon 1400-1900, Tue-Sat 1000-1230 and 1400-1900.
Opposite the Maison Carrée, this boutique specializes in *santons* and other traditional souvenirs from neighbouring Provence.

Food & drink
Les Caves du 41
191 chemin Mas de Cheylon, T04 66 36 20 36, caves-41.com.

Mon 1400-1900, Tue-Sat 1000-1230 and 1400-1900.
You'll need a car to get here – it's to the southwest of the centre off the N113 but Les Caves du 41 is a great place to stock up on wine, spirits and gourmet treats from across France.

Les Halles
5 rue des Halles, T04 66 21 52 49.
Daily 0700-1330.
Nîmes' covered market is chock-full of delights from the *garrigue* and the sea.

Maison Villaret
13 rue Madeleine, T04 66 67 41 79.
Mon-Sat 0700-1930.
Bakery founded in 1775 by Claude Villaret, inventor of the *croquants Villaret* – 'teeth-breaking' almond, lemon and orange blossom biscuits. They also offer marzipan and other sugary delights.

Oliviers & Company
3 rue des Broquiers, T06 11 46 48 14.
Mon 1400-1900, Tue-Sat 1000-1230 and 1400-1900.
Olive oils, *tapenades* and other olive-based products and cosmetics.

Interior design
Galerie Béa
4 place d'Assas, T04 66 21 19 34.
Mon 1400-1900, Tue-Sat 0930-1200 and 1400-1900.
A fun, eclectic mix of furniture and household items from around the world.

Listings

Ceramics
Galerie Terra Viva
14 rue de la Fontaine, St-Quentin-la-Poterie, T04 66 22 48 78, terraviva.fr.
Daily 1000-1900.
Exhibition area and boutique featuring delightful contemporary ceramics.

Poterie de l'Olivier
831 rte d'Anduze, Massillargues Atuech, T04 66 61 95 82, poterie-olivier.com.
Sep-Jun Wed-Mon 1000-1200 and 1400-1900, Jul-Aug daily.
For four centuries, Anduze has been renowned for its large Medici-inspired garden pots, and this is one of several manufacturers around town. Also sells antiques.

Clothing
Eyos
Monoblet, T04 66 77 93 61, eyos.fr.
Grefeuilhe's factory outlet-boutique near St-Hippolyte sells underwear for women and men, hand-painted scarves, etc, all made from Cévenole silk.

Food & wine
La Maison de la Truffe
27 place aux Herbes, Uzès, T04 66 63 86 45, lamaisondelatruffe. com.
Fresh truffles in season, oils and vinegars and other truffle-based products, as well as essentials such as truffle shavers.

Marché d'Uzès
Place aux Herbes and around.
Superb market held every Wednesday morning and all day Saturday.

Terroir Cévennes
Rte de Nîmes, St-Jean-du-Gard, T04 66 85 15 26.
Tue-Sun 0930-1300 and 1430-1900.
Chestnuts in all their forms, honey, organic produce, *pélardons* and other goodies.

Housewares
Design by C
21 rue Docteur Blanchard, Uzès, T06 82 68 54 10, celialindsell.com.
Tue-Sat 1000-1300 and 1500-1900.
Colourful things for the home, designed by Celia Lindsell.

Jewellery
Bénédikt Aïchelé
2 rue de la Calade, Uzès, T04 66 22 79 22, lebijou.net.
Tue-Sat 1000-1300 and 1500-1900.
Languedoc's award-winning jeweller makes rings like no one else.

Activities & tours

Golf
Golf De Nîmes Campagne
Rte de St-Gilles (7 km from Nîmes), T04 66 70 17 37, golfnimescampagne.fr.st.
Eighteen-hole par 72 tournament course, rated one of the most beautiful in France, plus a nine-hole pitch and putt.

Golf de Nîmes Vacquerolles
1075 Chemin du Golf, T04 66 23 33 33, opengolfclub.com/ vacquerolles.
Ten minutes from Nîmes in the *garrigue*, an 18-hole course and a nine-hole pitch and putt.

Water sports
Parc Aquatropic
39 Chemin de l'Hostellerie Ville Active, T04 66 38 31 00, vert-marine.com.
Jul-Aug Mon-Fri 1200-2000, Sat-Sun 1000-1900, Sep-Jun Mon, Wed and Fri 1000-2000, Tue and Thu 1000-1400 and 1600-2000, Sat-Sun 1100-1815.
€5.25 (€7.50 in summer), €1.41 child (under 8).
Southwest of Nîmes on the D6086 (take Bus D). A complex of outdoor heated pools, sauna, jacuzzi, rapids and lagoons.

Boat cruises
Arolles Marine
Port de Plaisance, Bellegarde (just south of Beaucaire), T04 66 01 75 15, camargue-fluvial.com.
Weekend to two-week cruises to Aigues-Mortes or down the Canal du Rhône à Sète to the Canal du Midi.

Children
Parc Historique de Beaucaire
1 rue des Anciens Combattants, Beaucaire, T04 66 20 27 76, parc-beaucaire.fr.
Mar-Sep 1000-1800. €9, €7 child (under 18), under 6s free.
Come here to see how the ancient Romans and medieval knights made their weapons and armour in various workshops and demonstrations, then watch gladiators, hoplites and knights use them in fights.

Nîmes to Bagnols-sur-Cèze

Canoeing/kayaking
Canoe Tourbillon
Chemin du Gardon, T04 66 22 85 54, location-canoe-kayak-gard-collias.canoe-kayak-gard-gorgedugardon.com.
Half- or full-day descents to the Pont du Gard.

Kayak Vert
Berges du Gardon, Collias, T04 66 22 80 76, canoe-france.com.
Kayak or canoe (up to four places) down to the Pont du Gard. Journeys range from two hours to two days.

Cooking classes
Miam-Miam
Aulas, Le Vigan, T04 67 81 75 74, stage-cuisine.com.
Learn to cook with 40 or even 80 spices and herbs, in a pretty country house. There are various classes on offer: Saturdays from 1400-2200, or from Thursday evening to Sunday afternoon for €480, including meals and accommodation.

Golf
Golf Club d'Uzès
Pont des Charettes, Mas de la Place, Uzès, T04 66 22 40 03, golfuzes.fr.
Flat, nine-hole par 36 course amid cypresses and pines.

Hot-air balloons
Les Mongolfières du Sud
64 rue Sigalon, Uzès, T04 66 37 28 02, sudmontgolfiere.com.
Float high over Uzès and the Pont du Gard.

Water sports
La Bouscarasse
Rte d'Alès, Uzès, T04 66 22 50 25, bouscarasse.fr.
Relaxing series of pools in a forest – their motto is "no slides, no waves". Bring a picnic.

La Petite Carmague

Horse riding
Abrivado Ranch
Rte de l'Espiguette, Le Grau du Roi, T04 66 53 01 00, abrivado-ranch.camargue.fr.
Ride white horses over the dunes and beaches of Espigette in the Petite Camargue.

Nature tours
La Maison du Guide
Montcalm (east of Aigues-Mortes), T04 66 73 52 30, maisonduguide.camargue.fr.
Nature tours, birdwatching treks, or a day riding and roping with the *gardians*. They also do Camargue weekends.

Safari Camargue: Le Gitan
Le Grau du Roi, T04 66 53 04 99, manade-safari.com.
Jeep safari tours in the Petite Camargue operated by authentic *manadiers*, as well as tours of the *manade* (cattle ranch).

Walking
Walking in Languedoc
T+44(870)-020 9900 (UK), T+1646-797 2887 (USA), walking-languedoc.com.
Walking holidays of all kinds in the Petite Camargue and elsewhere with French-based experts.

Canoeing by the Pont du Gard.

Contents

Lozère

Gorges du Tarn.

Introduction

A fter the olive groves and vineyards of Mediterranean Languedoc, the Lozère (or Le Gévaudan, as it was named under the *ancien régime*) offers a change of pace. Known as the 'Scotland of France' for its natural beauty, the Lozère is also the highest *département* in the country (with an average altitude of over 1000 m) as well as the least densely populated, counting only 15 Lozèriens per square kilometre. Museums and historic buildings are thin on the ground, but the Lozère's wide open spaces – austere, evocative and timeless – are perfect for rambling far from the madding crowds, an art pioneered here by Robert Louis Stevenson and his donkey. Historically it's a land of shepherds, where the long-distance trails follow ancient transhumance and medieval pilgrimage routes.

Mende is the capital and much of the land to the south belongs to the National Park of the Cévennes, the southern range of the Massif Central that the Lozère shares with the Gard, covered in gorse, heather and chestnut groves. To the west, the granite gives way before the massive limestone plateaux of the Grands Causses, sculpted by water over the eons to form dramatic subterranean wonders and one of Languedoc's star attractions: the spectacular Gorges du Tarn.

Early morning in the Lozère.

What to see in...

...one day
Start at La Malène, pack a picnic and paddle a canoe or kayak down the Gorges du Tarn. Spend a lazy afternoon in Mende or, if you have kids, an active one in Le Vallon du Villaret.

...a weekend or more
After the Gorges du Tarn, visit the Viaduc de Millau and the underground wonders along the Gorges de la Jonte. Visit the Cévennes and the belvedere of Mont Aigoual, and take one of the many stunning walks from Le Pont-de-Montvert. Alternatively, hire a donkey and follow Stevenson's 12-day walk through the Cévennes.

Mende & around

Lozère's capital, smack in the centre of the *département*, is not that well known, even in France, but its 12,000 inhabitants don't seem too bothered. Mende has a pretty 14th-century bridge spanning the River Lot called the Pont de Notre Dame and a cathedral big enough for a city with 10 times its population, surrounded by a medieval core with schist-roofed townhouses, fountains and little squares. That's about it, but it seems like big-time civilization in these parts.

Basilique-Cathédrale Notre-Dame-et-St-Privat.

Basilique-Cathédrale Notre-Dame-et-St-Privat

Place Urbain V.

Producing a pope was as good as winning the lottery in the Middle Ages, and the Lozère managed it with Urban V, one of the French popes in Avignon and the only one to be beatified. His statue stands in front of this gold-stoned cathedral, begun on his initiative (and funds) shortly before his death in 1370. What stands here today, though, is a near-complete rebuilding after the Wars of Religion. The taller of its strikingly asymmetrical towers originally contained a monster 25-tonne bell cast in 1517, named 'La Non Pareille'. At the time it was the biggest in Europe – until 1580 when it was melted down by the Protestants to make cannons. You can get an idea of its size from the 480-kg clapper kept just inside the porch.

In spite of its vicissitudes, the cathedral has some surprising treasures: eight 18th-century Aubusson tapestries on the *Life of the Virgin*, even if they are hung a bit too high to be seen clearly; beautiful 17th-century carved choir stalls; a 12th-century black Virgin, brought over from the Middle East by the Crusaders; and an organ in a lavish 17th-century case, saved from the destructive fury of the local sans-culottes when the organist began playing the *Marseillaise*.

Le Vallon du Villaret

Bagnols-les-Bains, T04 66 47 63 76, levillaret.fr. French school Easter holidays-Aug daily 1000-1845, Sep-Oct Sat-Sun 1100-1800, open daily during last week of Oct-1st week of Nov. Jul-Aug €10.50, after 1300 €11, Sep-Jun €9, after 1300 €9.50. Free for children under 1 m tall.

This adventure park in the Lozère's spa town, a 20-minute drive east of Mende and on the edge of the Parc National des Cévennes, was set up in 1993 as an artsy riposte to Euro Disney. It's in a valley near the restored medieval tower of the Villarets, the cradle of two Grand Masters of the Knights Hospitaliers: Guillaume and Foulques de Villaret,

Essentials

⊖ **Bus station** Place de la Gare, just northeast of Mende; local TUM bus No 1 provides a link with the town centre. For regional bus travel, see page 275.

🚋 **Train staion** Place de la Gare, just northeast of Mende. For regional train travel, see page 274.

💲 **ATM** BNP Paribas, 10 boulevard Soubeyran; Caisse d'Epargne, 1 place Chaptal.

⊕ **Hospital** Centre Hospitalier de Mende, avenue du 8 Mai, T04 66 49 49 49, ch-mende.fr.

⊕ **Pharmacy** Boutet, 7 rue des Clapiers, T04 66 49 19 43; Laune, 7 place du Blé, T04 66 49 11 07.

➲ **Post office** 6 boulevard du Soubeyran, T04 66 49 44 99.

❶ **Tourist information office** 14 boulevard Henri-Bourillon, T04 66 65 60 00, lozere-tourisme.com. Monday-Friday 0830-1200 and 1330-1730, Saturday 0830-1200 and 1330-1630.

Above: Mende's murals.

the latter famous for conquering Rhodes in 1309. Set among the trees you'll discover art installations designed by Keith Haring, Andy Goldsworthy and a hundred other artists, all designed for playing in, around and with. There are changing exhibitions and concerts. Allow at least three hours and come in the morning to avoid the crowds.

Parc des Loups du Gévaudan

St-Léger-de-Peyre, T04 66 32 09 22,
loupsdugevaudan.com.
Feb-Mar, Nov-Dec Mon-Fri 1000-1700, Apr-Jun,
Sep-Oct Mon-Fri 1000-1800, Jul-Aug Mon-Fri
1000-1900. Mid-Mar to Apr and mid-Nov to
mid-Dec Sat-Sun, but best to ring ahead. €7,
€3.50 child (3-11).

North of Marvejols, the Parc des Loups was set up
in 1985 by Gérard Ménatory to prove that wolves
are not so bad after all. Five species – from Poland,
Mongolia, Canada, Siberia and the Arctic – roam at
semi-liberty here; the original French wolves were
all killed in the early 20th century. Ménatory is an
author of several books about wolves and a firm
believer that the Bête de Gévaudan (see box,
below) was a serial-killing human psychopath.

Cirque de St Marcellin.

La Bête du Gévaudan

West of Mende, **Marvejols** is a peaceful country
town, but a bronze statue of a wolf-like monster on
the N9 is a reminder that between 1764 and 1767
the town and surrounding countryside were in the
grips of an ungodly terror, wrought by the blood-
chilling Beast of Gévaudan. By the time the Beast
had finished, 68 children, 25 women and six men
were dead. No one who ever saw it survived and its
savagery was such that people suspected it might
be the devil himself. The Bishop of Mende ordered
prayers in every church in the Lozère to deliver his
people from the monster, and the King of France sent
his dragoons and the best marksmen in France to
hunt and dispatch what many people believed must
be a wolf (although, unlike any other wolf in history
it only killed people, not sheep). The head of the
royal hunt, Antoine de Beaterne, bagged a huge wolf
and received an enormous reward of 10,000 *livres*
in Versailles, but the Beast of Gévaudan kept up its
murderous rampage around Marvejols. It continued
until 17 June 1767, when another hunter, Jean Chastel,
killed a wolf using specially blessed bullets. Then the
carnage stopped.

This is a story that resonates in the collective
unconscious and still gives the French frissons;
it inspired the 2001 film *Le Pacte des Loups*
(Brotherhood of the Wolf).

Five of the best

Day walks

❶ **Cirque de St Marcellin** Spectacular views and cliffs along the Gorges du Tarn; five hours, park 3.5 km north of Le Rozier. Relatively easy.

❷ **Pont du Tarn** A beautiful and varied walk in the Cévennes, partly along a 500-year-old canal (Béal); six hours, park in Le Pont-de-Montvert.

❸ **Esquina d'Ase Belvedere** Overlooking the Gorges du Tarn; 6½ hours, park near Le Ménial.

❹ **Les Corniches de Méjean** Sublime scenery over the Gorges du Tarn and de la Jonte; seven hours, park in Le Rozier. Only for the fit.

❺ **Cham des Bondons Menhirs** On Mont Lozère; six hours, leave from the car park on C35 above Le Pont-de-Montvert.

Parc National des Cévennes

The Gauls called these rugged granite and schist mountains the Cebenna, a name the conquering Caesar softened into the Cevenna, or Cévennes. Its lush valleys, laughing streams, rugged stone hamlets and farms are linked by age-old stone paths (*drailles*), and its 1200 species of flora and 350 species of fauna are protected in a 91,000-ha national park (80% in the Lozère; for the Gard section, see page 102). In 1985, UNESCO included the park in its list of biospheres. The enormous chestnut forests or 'bread trees' have provided basic food and fuel for centuries.

Parc National des Cévennes.

The Tarn is the main river in the Cévennes. Just down from Florac, the national park headquarters, it begins the most exciting stretch of its journey, carving its way through the Grands Causses to form the Gorges du Tarn, with its principal tributary, the Jonte, carving a similar cleft in the rock just to the south. Both meet near one of the greatest works yet built in the 21st century, the Viaduc de Millau.

Historically, the Cévennes are synonymous with the brutal War of the Camisards, round two in France's Wars of Religion. Many Protestants still live in the area, and here and there you'll also see mulberries, survivors of the once robust and mainly Protestant-run silk industry that supplied the stocking-makers in Nîmes. The industry is enjoying the beginning of a renaissance in the southern Cévennes, but silkworms aren't the only creatures to return: capercaillies, beavers and Griffon vultures have all been reintroduced.

Château de Florac & Centre d'Information du Parc National des Cévennes

6 bis place du Palais, Florac, T04 66 49 53 01, cevennes-parcnational.fr.
Oct-Easter Mon-Fri 0930-1230 and 1330-1730, Easter-Jun, Sep Mon-Fri 0930-1830, Jul-Aug daily 0930-1830. Château exhibit €3.50.

The attractive village of Florac is one of the Lozère's main tourist crossroads. It's located near the Gorges du Tarn and is a great base for visiting the national park; the central information office is based in its restored 17th-century château. Don't miss the unusual interactive introduction to the Cévennes, *Passagers du Parc* (with English commentary).

Tip...

Autumn is a beautiful time to visit the Cévennes, when the luminous valleys of chestnut, beech and oak forests change colour, the heather blooms and wild mushrooms are there for the taking (although note that you're 'limited' to 5 kg per day).

The highpoint (literally) in the Cévennes is the austere granite landmark of **Mont Lozère**, covered in snow in winter and often wrapped in fog and mist at other times; broom covers it in spring, and heather in autumn. Once the border between the Franks (north) and the Visigoths (south), it belonged to the Knights Templar, and after their downfall in 1307, to the Knights of Malta up until the Revolution – you can still see some of their crosses on the Mont Lozère 110-km walk, the GR68 (topo-guide available in Florac).

On the south slope of Mont Lozère, **Le Pont-de-Montvert** is a charming granite village named after its 17th-century hump-backed bridge spanning the baby River Tarn. The Templars had a fort here, and in 1309 Urban V (Guillaume de Grimoard) was born in the **Château de Grinzac**. It's also famous as the place that sparked the War of the Camisards: on 24 July 1702, Protestants besieged the house of the hard-line Abbé de Chayla (who had been sent to convert them by force), freed all his prisoners and, as they chanted psalms, stabbed him 52 times and left his body in the square. On a happier note, its Mairie is the seat of **L'Association 'Sur le Chemin de Robert Louis Stevenson'** (T04 66 45 86 31, chemin-stevenson. org), which provides information on all aspects of the trail. There's also the **Ecomusée du Mont**

Around the region

Lozère, devoted to all aspects of the big mountain (T04 66 45 80 73, Apr-May, Oct daily 1500-1800; Jun-Sep daily 1030-1230 and 1430-1830; Nov-Mar Sat 1500-1800, €3.50).

From Le Pont-de-Montvert you can drive to the pass and from there find the path to the 1699-m summit of Mont Lozère, the **Pic de Finiels**, or take the D35 to **Runes**, a hamlet with a famous waterfall. Nearby is the car park for the trails up to the **Cham des Bondons**, the most important megalithic site in Languedoc. Here 154 granite menhirs dating from around 2000 BC are spread out in various groupings over 10 sq km, on a landscape dominated by two distinct breast-shaped hills (the biggest collection in Europe after Carnac in Brittany).

Here 154 granite menhirs dating from around 2000 BC are spread out in various groupings over 10 sq km, on a landscape dominated by two distinct breast-shaped hills.

Observatoire de Mont Aigoual

Valleraugue, T04 67 82 60 01, aigoual.asso.fr. May-Sep 1000-1300 and 1400-1800, Jul-Aug 1000-1900. Free.

South of the Corniche des Cévennes, Mont Aigoual (1567 m) is the 'watery one'. With an average rainfall of 2250 mm per year, it's the wettest place in France and the source of the River Hérault. On its summit stands the country's last-surviving manned weather observatory, a castle-like structure built in 1894 where meteorologists not only study weather but test equipment in the extreme conditions. There's a meteorological museum, and if it's clear you can make out Mont Blanc, the Mediterranean and the Pyrenees. Bring a jacket, even in August.

Tip...

If you're short of time, drive along the 56-km **Corniche des Cévennes** (D9907-D983-D9-D260) over the mountain ridges between Florac and St-Jean-du Gard, taking in some of the most stunning scenery in the national park.

Opposite: Rest stop. Above: Along the Stevenson Trail.

Travels with a donkey in the Cévennes

"I have been after an adventure all my life, a pure dispassionate adventure, such as befell early and heroic voyagers; and thus to be found by morning in a random woodside nook in Gévaudan – not knowing north from south, as strange to my surroundings as the first man upon the earth, an inland castaway – was to find a fraction of my day-dreams realised".

Robert Louis Stevenson, *Travels with a Donkey in the Cévennes* (1879)

Because of, and often in spite of, his poor health, the young Robert Louis Stevenson was a frequent traveller to places sunnier than his native Edinburgh. He was 27 and an unknown when he met the American Fanny Osbourne in France; she was 10 years older, married, and the mother of three, but they became lovers. When she returned to California he was broken-hearted and decided to make a trek across the Cévennes in an attempt to get her out of his system. Why the Cévennes? Not only were they wild and remote, which appealed to Stevenson's sense of adventure, but for a Protestant Scot, the War of the Camisards had a special appeal and familiar ring.

Stevenson hired a stubbornly naughty donkey named Modestine and set off on 22 September 1878 from Le Monastier-sur-Gazeille to St-Jean-du-Gard, a 12-day 220-km trek now known as the Chemin de Stevenson (GR70). His humour-filled account, based on his notes, was his first book and in many ways the first of a genre; a solo journey 'to find himself' in the days before anyone regarded hiking and camping as something a person would do for leisure. The end result was that he earned enough money from the book to go to America to find Fanny and eventually marry her. Today, hundreds follow in his footsteps in the Cévennes, only the donkeys on hire have better manners than Modestine.

For companies that can organize transport, accommodation and baggage services, see page 141.

Gorges du Tarn

Pale reddish cliffs, sheer-sided swooping cirques and pinnacles in endless variations rising 600 m high, sliced by a blue-green ribbon of water; this magnificent canyon is one of the great natural wonders of France.

Beginning below Florac in **Ispagnac**, the Gorges du Tarn wind 65 km between the Causse de Méjean and the dolmen-dotted Causse de Sauveterre. If the *causses* are often buffeted by winds and cold, the sheltered gorges enjoy such a balmy microclimate that a century ago the Tarn was lined with almond groves. Among the other charms here are the riverside castles built by misanthropic *seigneurs*, now converted into luxurious hotels.

Ste-Enimie

The unofficial 'capital of the Gorges du Tarn', Ste-Enimie is a postcard vision of sandstone houses and cobbled lanes, rising in tiers above the river and a handsome 13th-century **bridge**. It looks peaceful enough on a summer day, but occasionally the Tarn bursts its banks in a big way. In 1992, the car park was 5 m under water.

The village is bound up with the legend of the beautiful Enimie, daughter of the sixth-century Merovingian king Dagobert. She prayed for ugliness so she wouldn't have to marry the nobleman chosen by her father and God granted her wish by giving her leprosy. In agony, Enimie prayed again, this time for relief, and an angel directed her to a miraculous spring, the **Fontaine de Burle** (behind the tourist office). As she started for home the leprosy returned, so she went back to the spring and was healed again; this happened several times before she realized she was meant to stay. She founded an abbey (only the crypt and chapterhouse remains) and spent her last days in the hermitage, a 90-minute walk up from the spring. An artist has illustrated the story of her life in ceramics, now displayed in the 12th-century church.

Pick of the picnic spots

The Lozère is so rural that it's not always easy finding picnic ingredients, but most hotel restaurants and *chambres d'hôtes* will make up picnic boxes if you ask early the day before. In Mende, pick up bread at Eric Kermès (see Shopping, page 139) and farm cheeses, *saucissons*, etc at the Saturday morning market. For breathtaking views try the Roc des Hourtous overlooking the Gorges du Tarn above La Malène (see page 132), or pick up a *capucin* and other goodies at the Aire du Viaduc de Millau (see page 135) and find a spot down on the grass overlooking the bridge.

Utopix

La Sivente (10 mins above Ste-Enimie on the Causse de Sauveterre), T04 66 48 59 07, utopix.lozere.org. Apr-Oct 1000-2000, Nov-Mar ring ahead. €7, €6 child.

Utopix is something completely different – a clutch of stone igloos resembling Languedoc's traditional dry-stone shepherds' huts. Since 1979, artist-owner Jo Pillet has been busily filling them with stone creatures, sculptures made of *objets trouvés*, dreamy surreal paintings and games, including mini-golf.

Gorges du Tarn, as seen from the Roc des Hourtous.

La Ferme de Boissets

Ste Enimie, T04 66 48 48 80.
Jul-Aug 1000-1900. €3, €1.50 child.

The *département* of the Lozère owns this stone hamlet, scarcely changed since the 17th century, high on the edge of the Causse de Sauveterre. Exhibits in seven of the buildings explain the life and landscapes of the area – its shepherds, geology, flora and fauna, and architecture. The farm also has a Parc de Mouflons, the big-horned wild sheep introduced in the 1970s from Corsica with so much success that they're now fair game for hunters.

In high season, the Petit Train des Causses will take you from Ste-Enimie to the farm; the tourist office (in the Mairie, T04 64 48 53 44, gorgesdutarn. net) has schedules.

Tip...

On Thursday evenings in July and August, Ste-Enimie holds a *marché nocturne*, where local producers set up picnic tables and stands selling ready-to-eat meats, salads, bread, wine, desserts, etc, allowing everyone to pick and choose. It's fun and a great option if you have fussy kids.

Down the Gorges du Tarn

Canoeing & kayaking

You can drive down the entire Gorges du Tarn in a few hours, but slowly drinking in the cliffs from the seat of a canoe or kayak as you paddle down is far more fun, and if it gets too hot you can hop into the drink to cool off. The only requirements are that you have to know how to swim, and children must be at least seven years old.

Although it fluctuates, depending on rains and water levels, the canoeing season runs from Easter to 1 November. If you can pick and choose, June and September are the best months, as the river flows gently, the weather is warm and you'll avoid rubbing shoulders with too many people – 800,000 visitors pass through the Gorges du Tarn every year, the bulk in July and August.

Come prepared: wear your swimming costume under your clothes and bring water, hat, sunglasses, submersible shoes, a towel and a snack or picnic. Start around 1000 for the best light, and be sure to get a general idea from your outfitter of how far you should be at any given time, so you aren't paddling like mad to catch the last shuttle bus back. Be aware that mobile phone coverage can be limited in the gorge.

There are quite a few courses to choose from. The classic stretches are on the relatively easy 9-km, three-hour descent from La Malène through the dramatic narrows – Les Détroits – to the Pas de Soucy (Baumes-Basses). If you have a full day (and you're fit) try the 23-km descent from Ste-Enimie to the Pas de Soucy, and if you have two days (and you're very fit) you can start from Ispagnac (45 km) or Montbrun (32 km) and camp by the river midway. Or if you just want to get a taste, try the 90-minute descent from Prades to Ste-Enimie.

Landmarks are many. After Ste-Enimie there's **St-Chély-du-Tarn**, with its clutch of houses under the cliffs and icy cold waterfall, surrounded by two huge bends in the gorge; and the **Cirque de St-Chély** and Cirque de Pougnardoires, where houses are built into the cliffs. There's also the magnificent **Château de la Caze**, now a luxury hotel, and **Hauterives**, a hamlet inaccessible by road. Pretty **La Malène** has long been a favourite stop along the river; it's the last village before the gorge narrows as it curves around the **Cirque des Baumes**, where the journey ends. A bit further on, the **Pas de Soucy** forms an impossible boulder-strewn barrier. For canoeing and kayaking operators, see Activities & tours, page 140.

Walking

The other way of exploring the Gorges du Tarn is on foot. Two major long-distance treks traverse the Grands Causses and the gorges: the 250-km **Sentier de la Vallée du Tarn** goes from Le Pont de Montvert all the way west to Albi, and the **GR60** follows the old muleteers' route from the Causse de Sauveterre to Ste-Enimie, then over to the Causse de Méjean towards Mont Aigoual. Local tourist offices are well supplied with maps and topo-guides, and can suggest local circuits and viewpoints if you don't have a week to wander.

Canoe down river along the Gorges du Tarn.

Around the region

This gorge, carved out by the Tarn's tributary, the Jonte, is less visited but no less ravishing than the Gorges du Tarn, especially between **Le Rozier** and **Meyruies**. There isn't enough water in the Jonte for canoeing, but geological wonders wait on either side, on the Causse Noir and the Causse Méjean.

Belvédère des Vautours

Le Truel (4 km from Le Rozier), T05 65 62 69 69, vautours-lozere.com.
Mid-Mar to mid-Jun, Sep to mid-Nov 1000-1800, mid-Jun to Aug 1000-1900. €6, €3 child (5-12).

Vultures were once abundant here but they disappeared in 1940, victims of mechanized farming (no dead horses or oxen to scavenge), trophy hunters and pesticides. In the 1980s, several pairs from Spain were introduced and today there are some 200 vultures, including the rare and enormous Cinereous or Eurasian black vultures, which are only slightly smaller than condors. This is the place to spot them, watch webcams of their nests and hatchlings, and learn all about them in the vulture museum.

Aven Armand

Meyrueis, T04 66 45 61 31, aven-armand.com.
Mar-Jun, Sep-Oct 1000-1200 and 1330-1700, Jul-Aug 0930-1800. €8.80, €7.20 young person (15-20), €6 child (5-15).

An *aven* is a swallow hole, and this is a remarkable one. It's an enormous karstic funnel hollowed out in the limestone Causse de Méjean, so big that the Cathedral of Notre-Dame would fit in the 120- by 60-m main chamber. The *aven* is decorated with a forest of 400 stalagmites, including a 30-m monster – the tallest in the world. Access is by funicular, but more adventurous types (on Fridays in summer, or by reservation) can make a dramatic descent by rope pulley down the natural well of the original entrance.

Gorges de la Jonte.

Grotte de Dargilan

7 km from Meyrueis, T04 66 45 60 20, grotte-dargilan.com.
Easter holidays to 1st week of Nov 1000-1730 (last visit), Jul-Aug 1000-1830. €8.50, €7.50 student, €5.80 young person/child (6-18), under 6s free.

Discovered in 1880 by an angry shepherd chasing a fox, this subterranean labyrinth is known as the 'pink cave'. There are richly coloured draperies in the 'petrified waterfall', 'bell tower', and other formations in the enormous central Hall of Chaos and along the bed hollowed by an underground river. The tour ends with a breathtaking vista over the gorge.

Abîme de Bramabiau

Camprieu, T04 67 82 60 78, abime-de-bramabiau. com.
Apr-Jun, Sep 1000-1730, Jul-Aug 0930-1830; Oct-1st week Nov 1030-1630. €7.50, €5 young person (13-16), €3.50 child (6-12).

The River Bonheur (Happiness) is born on Mont Aigoual, then plunges underground into this chasm before forming a sheer-sided 800-m tunnel in the limestone. It re-emerges in the daylight south of Meyrueis at Camprieu. A walkway has been fitted along its side; the waterfalls make such a thunderous echoing noise that the locals named it *brame biou*, the 'bellowing steer'. The temperature in the chasm is a constant 10°C, so wear something warm.

Millau

Viaduc de Millau

A75, Millau, leviaducdemillau.com.
Toll for a car Sep-Jun €6, Jul-Aug €7.70.

The A75 linking Paris to Languedoc passes down the west side of the Lozère, and used to peter out at Millau in the Aveyron before continuing into the rest of Languedoc. After years of studying several alternatives, the decision to build a bridge here was finalized in 1994. Bids were requested and the winning proposal was submitted by Michel Virlogeux, head engineer at the Ponts et Chaussées, with a stunning design by Sir Norman Foster.

Although the earth works took longer, the viaduct, with its 80,000 cu m of concrete and 20,000 tonnes of steel, took 600 workers a mere 23 months to build. This was thanks to cutting-edge technology, especially when you consider that the tallest of its seven pylons stands 19 m higher than the Eiffel Tower. When it opened in 2004, the Viaduc de Millau was hailed as the 'modern Pont du Gard', an audacious engineering epiphany, sailing 270 m over the River Tarn.

Tip...

There are great views of the bridge from the Aire du Viaduc de Millau on the north end of the viaduct. The motorway café here is run by top chef Michel Bras, so stop for lunch to try his *capucin*, a savoury pancake folded into a cone and stuffed with a choice of fillings all under €10.

Sleeping

Mende & around

Hotel de France €€
9 bd Lucien Arnault, T04 66 65 00 04, hoteldefrance-mende.com.
Originally a post house, this comfortable hotel in the centre of Mende has recently undergone a thorough refurbishment. The 27 spacious rooms have a mix of old stone walls and contemporary furnishings and are equipped with air conditioning and plasma TVs.

Hôtel le Commerce €
2 bd Henri Bourrillon, T04 66 65 13 73, lecommerce-mende.com.
Small and central, located on the boulevard that rings the medieval core of Mende, this hotel has rooms over the city's oldest café (in business since 1933 and renowned for its wide selection of beers). Rooms are tastefully designed, and a friendly welcome is guaranteed. Wi-Fi available.

Château de La Caze.

Self-catering
Le Columbier
Domaine du Chapitre, T04 66 49 50 50, gites-mende.com.
Just outside Mende, this clutch of 42 independent mountain cabins (sleeping two to 12) combine outdoorsy charm with conveniences like a bar, bakery, tennis courts, playing fields and a nearby outdoor pool. They also organize outings, concerts, kids' games, etc, and disabled access is available. Prices start at €252 per week for a cabin sleeping four.

Parc National des Cévennes

Château d'Ayres €€€
Meyrueis, T04 66 45 60 10, hotel-restaurant-meyrueis.com.
The most prestigious lodging in the Gorges de la Jonte began as a 12th-century priory, which was then rebuilt as a residential château in the 18th century. Set in a leafy 6-ha park with tennis courts and a pool, its ivy-clad walls contain 22 tranquil bedrooms decorated in a country style, and a monastic dining room.

Château de la Caze €€€
Rte des Gorges du Tarn, La Malène, T04 66 48 51 01, chateaudelacaze.com.
A 15th-century castle in a fairytale setting, this is the only four-star hotel in the Lozère and a lovely place to get away from it all. The 10 rooms are replete with castle character, and the leafy park has a pool if you don't feel like a dip in the Tarn. The adjacent 19th-century Maison de Martine has six spacious suites for families and groups of friends. There's an excellent restaurant on site as well, where owner Jean-Paul Lecroq prepares delights like saddle of lamb with olives and wild mushrooms, and chestnut cake.

Grand Hôtel de la Muse et du Rozier €€€
Le Rozier, T05 65 62 60 01, hotel-delamuse.fr.
This idyllic 35-room hotel, built over a century ago at the confluence of the Jonte and Tarn, has recently had a thorough makeover to promote a Zen-like state of serenity. Big windows in the salon and the excellent restaurant overlook a large, lush park with a heated pool. All bedrooms have views over the Tarn, and there's a boules court, a billiards room and satellite TV.

Le Mas de Coupétadou €€
Lieu-dit Souteyrannes, Vialas, T04 66 41 05 49, chambre-hote-cevennes.fr.
This handsome stone house is set in 3 ha of land and is owned by Stéphane and Fred, who have created three cosy rooms with wooden floors, stone walls and beams. Lovely breakfasts are served on the veranda and *table d'hôte* meals can be enjoyed under the wisteria. Stéphane was a nutritionist in Paris, and serves healthy, creative dishes.

Le Mas Nouveau €€

Génholhac, T06 84 07 00 51, masnouveau.com.

At the foot of Mont Lozère along the Voie Régordane, this farmhouse dates from the 12th century and even has carvings in the floor left behind by the Knights Templar. Beautifully restored by owner Christine Gerbino, it's surrounded by 25 ha of orchards and chestnuts. Ask for one of the rooms or suites with huge solid granite tubs, constantly replenished with warm spring water. Chinese and Ayurvedic massages are available for total relaxation.

Maison Victoire €€

Finiels, Le Pont-de-Montvert, T04 66 45 84 36, gites-mont-lozere. com.

Near the summit of Mont Lozère, close to the Chemin Stevenson, this stone-built B&B set in the wild granite landscape guarantees atmospheric peace and quiet. There are five big rooms sleeping up to three people, and rates include a hearty breakfast and dinner by the fireplace.

Manoir de Montesquiou €€

La Malène, T04 66 48 51 12, manoir-montesquiou.com. Mid-Apr to mid-Oct.

The picturesque 15th- to 16th-century château has 10 bedrooms of varying sizes, with evocative names and a mix of antique and contemporary furnishings. Also on offer are two studio flats sleeping up to four.

There's an intimate gastronomic restaurant with a terrace, serving dishes such as avocado and smoked trout purée, endive tatin with goat's cheese, and a delicious walnut and chocolate gâteau (menus from €27). The brasserie is open all day and serves simple dishes and excellent ice cream.

Hôtel Burlatis €

Ste-Enimie, T04 66 48 52 30, monsite.orange.fr/hotelburlatis. Mar-Nov.

This sturdy stone hotel has nine simple, en suite rooms with double-glazed windows and internet access. There are also two family rooms. Free parking for bikes and motorcycles is available and the owners are a goldmine of information on local activities.

Hôtel du Gorges du Tarn €

48 rue du Pêcher, Florac, T04 66 45 00 63, hotel-gorgesdutarn.com. Easter-Oct.

Impeccably run, this Logis de France has a wide choice of rooms – some are pricier, newly renovated and equipped with flat-screen TVs. The hotel is good for families, as many rooms (and self-catering studios) can sleep up to four people. Note, however, that there's no lift.

Hôtel Restaurant Le Sully €

28 place de Sully, Meyrueis, T04 66 45 68 38, hotel-meyrueis.com. Recently renovated and in the centre of the village, Le Sully offers a choice of 30 en suite

rooms (many overlooking the courtyard or the pool) in the main hotel and its annex La Renaissance. The restaurant is good, and in the summer you can eat next to the Béthuzon river.

La Ferme de Vimbouches €

St-Frézal-de-Ventalon, 20 mins south of Le Pont-de-Montvert, T04 66 31 56 55, causses-cevennes.com/ferme-vimbouches.

This farm offers four rustic en suite rooms, with chestnut beams and a magnificent terrace with stunning views over the hills. It's perfect for active families: you can swim in the river, canoe, rent a mountain bike or donkey, or participate in farm activities. They also offer *table d'hôte*.

L'Oustaou de Bigan €

Serviès, T04 66 47 49 80, vacances-cevennes-lozere.com/ anglais/bb-guestrooms-france. htm.

At 1300 m and 15 minutes from Bagnols-les-Bains, this delightful and well-equipped B&B is run by Fabienne and Jean-Luc. They offer a handful of pretty rooms in cosy wood and stone that sleep up to four. Don't miss the delicious meals prepared with vegetables from their garden.

Listings

Self-catering

Le Merlet

Le Pont-de-Montvert, T04 66 45 82 92, lemerlet.com.

In a remote setting outside Le Pont-de-Montvert, the award-winning Le Merlet is a beautifully restored granite farm complex (1593) that once belonged to the Camisards. Today it is dedicated to sustainable tourism and produces honey, lamb, terrines, etc. The mill and other outbuildings have been converted into gîtes (from €320 per week for two people in the off season) and six *chambres d'hôtes* (€52); the hosts also serve excellent meals around their big oak table.

Chestnut cake.

Eating & drinking

Mende & around

Hotel de France €€€

9 bd Lucien Arnault, T04 66 65 00 04, hoteldefrance-mende.com.

Mon for dinner, Tue-Fri for lunch and dinner, Sat for lunch.

This popular hotel (see Sleeping, page 136) has one of the best restaurants in town, with tables by an open fire in winter or out on the terrace in summer. You'll find a good choice of seafood and meat (try the traditional slow-roasted lamb), and arty desserts such as apricots in puff pastry with grilled almonds. Menus €28-31.

La Safranière €€€

Chabrits (5 km west of Mende), T04 66 49 31 54.

Tue, Thu-Sat for lunch and dinner, Wed for dinner, Sun for lunch.

There are only five tables in this old stone farm in the hills above Mende, but the fresh, light, Mediterranean cuisine and peaceful rural setting of Chabrits make it a great choice for a special meal. The vegetable dishes, the asparagus, the aubergine caviar and the lamb are especially good, and the wine cellar is one of the best in the area. Weekday menu €22.

Les Voûtes €

13 rue d'Aigues Passes, T04 66 49 00 05, les-voutes.com.

Sep to mid-Apr Tue-Sun for lunch and 1900-2300, mid-Apr to Aug for lunch and 1900-2300.

In the heart of Mende, the 'Vaults' has three dining rooms in an 18th-century convent and features tasty pizza baked in a wood-burning oven. The varied menu changes every three months; try local favourites such as *aligot* (mashed potatoes with garlic and Tome cheese), *salades composées* and *maigret de canard*. In summer eat out on the cool, shady terrace.

Parc National des Cévennes

La Lozerette €€€

Cocurès (6 km from Florac), T04 66 45 06 04, lalozerette.com.

Palm Sunday-1 Nov Wed for dinner, Thu-Mon for lunch and dinner.

Cocurès is a sweet little village and this charming restaurant is one of the best in the Lozère. The chef makes imaginative use of the local products, with dishes such as chestnut-flour ravioli filled with escargots, tuna with *jambon de pays* and duck breasts stuffed with fruit in a foie gras sauce. The enormous wine cellar has over 300 wines, many sold by the glass. Menu du jour €25.

Auberge du Moulin €€
Rue de la Combe, Ste-Enimie, T04 66 48 53 08, aubergedumoulin. free.fr.
Mid-Mar to mid-Nov for lunch and dinner.
This hotel-restaurant in an old stone mill has a lovely summer terrace overlooking the river. It has a good reputation for its traditional dishes, such as home-made game terrines, fresh crayfish *à la bordelaise* and lamb from the *causse*.

L'Adonis €€
48 rue du Pêcher, Florac, T04 66 45 00 63, hotel-gorgesdutarn.com.
Easter-Jun, Sep-Oct Thu-Tue for lunch and dinner, Jul-Aug daily for lunch and dinner.
Fresh, seasonal dishes have made this restaurant a favourite

Goat's milk cheese.

in Florac: asparagus in spring, ravioli filled with *pélardons* in a mushroom sauce in the autumn. Try the tasty river fish or duck fillet, and the decadent, gooey chocolate cake with violet ice cream. Menus from €18.

Le Mont-Aigoual €€
34 quai de la Barrière, Meyrueis, T04 66 45 65 61, hotel-mont-aigoual.com.
Apr-Jun, Sep-Oct Wed-Mon for lunch and dinner. Jul-Aug daily for lunch and dinner.
A very pleasant, relaxing Logis de France hotel in the Gorges de la Jonte with a good restaurant that's much appreciated by the locals. Features chef Daniel Lagrange's *cuisine de terroir* – fresh trout with chorizo, crayfish *a la plancha*, seven-hour lamb – with a good choice of Languedoc wines to wash it down.

Tables de la Fontaine €€
31 rue du Thérond, Florac, T06 81 44 89 56, tables-de-la-fontaine. com.
Thu-Tue for lunch and dinner.
With its garden patio in the historic centre, this family-run restaurant is a lovely place to dine on dishes such as chicken grilled on a skewer with dried tomatoes, millefeuille of potatoes with goat's cheese, and home-made ice cream. They also have four pretty *chambres d'hôtes*.

Shopping

Mende & around

Food & wine
Eric Kermès Boulangerie-Pâtisserie
3 rue du Soubeyran, T04 66 49 09 51.
Mon-Sat 0830-1200 and 1500-1900.
Bakery celebrated for its traditional bread made from locally grown wheat and rye and crunchy almond *croquants de Mende*.

Pâtisserie Majorel
1 rue de la République, T04 66 65 17 85.
Among the specialities here are chocolate bells, recalling the cathedral's Non Pareille.

Wood
Jean-Louis Sirvins
12 rue des Cytises, Les Pousets, T04 66 65 39 47.
Ring to visit.
Woodworker Jean-Louis Sirvins makes beautiful bowls, plates, cheeseboards, etc, as well as chestnut *bouffadous* – special pipes to blow through to keep a fire or barbecue going. He also makes things to order.

Parc National des Cévennes

Arts & crafts
Les Confidences du Terroir
Ste-Enimie, T04 66 48 51 18.
Jul to mid-Sep 1030-1230 and
1400-1900.
A beautiful, three-storey
16th-century house near the
medieval Halles des Grains,
offering the works of 50 artists
and craftspeople from across the
Lozère.

Food & wine
Au Gré... des Saveurs
Ste-Enimie, T04 66 48 46 55.
Apr-Sep 1000-1900, Oct-Nov
1100-1730.
Vast selection of spirits and
wines, including some
little-known wines from the
Lozère. They also do tastings.

La Maison du Pays Cévenol
3 rue du Pêcher, Florac, T04 66 45
15 67, maisonpayscevenol.fr.
Mar-Dec Tue-Sat 0930-1230 and
1500-1730, Sun 0930-1230.
From jams and cheeses to
baskets and mohair scarves,
sourced from some 35 producers
across the region.

Activities & tours

Fishing
Clubfish France
T+44(20)-8874 6717 (UK),
*clubfishfrance.co.uk/lozere_*
rivers.htm.
This UK-based company
organizes trips on the Lozère,
which, with 2700 km of limpid
trout streams, offers some of the
best fly fishing in France

Mende & around

Cycling
The Lozère has over 200 km of
mountain bike paths, and cycle
touring on its empty roads is very
popular. Go late in the spring if you
can, when temperatures are ideal.

Cycloclub Mendois
Contact Pierre Lusson, 10 rue du
Chastel, Mende, T04 66 94 07 63.
Promotes the six-stage 595-km
Tour de la Lozère.

Espace Bike
1 bd Soubeyran, Mende, T04 66
65 01 81, cycles-lozere.com.
For road or mountain bike rentals.

Planète 2 roues
5 av du Pont Roupt, Mende, T04
66 49 17 00, planete2roues.com.
Hires out road and mountain bikes.

Golf
Domaine de Barres
Rte de Mende, Langogne, T04 66
46 08 37, domainedebarres.com.
Located 30 km north of Mende,
this nine-hole par 36 course is
1000 m above sea level. It has big
greens, wide fairways and lovely
views. It also boasts a swimming
pool and a sauna

Wellbeing
Station Thermale
Bagnols-les-Bains, T04 66 47 60
02, bagnols-les-bains.com.
By the hot springs near the
source of the Lot, this spa offers
a choice of relaxing baths and
treatments. €28 for a half day.

Parc National des Cévennes

Boat trips
Les Bateliers de La Malène
La Malène, T04 66 48 51 10,
gorgesdutarn.com.
Since the 19th century, the
boatmen of Màlene have punted
visitors 8 km past some of the
Tarn's best scenery. Cost is €80
for four people, including the
return to La Malène by minibus
(Apr-Oct).

Les Bateliers du Viaduc
Place du 19 mars, Creissels, T05 65
60 17 91, bateliersduviaduc.com.
A 1½-hr journey down the Tarn
and under the extraordinary
Viaduc de Millau – it's a great way
to appreciate its astonishing
dimensions.

Canoeing/kayaking
The following outfits rent canoes
and kayaks. Prices start at €28 for
a two-person canoe (€17 for a
kayak) for 8 km:

Au Moulin de La Malène
La Malène, T04 66 48 51 14, www. canoeblanc.com.

Canoë 2000
La Malène, T04 66 48 57 71, location-canoe-kayak-lozere-gorges-du-tarn.location-canoe-kayak-lozere.com.

Méjean Canoë
Ste-Enimie, T04 66 48 58 70, canoe-mejean.com.

Canyoning & rock climbing
Bulledo
Quézac, T04 66 32 28 15/T06 78 16 00 20, bulledo.fr.
Offers canyoning, rock climbing and Via Corda for high-adrenalin thrills.

Cévennes Evasion
6 place Boyer, Florac, T04 66 45 18 31, cevennes-evasion.com.
Specialists in caving, canoeing, mountain biking, rock climbing, canyoning or whitewater rafting. Offer 24 different excursions, including accompanied walks on the Chemin de Stevenson.

Donkey trekking
If you want to follow the Chemin de Stevenson step by step, you need to start in the Haute-Loire just north of the Lozère:
Les ânes à Gilles, Ecuries du Musée Rocher de Grelet, Pradelles, T04 66 69 49 35, lesanesagilles.com, or **Rando-Âne Gaëlle Bruchet**, 4 rte du Monastier, Arsac-en-Velay, T04 71 03 99 32, bourricot.com, can organize things for you. If you

don't want to backtrack with your *burro*, they provide donkey transport services as well.
See also page 127 and Walking, below.

Badjâne
Cessénades, Malons-et-Elze, T04 66 56 71 54, badjane.org.
Hire out donkeys for autonomous or guided journeys on a variety of paths, including the long-distance Chemin de Stevenson and the Régordane (GR700).

Golf
Le Golf du Gorges du Tarn
Complexe du Val d'Urugne, La Canourgue, T04 66 32 84 00, lozereleisure.com.
A technical 18-hole par 71 course with narrow fairways in a deeply wooded valley. They also have chalets and a campsite.

Hang-gliding
Antipodes
39 av Jean Jaurès, Millau, T05 65 60 72 03, antipodes-millau.com.
Soar with the vultures over the *causses* and the Viaduc de Millau. Anyone over the age of five can have a go.

Bulledo
Quézac, T04 66 32 28 15/T06 78 16 00 20, bulledo.fr.
Hang-gliding over the Gorges du Tarn.

Horse riding
La Périgouse
Ste-Enimie, T04 66 48 53 71, perigouse.com.

Specialists in endurance riding, this stable offers weekend and longer excursions for experienced riders. Also has B&B rooms.

Skiing
Le Bleymard-Mont Lozère
Le Bleymard, T04 66 48 66 48, lemontlozere.com.
Downhill (two green, one blue, three red and one black piste), cross-country skiing, snow-shoeing and luge on Mont Lozère.

Prat Peyrot
Pray Peyrot (near Valleraugue), T04 67 73 19 80, pratpeyrot.info.
Downhill (five green, six blue and four red pistes) and 60 km of cross -country skiing on Mont Aigoual.

Walking
The best-known long-distance path through the Cévennes is the Chemin de Stevenson (see 129) and the 242-km Voie Régordane or Chemin de St-Gilles (GR700), following the ancient transhumance and pilgrimage route to St-Gilles-du-Gard (see page 105). Cévennes Evasion (see Canyoning & rock climbing, above) can organize accommodation. Two companies provide taxi and baggage transport services:

Stevenson Bagages
T06 07 29 01 23, stevenson-bagages.com.

Transbagages
T04 66 65 27 75, transbagages. com.

Contents

Canal du Midi.

Introduction

Y ou could spend your whole holiday in the Hérault and never be bored. Montpellier, Languedoc-Roussillon's edgy, adrenalin-charged capital is urbane and sleek, enlivened by a huge student population, while its 17th-century predecessor Pézenas, the golden-stoned 'Versailles of Languedoc', daydreams of Molière. For seaside frolics you can choose between the futuristic resort of La Grande-Motte or fashionable Cap d'Agde, home to the excellent Musée de l'Ephèbe, which houses the region's finest antiquities. For salty character and delectable crustaceans, there's Sète and the fishing villages around the vast oyster nursery that is the Bassin de Thau.

Picturesque Béziers is the Hérault's second city, and nearby is the ancient oppidum of Ensérune, one of the best-preserved pre-Roman sites in France. Many of the *département*'s finest vineyards are not far away in the Minervois, set between the languid meanders of the Canal du Midi – a magical 17th-century marvel of engineering. The sparsely populated mountains and *garrigue* in the northern Hérault have their splendours too – wild gorges, caves and rivers – and it's ideal country for trekking and canoeing. It's also worth exploring the cache of exceptional medieval villages here, headlined by St-Guilhem-le-Désert, Roquebrun, Minerve and Olargues.

Cathédrale St-Nazaire, Béziers.

What to see in...

...one day
Take a walk in Montpellier's Ecusson and visit the 19th-century masterpieces in the Musée Fabre, then drive out to Bouzigues on the Bassin de Thau for the freshest of seafood lunches. Go for a swim at Cap d'Agde and visit the Museé de l'Ephèbe before indulging in an evening stroll and dinner in Pézenas.

...a weekend or more
After taking in Montpellier, spend a day or weekend on a barge on the bucolic Canal du Midi, or hire a bike and go for a pedal along the towpath – an activity easily combined with winetasting in the Minervois. Alternatively, go up the rivers Hérault or Orb and visit their picturesque medieval towns. These are great bases for swimming or kayaking, or for fragrant walks in the *garrigue*.

Montpellier & around

Languedoc's capital, Montpellier (population: 240,000) is currently France's eighth largest city and growing like a weed, with 1000 new residents arriving every week. This is astounding considering it was number 25 back in 1977, when its controversial, go-getting mayor Georges Frêche was elected (he left in 2004, only to become president of the Languedoc-Roussillon region). Home to a major university, research institutes and 70,000 students, its historic core, L'Ecusson, offers a buzzing urbane cocktail of elegant *hôtels particuliers*, boutiques and restaurants. Although it's one of the very few French cities without ancient roots, Montpellier (founded in 985) has made up for this lack with an array of 'new' classics – Antigone, the Corum, the Odysseum and Mare Nostrum aquarium, the results of a building spree few can match.

The Rockstore, Rue de Verdun.

Essentials

❶ Getting around Montpellier's historic centre, L'Ecusson, is the biggest pedestrian zone in France. Car parks and garages are signposted on the periphery, especially on the south side and towards Antigone. There are cheaper car parks along the city's two tramlines.

By public transport The city's two tramlines are Hirondelles (Line 1) and Fleurs (Line 2); the future Line 3, Haute Couture (designed by Christian Lacroix) will go as far as Lattes-Pérols and the sea. Tickets cost €1.30 (€2.40 return) and are valid for one hour on both buses and trams. From Thursday to Saturday (2400-0500), Amigo buses provide a service which runs from Gare St-Roch to the nightclubs (for timetables, see Transports de l'Agglomération de Montpellier TaM, T04 67 22 87 87, montpellier-agglo.com).

By bicycle The Vélomagg scheme allows you to hire a bike in one of 50 locations. It costs €1 for up to four hours or €2 for a day.

By Taxi There are taxi ranks at the train station and in Place de la Comédie; alternatively, ring T04 67 58 10 10.

☺ Train station Gare St-Roch, five-minute walk south of the Place de la Comédie, T36 35. For regional rail travel, see page 274.

☻ Bus station Rue du Grand-St-Jean, 200 m from the train station, T04 67 92 01 43. For regional bus travel, see page 275.

💲 ATM Banque Populaire, 11 place de la Comédie; BNP Paribas, 8 rue Maguelone.

⊕ Hospital CHU-Hôpital Lapeyronie, 191 avenue Doyen-Gaston-Giraud, T04 67 33 67 33.

✚ Pharmacy Place de la Comédie, 1 rue Verdun, T09 62 20 91 01; Foch, 20 rue Foch, T04 67 60 69 23.

✎ Post office 15 rue Rondelet, T04 67 34 50 00.

ℹ Tourist information 30 allée Jean de Lattre de Tassigny, T04 67 60 60 60, ot-montpellier.fr. Monday to Friday 0900-1930, Sat 0930-1800, Sunday and national holidays 0930-1300 and 1430-1800.

Place de la Comédie & around

The Place de la Comédie, poised between the historic centre and the 'new' Montpellier, is the vortex where everyone and everything converges. With the **Fountain of the Three Graces** (1796) splashing in the centre, this is a square that would look at home in Paris, embraced as it is by the elegant 19th-century **Opéra Comédie** and Second Empire buildings sporting Mansard roofs, froufrou balconies and grand cafés. Cars were banned in 1985, but sleek trams glide along the edge.

The square extends north into the leafy **Esplanade Charles de Gaulle** and the **Jardin du Champ du Mars**, a popular city park with duck ponds and arty playgrounds anchored by one of Georges Frêche's pricey grands projets: the pink marble Corum (1988) housing a conference centre and the **Opéra Berlioz**.

Musée Fabre

39 bd de Bonne Nouvelle, T04 67 14 83 00, museefabre-en.montpellier-agglo.com.
Tue, Thu, Fri and Sun 1000-1800, Wed 1300-2100, Sat 1100-1800. €6, €4 young person/child (6-18), family ticket €12. Free on 1st Sun of every month. Map: Montpellier, C4, p148.

One of France's top provincial collections, the Fabre was founded in 1825 and re-opened in 2007 after a superb four-year restoration. There are some fine Dutch and Flemish Grand Masters, Veronese's richly coloured *Mystic Marriage of St Catherine*, Zurbarán's *St Agatha* and several works by Nicolas Poussin, including a poetic *Venus and Adonis* (1624) – or half of it. Recently, the rest of the painting was discovered in a private American collection and the museum is currently raising funds to buy it.

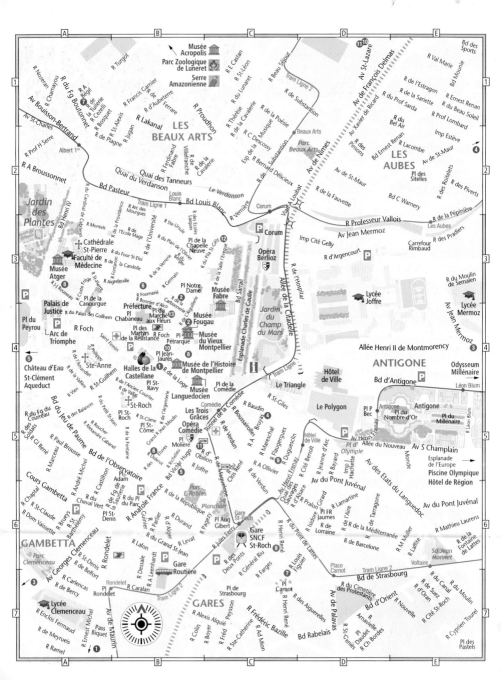

The Fabre is best known, however, for its 19th-century French art, donated by local benefactor Alfred Bruyas, who had his portrait painted by Delacroix, Courbet and every other artist he ever met. He also co-stars in the museum's best-known work: Gustav Courbet's jaunty *The Meeting*, celebrating the artist's arrival in Montpellier, but better known as *Bonjour, Monsieur Courbet* for the artist's prominent self portrait. Another featured canvas by Courbet, *Les Baigneuses*, caused such a scandal at the Paris Art Salon of 1853 that Napoleon III ordered it removed. Bruyas, who knew more about painting than the emperor, bought it. Soon artists were making pilgrimages to Montpellier to study what is now recognized as a pivotal work in the history of art.

Other highlights of the museum include luminous paintings by Montpelliérain Frédéric Bazille (a proto-Impressionist who died young) and works by Géricault, Ingres, Fragonard, David, Morisot, Sisley and Matisse. A new wing holds 20 paintings by contemporary artist Pierre Soulages, while just around the corner at 6 bis rue Montpellieret, the **Hôtel de Cabrières-Sabatier d'Espeyran** opened in 2010 with a collection of furniture and decorative arts.

Fountain of the Three Graces, Place de la Comédie.

Montpellier listings

➊ Sleeping

1 Appart'City Montpellier l'Orangerie *29 bd Berthelot* **A7** (off map)
2 Baudon de Mauny *1 rue de la Carbonnerie* **B3**
3 Château Résidence de Bionne *225, rue de Bionne* **A7** (off map)
4 Hôtel d'Aragon *10 rue Baudin* **C5**
5 Hôtel des Arts *6 bd Victor Hugo* **B5**
6 Hôtel des Etuves *24 rue des Etuves* **B5**
7 Hôtel du Parc *8 rue Achille Bégé* **A1**
8 Hôtel Le Guilhem *18 rue Jean-Jacques Rousseau* **A3**
9 Hôtel le Mistral *25 rue Boussairolles* **C5**
10 Le Jardin des Sens *11 av St-Lazare* **D1**
11 New Hotel du Midi *22 bd Victor Hugo* **B5**

➊ Eating & drinking

1 Cocco e Fragola *8 rue de la Loge, place Jean-Jaurès* **B4**
2 La Maison de la Lozère: Cellier-Morel *27 rue de l'Aiguillerie* **B4**
3 La Pause Mermoz *890 av Jean Mermoz* **E4**
4 La Réserve Rimbaud *820 av St Maur* **E2** (off map)
5 L'Assiette aux Fromages *17 rue Gustave* **A4**
6 La Tavola da Pépé *8 rue de l'Université* **B3**
7 Le Ban des Gourmands *5 place Carnot* **C7**
8 Le Circus *3 rue Collot* **B4**
9 Le Dilemme *12 rue Farges* **C6**
10 Le Huit *8 rue de l'Aiguillerie* **B4**
11 Le Jardin des Sens *11 av St-Lazare* **D1**
12 Morceau de la Lune *14 rue du Pila St-Gély* **C3**
13 Tamarillos *2 place du Marché aux Fleurs* **B4**

Around the region

Old Montpellier, named after its escutcheon shape on the map, is a fascinating tangle of streets, bijou squares, lovingly preserved *hôtels particuliers,* boutiques and little restaurants. From Place de la Comédie, head up **Rue de la Loge**, the city's high street, and midway you'll see a statue of assassinated Socialist Prime Minister Jean Jaurès standing like a benevolent guardian over the bustling pavement cafés in **Place Jean-Jaurès**. This square was once the site of the city's most important church, Notre-Dame-des-Tables, the 'tables' belonging to the money changers who did business with pilgrims to Compostela. Although the church was destroyed in the 16th-century Wars of Religion, the crypt survives and you can take a bizarre 'virtual tour' of the church and city in the **Musée de l'Histoire de Montpellier** (Tue-Sat 1030-1230 and 1330-1800, €1.55).

At the top of Rue de la Loge, the covered market, or the **Halles de la Castellane** (1869) stand at an important crossroad. To the left, busy Rue St-Guilhem runs past some of Montpellier's most picturesque medieval lanes: one, Rue Ste-Anne, leads to the tall neo-Gothic **St-Anne**, a church now used for art exhibitions.

If you're in a hurry, however, turn right at the top of Rue de la Loge, towards the Préfecture flanked by pretty squares. You'll find **Place du Marché aux Fleurs** and lovely little **Place Chabaneau**, both filled with popular pavement cafés.

In 1878, a section of the medieval town west of here was razed for broad **Rue Foch** and a Greek temple of Justice or a Palais de Justice. Near this, Rue Astuc leads just north to one of the city's best-loved squares: the tree-lined 17th-century **Place de la Canourgue** with a unicorn fountain.

Arc de Triomphe & Place du Peyrou
Map: Montpellier, A4, p148.

If Montpellier's Place de la Comédie echoes Paris, Paris also echoes Montpellier. Rue Foch, like a mini Champs Elysées, is closed off by an Arc de Triomphe that pre-dates Paris's by a century. It was erected to replace a medieval gate and to celebrate the triumphs of Louis XIV over heresy, England and the Holy Roman Empire, as well as the construction of the Canal du Midi.

Through the arc, at the city's highest point are the gardens of the Place du Peyrou, with their century-old magnolias and an equestrian statue of Louis XIV. The original was cast in Paris, but by the time it made it to Montpellier after the boat carrying it sunk in the Garonne, the Roi Soleil was dead. During the Revolution it was smashed to bits; the current copy dates from 1838. Behind it stands the hexagonal water tower or **Château d'Eau**, into which flowed the waters of the 18th-century **St-Clément aqueduct** that stretches majestically to the west on arches inspired by the Pont du Gard.

Cathédrale St-Pierre

Place Cathédrale St-Pierre.
Daily 0900-1200, Mon-Sat 1430-1900.
Map: Montpellier, A3, p148.

Tall, austere St-Pierre was the college of St-Benoît's church before it was converted into a cathedral in 1563, only to be wrecked during the Wars of Religion and the Revolution. The striking porch with its rocket-like towers is the only original feature to survive. Of the paintings inside, the best is Montpellier-native Sébastien Bourdin's *Fall of Simon Magus* (1657) in the right transept.

Tip...

Save money by purchasing a **City Card** at the tourist office for 24, 48 or 72 hours (€15, €22, €28, half price for children). It offers free transport, guided tours and free or reduced entry to Montpellier's main sites.

Place de la Comédie.

Five of the best

Squares for people-watching

❶ Place de la Comédie

❷ Place Jean-Jaurès

❸ Place de la Canourgue

❹ Place Marché des Fleurs

❺ Place Castellane

Faculté de Médecine.

Faculté de Médecine

Rue de l'Ecole-de-Médecine.
Currently closed to visitors, check with the tourist office to see if their guided tours have resumed.
Map: Montpellier, A3, p148.

Montpellier has long had a medical vocation: its medical school was founded in 1220 by teachers who had learned their profession through the city's trading contacts with the Levant and the famous medical school in Salerno, Italy. In 1289 Pope Nicolas issued a bull that put Montpellier's Studium Generalis – its university of medicine, law and the arts – on the same level as those of Paris and Bologna.

The current building began as the monastic college of St-Benoît, built in 1364 by Pope Urban V (a former teacher), who employed the same architects as had designed Avignon's Papal Palace: during the Revolution, it all became strictly secular.

The most famous alumni were Rabelais and Nostradamus, neither of whom were known, however, for their doctoring. At the time of writing the collections and building, with its portraits of 200 great doctors and the rather stomach-churning Anatomy Museum, were being restored.

Musée Atger

2 rue de l'Ecole-de-Médecine, T04 67 41 76 40.
Mon, Wed and Fri 1330-1745. Free.
Map: Montpellier, A3, p148.

Located within the Faculté de Médecine, this is the oldest museum in Montpellier, the home to a superb collection of French, Flemish and Italian drawings and prints (on sliding panels). All were donated by Xavier Atger in the early 19th century. Fragonard and Rubens are present, but the most beautiful are the 26 drawings by the great baroque Venetian Giambattista Tiepolo.

Jardin des Plantes

163 rue Auguste Broussonnet, T04 67 63 43 22, univ-montp1.fr.
Jun-Sep Tue-Sun 1200-2000, Oct-May Tue-Sun 1200-1800.
Map: Montpellier, A2/A3, p148.

This romantic, luxuriant 4.5-ha garden, beloved of artists and poets (Paul Valéry was a regular *habitué*) is the oldest botanical garden in France. It was founded in 1593 by Henri IV and laid out by Pierre Richer de Belleval, so the future doctors of France would know their medicinal plants.

Some of the trees here are unique, for example the massive Ginkgo biloba, the oldest of its kind in France, which has female branches grafted on to a male trunk. Don't miss the statue of Rabelais, with a motto on the back exhorting passersby to "live joyfully".

Musée Languedocien

7 rue Jacques Coeur, T04 67 52 93 03, musee-languedocien.com.
Mid-Sep to mid-Jun Mon-Sat 1430-1730, mid-Jun to mid-Sep Mon-Sat 1500-1800, closed Sun and national holidays. €6, €3 student/child.
Map: Montpellier, B4, p148.

This museum is located in the Renaissance *hôtel particulier* of Jacques Coeur, the fabulously wealthy treasurer of Charles VII who, when charged with getting more taxes out of Languedoc, did so in a then-novel way, by investing in local projects so people would have more money in their pockets. That was until his downfall in 1451, when he was accused of poisoning the king's mistress.

The mansion was remodelled in the 17th century, when it was given the grandest staircase in Montpellier, but it still maintains Coeur's 'alchemist' coat of arms on a pillar and painted ceiling. Exhibits include prehistoric artefacts, Greek and Gallo-Roman finds, medieval paintings, ivories and sculpture, mule bridles from the Cévennes and an exceptional collection of ceramics, including some made in Montpellier.

Musée du Vieux Montpellier

1 place Pétrarque, T04 67 66 02 94.
Tue-Sat 0930-1200 and 1330-1700. Free.
Map: Montpellier, B4, p148.

Installed in the beautiful Hôtel de Varennes, this five-room museum displays a hodgepodge of sculpture, religious artefacts (including the 13th-century statue of the Black Virgin that once presided on the altar of Notre-Dame des Tables), prints, watercolours, plans, a model of the Bastille and the mallets for the *jeu de mail*, a 15th-century version of croquet played in Montpellier until the First World War.

Musée Fougau

Place Pétrarque, T04 67 84 31 58.
Mid-Aug to mid-Jul Wed and Thu 1500-1800. Free.
Map: Montpellier, B4, p148.

Fougau, means 'foyer' in Occitan, and this museum recreates an 18th-century apartment in the Hôtel de Varennes. It is furnished entirely by local donations and run by volunteers. There are some rare items (they have a *jeu de mail*) and frequent special exhibitions.

Antigone

From Place de la Comédie, walk through the shopping funnel that is Le Triangle to the ziggurat-style shopping centre **Polygone** (built in the early 1970s). There, you'll find yourself in former mayor Georges Frêche's most audacious project: the monumental, post-modern, neoclassical quarter of **Antigone**. Begun in 1983, it is a serenely classical antidote to Polygone's mercantile crassness.

On the map it looks like a key – a key to the future. *"Changer la ville pour changer la vie"* (Improve the city in order to improve life) was Frêche's motto, and he hired Barcelona architect Ricardo Bofill to build this pendant to l'Ecusson on 50 ha

What the locals say

First, coffee on the terrace of the Grand Café Riche, with the sunlit spectacle of city life flowing across the Place de la Comédie – provincial France's most desirable central square.

Then a dose of culture at the nearby **Musée Fabre**, where the first-class collections including 19th-century greats Delacroix, Géricault and Courbet – now have a decent setting.

From there to the **Arc de Triomphe** and **Promenade du Peyrou**. Both were built to demonstrate that once-Protestant Montpellier was once again in awe of Catholic royalty. Louis XIV looks suitably gratified up on his horse on the Prom.

Now filter back through the magnificent old town, crammed with bourgeois townhouses, restaurants and shops of all stripes. Lunch in the labyrinth at the good-value **Bouchon St Roch** (15 rue Plan-d'Agde, three courses for €10), before nipping over to **Antigone**, an extraordinary modern development in monumental bounds of neoclassical imagination, humanized with bistros, walk-through fountains and playing children.

Next, hop on a tram and a bus to reach the **Lunaret Zoo**, a Mediterranean forest studded with animals. The attendant **Amazonian hot-house** costs, but the assembly of exotic plants and beasts is worth €6 of anyone's cash.

Back to the centre for an aperitif on **Place Jean-Jaurès**, the epicentre of early nightlife. A short walk away, **Kinoa** (Place St Roch, T04 67 15 34 38) serves great Med fare with a contemporary twist. Allow €30 per person, including wine.

And so to bed. Or, if not, to **Le Rockstore** (20 rue Verdun), a rugged, blast-from-the-past rock music club. You can't miss it. It's got the back end of a Cadillac sticking out of the wall.

Anthony Peregrine, local travel writer.

Hôtel de Région.

purchased from the army and the Church. Under Bofill's exaggerated cornices (set apart from the walls to provide views of the ever-changing sky), the goal was to create a humanist middle-income district. The place names – Place du Nombre d'Or (Golden Number Square), Place Marathon, Place Dionysos, etc – play on classic themes, as do the copies of famous Greek bronzes. Place du Millénaire celebrates Montpellier's first, and next, 1000 years.

Over the years, the trees have grown and amenities have been added along Antigone's 1.5-km axis, including the Mediathèque Federico Fellini with a library of 7000 films, the Mediathèque Emile Zola, the regional library and an Olympic-sized pool. Antigone reaches a grand finale with an enormous hemicycle, the **Esplande de l'Europe**, where a copy of the Victory of Samothrace presides over the banks of the Lez. On the far bank the vista is framed by the **Hôtel de Région**, Frêche's HQ as President of Languedoc-Roussillon. It's shaped like a glass arch, echoing the Grande Arche in Paris and reflecting the waters of the Lez.

Antigone is only the beginning of a master plan to expand Montpellier east of and along the Lez to the Mediterranean, and a new tram line is already in the works. One of the many projects already completed is the **Odysseum**, a 50-ha entertainment complex that includes a multiplex cinema, an ice skating rink, a planetarium and an aquarium. **Port Marianne** is an urban water sports centre just down from the Hôtel de Région, where a new town hall is planned along with the **Jardins de la Lironde**, a 21st-century garden city designed by Christian de Portzampac.

Aquarium Mare Nostrum

Odysseum, allée Ulysse, T04 67 13 05 50, aquariummarenostrum.fr.
Oct-Apr Sun-Thu 1000-1900, Fri-Sat 1000-2000, closed Mon except during French school holidays, May-Jun, Sep Sun-Thu 1000-2000, Fri-Sat 1000-2200, closed Mon in May and Sep except during French school holidays, Jul-Aug daily 1000-2200. €12.50, €9 child (3-12), under 3s free. Free parking, or take the tram (Line 1).

Montpellier is proud of this huge state-of-the-art aquarium in the Odysseum leisure centre. Some 300 different marine species from sharks to penguins are on display, many in the 'balcony of the Ocean', one of the biggest and deepest pools in any aquarium. There's plenty for kids to enjoy, including an ice cave, a realistic cargo boat ride through a storm, and a simulated descent into an ocean abyss.

Parc Zoologique de Lunaret & La Serre Amazonienne

50 av d'Agropolis, T04 67 54 45 23, zoo.montpellier.fr.
Apr to mid-Oct Tue-Sun 1000-1900, mid-Oct to Mar 1000-1700, closed Mon except national holidays. The zoo is free, the Serre Amazonienne is €6, €4 concession/child (6-12), under 6s free. To get there by public transport, take shuttle bus No 9 from the St-Eloi station (Tram 1).

Montpellier's excellent zoo, north of the Ecusson, has a new attraction. Set up in conjunction with a park in Guyenne, the Amazonian greenhouse is dedicated to preserving endangered species (two-toed sloths, armadillos, ocelots) in mangroves, mountain forests, rainforest canopies and other specially reconstructed tropical environments.

Aquarium Mare Nostrum.

Château de Flaugergues.

Musée Agropolis

951 av Agropolis, T04 67 04 75 00, museum.
agropolis.fr.
Mon-Fri 1000-1230 and 1400-1800. €5, €2.50
concession, under 10s free.

Near the zoo, Agropolis is a research centre
dedicated to agriculture, biodiversity and the
environment. The museum itself explores the
history of food and farming around the world.

Tip...

Montpellier's tourist office offers two-hour guided
tours (€7) on different themes every Wednesday,
Saturday and Sunday at 1500 (1700 in summer).
These are your only chance to see inside the Arc
de Triomphe, the Faculté de Médecine, the Mikveh
(Jewish ritual baths) or the Hôtel Montcalm (home of
the general who lost the Battle of Quebec in 1759).

Outside the city

Château de Flaugergues

1744 av Albert Einstein, T04 99 52 66 37,
flaugergues.com.
Jun-Jul, Sep Tue-Sun 1430-1900, otherwise by
appointment. Park and wine cellar Jun-Jul, Sep
Mon-Sat 0900-1230 and 1430-1900, Sun and
national holidays 1430-1900. Guided tours of the
interior €6.50, €4 concession. Park €4. For wine
tastings, ring ahead. To get there by public
transport, take Bus No 9 and get off at the
Evariste Gallois stop.

In the late 17th century, Montpellier's grandees
built large summer residences or 'follies' in what
was then the countryside. This château, begun in
1695 by Etienne de Flaugergues (advisor to the
count of Montpellier), is the biggest of them all and
is filled with 17th- and 18th-century furnishings,

Flemish tapestries, ceramics and antique scientific and optical instruments. The park's box hedges and alleys are a fine example of 18th-century French gardens. The château's own AOC Coteaux du Languedoc is on sale in its caves.

Château de la Mogère

2235 rte de Vauguières, T04 67 65 72 01, lamogere.fr. Jun-Sep daily 1430-1830 (ring ahead on Sat), Oct-May Sat-Sun, national holidays 1430-1800. €5.

The Château de la Mogère, another of Montellier's grand follies, is located just southeast of the Odysseum. It was begun in 1719 and is set amid French gardens, massive cypresses and parasol pines. The owner, the Vicomte Gaston de Saporta, is often on hand to lead tours of the château's period furnishings, elegant plasterwork, paintings and family portraits. A lovely baroque *buffet d'eau* (a fountain built into a wall) overlooks the old kitchen garden.

L'Abbaye de Valmagne

On the D5, Villeveyrac, T04 67 78 06 09, valmagne.com. Mid-Jun to Sep Mon-Fri 1000-1800 and Sat-Sun 1000-1800, Oct to mid-Jun Mon-Fri 1400-1800 and Sat-Sun 1000-1800. Closed Tue from mid-Dec to mid-Feb. Guided tour and wine-tasting €7, €5.50 child, under 10s free.

St Marie de Valmagne (40 km west of Montpellier) was founded in 1138 by Raymond Trencavel, Viscount of Béziers, Nîmes and Carcassonne. After joining the stricter Cistercian order in 1159 it became one of the most powerful abbeys in the region, growing so quickly that a new church was begun in 1257, modelled on the Gothic cathedrals in the Ile de France, with a 112-m nave just to contain the many monks. Valmagne soon became known for its parties rather than its piety, and in 1575 its own abbot switched over to the Protestant camp and led the attack against it. It limped on until the Revolution, when many of France's great religious houses were used as stone quarries – a fate Valmagne avoided by being converted into a winery in 1791.

Owned since 1838 by the descendants of the Count of Turenne, wine (AOC Coteaux du Languedoc and Grès de Montpellier) is still the abbey's main concern. The church, under its 24-m vaulted ceiling, is more lavish than the typically austere Cistercian edifice, and decorated (rather appropriately) with reliefs of vines. The cloister, planted with special Cistercian (Cîteaux) roses, has an utterly enchanting octagonal Gothic pavilion crowned with trellises, with a tall fountain in the centre. It's a lovely venue for the classical music festival in July and August.

L'Abbaye de Valmagne.

Around the region

Pézenas

In 1261, Louis IX purchased a down-at-heel former Roman colony called *Piscenae*, famous for its soft wool. In 1456 it became the seat of the governor and the Three Estates of Languedoc, making it the de facto regional capital before Louis XIV hustled the nobles and jurists off to Montpellier. Only princely Uzès can rival the old capital's streets of elegant *hôtels particuliers*, with their beautiful courtyards and external stairs. But Pézenas is proudest of Jean-Baptiste Poquelin, better known as Molière, whose company came to entertain the governor, the Prince of Conti, for three-month stints every summer from 1650-1656.

Musée de Vulliod-St-Germain

3 rue Albert-Paul Alliés, T04 67 98 90 59, ville-pezenas.fr.
Jul-Oct Tue-Sun 1000-1200 and 1500-1900, Sep-Jun Tue-Sun 1000-1200 and 1400-1700.

This magnificent *hôtel particulier* houses the kind of aristocratic accessories you might expect to find in Pézenas: 17th-century tapestries, ceramics, period furnishings and paintings, and items somewhat tenuously linking Molière to the town. Not surprisingly, the whole town was abuzz in June 2009 when the newest exhibit acquired by popular subscription finally arrived to take its place: Molière's Chair. When in Pézenas the playwright used to sit in the shop of his friend the barber, Gély (1 place Gambetta), and eavesdrop on conversations about local characters, inspiring at least two of his plays – *Dom Juan* and *Tartuffe*.

Scénovision Molière

Place des Etats-du-Languedoc, T04 67 98 35 39, scenovisionmoliere.com.
Sep-Jun Mon-Sat 0900-1200 and 1400-1800, Sun 1000-1200 and 1400-1800, Jul-Aug Mon-Tue, Thu, Sat-Sun 0900-1300 and 1500-1900, Wed and Fri 0900-1300 and 1500-2200. The last show is 1 hr 15 mins before closing. €7, €5 concession.

Sharing the 17th-century Hôtel de Peyrat with the tourist office, this is a high-tech audiovisual evocation of Molière's life and work in five 'acts', ending with his death on stage while playing the *Malade Imaginaire* in Paris. Be warned, it's in French and the 3D glasses come in a comedy mask; you may feel silly but no one should recognize you.

Pézenas tourist map.

Tip...

Many *hôtels particuliers* now house antique shops, *ateliers* and art galleries. Pick up a free directory and map at the tourist office (Place des Etats du Languedoc, T04 67 98 36 40, pezenas-tourisme.fr).

Pézenas makes a good base for visiting the villages of Haut Languedoc.

Inland from Montpellier

This is classic *garrigue* country, green with aromatic scrub, and even the wines produced here have a certain earthy herbal essence. West and north of Montpellier, the *garrigue* is steeply sliced by rivers and otherworldly caves and gorges and dotted with medieval churches, including two famous ones along the road to Compostela.

St-Guilhem-le-Désert.

Le Pic St-Loup & St-Martin-de-Londres

At 644 m, Le Pic St-Loup is one of the great landmarks of the *garrigue* – a bluish limestone ridge that from certain angles appears to come to a needle-sharp point. It's the centrepiece and namesake of a small but emerging wine region, the northernmost pocket of the Coteaux du Languedoc. In the Middle Ages it signalled to pilgrims en route to Compostela that they were approaching St-Martin-de-Londres; this is the French for London, but it's also the Celtic word for the now dry swamp that surrounded this pretty village. St-Martin-de-Londres was built over a prehistoric settlement and named after a handsome church founded in the time of Charlemagne in a picture-perfect setting, encircled by old stone houses in an exquisite, arcaded medieval square. Part of the ensemble once belonged to a priory set up by the Abbaye de Gellone, the pilgrims' next major stop.

A pilgrimage destination even before Compostela, St-Guilhem-le-Désert is a gem of a honey-stoned village with narrow cobbled lanes and flower-filled balconies surrounding a World Heritage Site abbey. Just don't visualize sand and palms – the 'desert' in its name means deserted. Be warned though, in summer and at weekends it's anything but.

L'Abbaye de Gellone

Place de la Liberté, T04 67 57 44 33.
Cloisters Sep-Jun Mon-Fri 0800-1200 and 1400-1800, Sat, Sun and national holidays 0800-1100 and 1430-1800, Jul-Aug daily 0800-1200 and 1430-1830. Refectory museum €2.

Guilhem, Count of Toulouse and grandson of Charles Martel, was one of the great paladins of his cousin Charlemagne. He defeated a large Saracen army led by Hisham I near Narbonne and liberated Barcelona in 803; some say he captured Orange as well. In gratitude, Charlemagne gave Guilhem a piece of the True Cross and he retired here in 804, founding an abbey of Gellone (the old name of the River Hérault) under the spiritual guidance of his friend, St Benedict of Aniane. Soon after his death he was canonized and pilgrims began to arrive, including the very first Crusaders to the Holy Land; other pilgrims flowed in from Spain. In 1050, the great abbey church was built in the Lombard style, decorated with blind arcading, notably around its splendid apse, and in 1066 Guilhem was canonized again – a rare honour. The tower was added in the 14th century; the huge plane tree in the charming Place de la Liberté was planted in 1855.

Once again home to a community of monks, Guilhem's abbey is sombre and beautiful. It has been stripped of much of its original decoration: its reliquaries, saintly sarcophagus and once-famous library were sacked by the Protestants during the Wars of Religion, and its cloister was sold in the early 20th century to the Cloisters Museum in New York. There are traces of frescoes, and you can see fragments of the capitals and other stonework in the refectory. The best time to hear the 18th-century organ is during the July Festival of Baroque Organ and Choral Music.

St Guilhem

Guilhem was the subject of several popular 12th-century *Chansons du Geste* that combined his career with that of a dozen real and legendary warriors. According to legend, his nickname was Guilhem de Court-Nez ('of the Short Nose') after he lost a bit of it in battle with a giant Saracen. In 1972, American historian Arthur Zuckermann wrote *A Jewish Princedom in Feudal France*, suggesting Guilhem was a Jew from the Royal House of David, a descendant of the Merovingians through his father Thierry, which places him in the great web of Rennes-le-Château secrets (see page 206). Some also associate Guilhem with 'Kyot of Provence', the source of the Grail legend in Wolfram von Eschenbach's masterful *Parzifal* and the subject of his other epic poem *Willehalm*.

Around the region

Pont du Diable & La Maison du Grand Site

Aniane, T04 99 61 73 01, saintguilhem-valleeherault.fr.
Maison du Grand Site open Easter-Nov half-term holiday 1000-1900. The brasserie is open mid-Apr to mid-Jun and mid-Sep to Nov half-term Mon-Fri 1130-1800, Sat-Sun and French school holidays 1130-2200, mid-Jun to mid-Sep 1100-2300.

Three kilometres south of St-Guilhem, the road parallels the Pont du Diable, the spectacular bridge built in the 11th century to help pilgrims over the Gorges de L'Hérault. To take a good look or to picnic or swim, park by the Maison du Grand Site where there's a tourist office, a shop selling local products and wines and a brasserie.

Grotte de Clamouse

Between St-Jean-de-Fos and St-Guilhem-le-Désert, T04 67 57 71 05, clamouse.com.
Feb-May and Oct to mid-Nov 1000-1700, Jun and Sep 1000-1800, Jul-Aug 1000-1900. €8.70, €5.50 child (4-14), under 4s free.

At a constant 15°C even in August, this living cave is one of the most beautiful in France. It has recently been fitted with LED lighting and music, and a video explains its history and geography. One highlight is the Cathedral of Time with a pair of giant stalagmite 'organs'; another is the glittering White Corridor of spiky aragonite crystals.

Prieuré St-Michel-de-Grandmont

Soumont (west of St-Guilhem, towards Lodève), T04 67 44 09 31, prieure-grandmont.fr.
Guided tours mid-Jan to May and Oct to mid-Dec 1500, Jun-Sep 1030, 1500, 1600 and 1700. €10.

This 13th-century priory has an animal park and grand views down to the sea, but the site is essential viewing for anyone who loves Neolithic megaliths. It's home to the 2-m-high **Dolmen Coste-Rouge** (c 2000 BC), one of the most spectacular anywhere and it has a unique 'oven door'.

Ganges & the Upper Hérault

A market town at the confluence of the Rieutord, Vis and Hérault rivers, Ganges offers a good base for exploring the northern *garrigue*. People come to canoe down the gorges of the Hérault from the little fortified village of **Laroque** (just to the south) or **St-Bauzille-de-Putois** (just to the north); walk along the watermill-lined 13th-century irrigation canal at **Cazilhac**; or swim in the waterfalls of the Vis at **St-Laurent-du-Minier**. They also come to see two tremendous holes in the ground: the Grotte des Demoiselles and the Cirque de Navacelles.

Grotte des Demoiselles

St-Bauzille-de-Putois, T04 67 73 70 02, demoiselles.com.
Tours Nov-Feb Mon-Sat 1400-1600, Sun and French school holidays 1000-1600, Mar and Oct Sun and French national holidays 1000-1630, Apr, May-Jun Mon-Sat 1000-1730, Sun and French school holidays 1000-1730, Jul-Aug daily 1000-1800. €8.90, €6.60 young person (12-17), €5 child (6-11), €1 child (3-5).

A funicular does the hard work, taking visitors to the entrance of this spectacular stalactite cave, the legendary home of beautiful fairies, the *demoiselles*. The cave also has a long local history as a hideout for the Protestants in the early 18th-century War of the Camisards, and for priests during the Revolution.

Cirque de Navacelles

You'll begin to wonder if the signs are pulling your leg as you follow them up to a vast empty stretch of *causse*, and then suddenly, breathtakingly there it is yawning at your feet: a spectacular canyon, where the limestone has been carved over millions of years by the tight meander of the River Vis. After drinking in the views from the tops of the cliffs (**St-Maurice Navacelles** has the best views, and a restaurant) take the winding drive down to **Navacelles**, the sweet little village that from high above resembles an island on the canyon floor, where you can jump off the rocks into the cool waterfall.

Pont du Diable.

Tip...

In July and August don't even try to park in St-Guilhem. Instead, leave your car at the car park of **La Maison du Grande Site** (€3), a short walk from the Pont du Diable, and there's a free shuttle bus to the village and the Grotte de Clamouse.

Coastal Hérault

Lined with big lagoons and sandy beaches, the Hérault's long stretch of sea shore is full of surprises: there's La Grande-Motte, a cross between the 1964 New York World's Fair and a Babylonian ziggurat, and Le Cap d'Adge, a colony founded by the ancient Greeks, who would probably approve that half of the beaches are for naturists. Although the main Montpellier beach, Palavas, is low on charm, there's Maguelone (the 'cathedral of the sands'), Roman mosaics, dinosaur eggs, lagoons full of shellfish and the salty, lively Sète.

La-Grande-Motte.

City Hall Square, La Grande Motte.

La Grande Motte

This easternmost end of the Hérault coast was always known as the 'Big Lump', and the name stuck in 1963, when the French decided to make this grassy knoll into the seaside resort of the future. Architect Jean Balladur (brother of former Prime Minister Eduard Balladur) took charge, designated a 'Point Zero' and radiated out from there, presenting the French with (what seemed at the time) a dream of the future, full of 1960s go-go panache: brightly coloured curving holiday flats, ziggurat hotels, groovy shopping plazas, a casino, a thalassotherapy spa, and golf courses and tennis courts galore on the sandy beaches. It was a huge hit, and it still is. It's kept gleaming and is busy all year round, intermingled with 43,000 trees, pedestrian walkways and a huge marina.

Cathédrale de Maguelone

From Villeneuve-lès-Mageulone, cross the bridge from the car park (€4) and walk 2 km around the Etang de l'Arnel. In summer there's a free train to the cathedral and beaches, for information T04 67 69 75 87. Open 0900-1900.

The roots of Montpellier lie in Maguelone, a thin vine-covered volcanic strip linked to the mainland by a causeway. Originally a Phoenician or Etruscan trading post, it became a Visigoth bishopric, one of the seven cities of Septimania. The sixth-century cathedral was rebuilt in the 11th century, part church and part fortress against marauding pirates. Pirates, however, weren't as deadly as the tensions between Catholics and Protestants during the Reformation. In 1536, the bishop moved to higher ground in Montpellier, leaving the town of Maguelone to become a Protestant stronghold. In 1622, Richelieu ordered it razed to the ground to keep them from ever coming back – except for this church, which was left evocatively alone amid the vines on a lido. It's an austere place, relieved only by the scene over the door showing Christ and the Four Evangelists, some sculpted capitals and tombs. You can climb the bell tower for the view. Another reason to visit is Maguelone's beach, which is lovely and rarely crowded even in summer, except during its prestigious June festival of medieval and baroque music.

Musée International des Arts Modestes.

Sète & the Bassin de Thau

Squeezed on a narrow strip between sea and lagoon, Sète is a likable, salty port that works and parties hard. It was founded in 1666 by Colbert, Louis XIV's powerful finance minister, who saw that the new Canal du Midi needed a proper seaport, and that this hill on a sandy strip along the Bassin de Thau provided a perfect, defensible site. To encourage people to move here, Colbert showed them what was possible by building a fake city out of wood and cardboard. The ploy worked, and a real Sète was soon built, a town that calls itself the 'Venice of Languedoc' for its many canals. Vibrant festivals fill the summer calendar, and the unusual museums are fun. Sète's speciality is a unique snack called a *tielle sètoise*, a pie filled with a delicious mix of cuttlefish, onion and tomato.

Musée International des Arts Modestes

23 quai du Maréchal de Lattre de Tassigny, T04 99 04 76 44, miam.org.
Sep-Jun Wed-Mon 1000-1200 and 1400-1800, Jul-Aug daily 1000-1200 and 1400-1800. €4, €1.50 young person/child (12-18).

'Modest Arts' are everyday knick-knacks and gadgets that make you smile, whether they are mass-produced or a one-off. This delightfully kitch museum is run by artist-brothers Richard and Hervé Di Rosa (inventors in the 1980s of Figuration Libre, an art influenced by comic books), who display treasures accumulated over the past three decades in an organized chaos. It's fun for kids and adults and there are frequent special exhibits on Elvis and other kitsch-magnets.

Musée Paul Valéry

Rue François Desnoyer, T04 99 04 76 16.
Sep-Jun Wed-Mon 1000-1200 and 1400-1800,
Jul-Aug daily 1000-1200 and 1400-1800. €4,
€1.50 young person/child (12-18).

Sète's poet and scientist Paul Valéry (1871-1945)
wrote one of his most famous poems about the
Cimetière Marin, adjacent to this museum on the
steep slopes of Mont St Clair. Besides 18th- to
20th-century paintings by such artists as Courbet,
Jongkind, Desnoyer and Sarthou, there are
exhibitions of contemporary works. Other rooms
are dedicated to Valéry's life and art and to the
Joutes Nautiques, with paintings and models,
costumes and attempts to explain the rules,
which vary from city to city.

Espace Brassens

*67 bd Camille Blanc, T04 99 04 76 26, sete.fr/
brassens.*
Jun and Sep daily 1000-1200 and 1400-1800, Oct-
May Tue-Sun 1000-1200 and 1400-1800, Jul-Aug
daily 1000-1200 and 1400-1900. €5, €2 young
person/child (10-18), under 10s free.

A short drive west of the centre along the Corniche
de Neuburg, this homage to Georges Brassens
(1921-1981) is a must for lovers of *la chanson
française*. Brassens was a beloved chansonnier/

songwriter/poet and a sometime bad boy who
was born in Sète. An audio tour tells the story of his
life and music, including a video of his 1972 concert
in Paris.

Around the Bassin de Thau

The largest and deepest of all Languedoc's coastal
étangs, the Basin de Thau is a famous nursery for
oysters and 17 other kinds of shellfish. On
weekends and summer evenings its seafood
restaurants, which tend to be better and cheaper
than the more touristy offerings in Sète, are
packed. Try one in **Bouzigues**, a pocket-sized port
synonymous with some of France's best oysters,
which has spectacular views of the oyster beds –
neat rows of wooden tables set in the water like a
vast mermaid restaurant. Or head to calmer **Mèze**
to the west, or pretty **Marseillan**, a sweet fishing
village at the beginning of the Canal du Midi,
where the Bassin de Thau has a channel to the sea.

Tip...

Visit Sète's fascinating wholesale fish market and
auction (Criée aux Poissons) by booking ahead with
the tourist office (60 Grand'Rue Mario Roustan,
T04 67 74 71 71). Tours start at 1530, take one
hour and cost €6, €3 child (3-12).

Bassin de Thau.

Around the region

La Villa Loupian

Loupian (4.5 km west of Bouzigues), T04 67 18 68 18, villaloupian.free.fr.
Sep-Jun Wed-Mon 1330-1800, Jul-Aug daily 1330-1800, last admission 1700. €4.60, €3.05 student.

Located along the Via Domitia, this luxurious Gallo-Roman villa, inhabited from the first century BC to the sixth century AD, was subject to a 30-year excavation. The patrician owners (whose initials were MAF) owned a vast tract of vines, and a pottery that made the amphoras used to import their wine across the Mediterranean. In the fourth century the villa was rebuilt with lavish mosaic floors, attributed to Syrian artists. Visits include the museum and a guided tour of the villa, now sheltered under a large roof.

Les Joutes Nautiques

Every year since 1666, the Sétois have competed for glory in the Joutes Nautiques (nautical jousts). The sport, played up and down the ports of Languedoc, was invented in the 13th century by St Louis' knights at Aigues-Mortes; short on horses, they amused themselves by charging at each other from fishing boats. The rules are complex, but this is the way they play today: each nautical knight, armed with lance and shield, stands on an elevated platform of a long boat as teams of eight to ten rowers provide the momentum for the collision to the tune of drum and oboe. The loser tumbles into the drink; seven times the boats pass, and whoever has more dry men at the end wins. Sète alone has 17 teams, and there are others from up and down the coast. Beginning on weekends in late June, jousts take place in the Canal Royal before climaxing in a grand finale between the best teams of the year on St Louis' Day, 25 August. There are parades, music and feasts of pastis and macaronnade (pasta baked with shellfish and tomatoes).

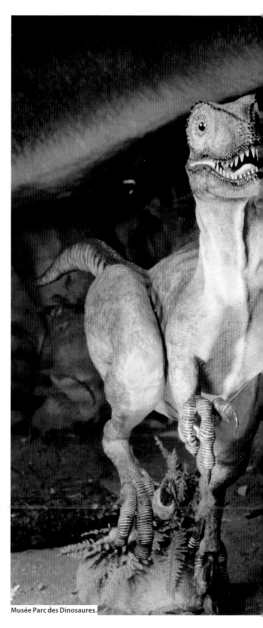
Musée Parc des Dinosaures.

I've done lots of experiments with white wines for fish sauces and I've come to the conclusion that Noilly Prat is the best.

French Odyssey, Rick Stein

Musée Parc des Dinosaures

Mèze, T04 67 43 02 80, musee-parc-dinosaures. com.
Feb-Jun and Sep daily 1400-1800, Jul-Aug daily 1000-1900, Oct-Dec daily 1400-1700, Jan Sat-Sun 1400-1700. €8, €6.50 child (5-12).

Kids love this place. The park features life-sized models of dinosaurs (including a 25-m brachiosaurus) in a 5-ha park, where clutches of dinosaur eggs and other fossils were discovered in the 1990s.

Noilly Prat

Marseillan Port, T04 67 77 20 15, noillyprat.com.
Mar-Apr, Oct-Nov daily 1000-1100 and 1430-1630, May-Sep 1000-1200 and 1430-1900. €3.50, €2 young person/child (12-18), under 12s free, family €7.

The straw-coloured Noilly Prat, the 'Rolls Royce of Vermouths' and one of France's distinctive tipples, has been distilled in Marseillan since 1813. This popular guided tour takes you through the manufacturing process, which includes leaving wooden casks of wine out in the sun for a year.

Tip...

The Route des Vignerons et des Pêcheurs has been set up to enable wine and seafood lovers to visit local producers. Pick up a map with addresses at the Agde tourist office (Rond-point du Bon Accueil, Le Cap d'Agde, T04 67 01 04 04).

Agde & Le Cap d'Agde

Founded near the mouth of the Hérault by the Greeks in the fifth century BC, *Agathé Tyché* (Good Fortune) was an important ancient port of call for ships sailing between Italy and Spain. Rebuilt in the Middle Ages, the old town of Agde looks like no other town in France. Positioned on top of a volcanic bubble, its buildings are made of blocks of black basalt, including the rugged 12th-century fortress of a church, the **Cathédrale de Saint-Etienne**, built over a Temple of Diana.

Le Cap d'Agde, Agde's modern beach-lined resort extension, draws a large contingent of Parisian fashion victims. A large swathe of land and beach is given over to the biggest (discreetly fenced) naturist resort in Europe. If it's all too busy though, head to dreamy, dune-tufted **La Tamarissière**, shaded by a 200-year-old pine forest, just west at the mouth of the Hérault.

Musée de l'Ephèbe

Mas de la Clape, Le Cap d'Agde, T04 67 94 69 60, ville-agde.fr.
Nov-Mar Mon, Wed-Sat 0900-1200 and 1400-1700, Sun 1400-1700, Sep-Oct and Mar-Jun Mon, Wed-Sat 0900-1200 and 1400-1800, Sun 1400-1800, Jul-Aug Mon-Fri 0900-1915, Sat-Sun 1200-1900. €4.50, €1.80 young person/child (10-18), under 10s free.

This excellent museum, built in 1984 near the port, was the first in France dedicated to underwater archaeology, and the nearby seas and river have yielded some choice finds. On display is an ornate Etruscan bronze tripod, one of only five ever found, and a bronze Eros and 'royal child' (identified as the son of Caesar and Cleopatra), both discovered in 2001.

The prize, however, is a Hellenistic bronze of a youth (*ephèbe*), identified as a young Alexander the Great, discovered in 1964 in the Hérault. There's also a vast collection of amphoras, pots, anchors, marbles and remains of ancient ships and finds from more recent wrecks, up to the 19th century.

Musée Agathois

5 rue de la Fraternité, Le Cap d'Agde, T04 67 94 82 51, ville-agde.fr.
Nov-Mar Mon, Wed-Sat 0900-1200 and 1400-1700, Sun 1400-1700, Sep-Oct Mar-Jun Mon, Wed-Sat 0900-1200 and 1400-1800, Sun 1400-1800, Jul-Aug Mon-Fri 0900-1915, Sat-Sun 1200-1900. €4.50, €1.80 young person/child (10-18), under 10s free.

Housed in a Renaissance *hôtel particulier*, this surprisingly large collection covers the history of Agde from medieval times to the present day. There are costumes, lace, headdresses, furnishings, paintings and more.

Le Cap d'Agde.

Le Monde des Santons du Monde

1 rue Rabelais, Le Cap d'Agde, T04 67 11 04 65, santonsdumonde.com.
Sep-Jun daily 1400-1830, Jul-Aug daily1000-2000, Christmas 1000-1830. €5.70, €4.70 concession, €4.20 young person/child (4-15).

Santons, the traditional figurines, populate Nativity scenes in the south of France, but this child-friendly museum shows they are made around the world, in all shapes and sizes, and that occasionally they take time off from the manger scene to play cards or eat pizza.

Béziers & around

Founded by Caesar as the *Colonia Victrix Julia Septimanorum Baetarae*, Hérault's second city, Béziers, unlike Montpellier is still the old Languedoc. It's a mix of genteel and scruffy (although the latter is perhaps endangered by the new slew of direct flights from the UK and the house bargain-hunters who follow), and its passions are wine, rugby (the Biterrois are 12-time French national champions) and bullfights. The August feria is the biggest festival in Languedoc.

Cathédrale St-Nazaire, Béziers.

Allées Paul Riquet

This is the heart of Béziers, a shady café-lined promenade named after the local who dug the Canal du Midi. On Fridays it's the scene of a colourful flower market. The bottom of the Allées gives onto a beautiful romantic garden, the **Plateau des Poètes**, planted in 1865 and adorned with busts of the poets (Victor Hugo being the only non-southerner). At the top, the delightful 19th-century **Théâtre Municipal** has recently been restored.

From the theatre, Rue de la République carries on to Place de la Madeleine, site of the recently restored Romanesque church of **St-Madeleine**. Nearby are the **Halles**, with a collection of arty camels inside. Camels became the symbol of Béziers after the city's first bishop, St Aphrodise, arrived on one in the first century AD.

The massacre of 1209

Ruled by the tolerant Viscount Roger-Raymond Trencavel, Béziers had an important Cathar population. In 1203, Pope Innocent III suspended the Bishop of Béziers for refusing to excommunicate them, and not long after, the Papal Legate Pierre de Castelnau who was sent to convert them, fled Béziers fearing for his life – only to be assassinated in 1208. The Albigensian Crusade was on, and from the very beginning Béziers was a prime target.

When Simon de Montfort appeared with his siege engines and demanded that the Catholics leave before he attacked, they stalwartly refused and defended the walls side by side with their Cathar neighbours. The city fell on 22 July and was put to the sack, as men, women and children sought refuge in the cathedral and church of St-Madeleine.

The order was then given to massacre the Cathars, and when asked how to tell them apart from the Catholics, the new Papal Legate Arnaud-Amary famously (and perhaps apocryphally) replied: "Kill them all; God will know His own". The churches were set ablaze, the blood flowed and in his report to the pope, Arnold-Amary boasted of sending 20,000 new souls to God for sorting.

Cathédrale St-Nazaire

Place des Albigeois.
Sep-Jun daily 0900-1200 and 1430-1730,
Jul-Aug daily 0900-1900.

Perched on top of the city, Béziers' landmark cathedral fills the skyline, its commanding presence acting as a perpetual reminder of just who was in charge after the Albigensian Crusade. The original church was filled with refugees on 22 July 1209, set alight by the Crusaders and then 'split in half like a pomegranate' (see box, below). Rebuilding began soon after, this time in the conquerors' Gothic style, with a fortress façade and a huge rose window. Inside, it's not quite as severe, especially around the ornate organ and the baptismal chapel where playful angels sit on the upper balustrade; on the left wall of the nave you can make out some faded 15th-century frescoes. The handsome cloister dates from the 14th century.

Musée des Beaux-Arts: Hôtel Fabrégat

Place de la Révolution, T04 67 28 38 78.
Nov-Mar Tue-Sun 0900-1200 and 1400-1700,
Apr-Jun, Sep-Oct Tue-Sun 0900-1200 and 1400-1800, Jul-Aug Tue-Sun 1000-1800. €2.70,
€1.90 concession (ticket also valid for the Hôtel Fayet, see below).

Near the Cathedral, this grand *hôtel particulier* was once the residence of Béziers' mayor. It is packed with an eclectic collection of art donated to the city, from a masterful 16th-century *Virgin and Child* by Martin Schaffner, to a portrait by Holbein the younger, to works by Corot and Delacroix. Most of the 20th-century works once belonged to Jean Moulin, a native of Béziers (1899-1943) and the most famous leader of the Resistance, who posed as an art dealer before he was captured and tortured to death by the Nazis. There are paintings by De Chirico, Soutine, Dufy and others, and drawings by Moulin himself.

Around the region

Musée des Beaux-Arts: Hôtel Fayet

Rue du Capus, T04 67 49 04 66.
Nov-Mar Tue-Sun 0900-1200 and 1400-1700,
Apr-Jun, Sep-Oct Tue-Sun 0900-1200 and
1400-1800, Jul-Aug Tue-Sun 1000-1800. €2.70,
€1.90 concession (ticket also valid for the Hôtel
Fabrégat, see above).

Set in a delightful 17th-century townhouse, this
branch of the art museum is filled with works by
local sculptor Jean Antoine Injalbert (1845-1933),
who carved most of the statues in the Plateau des
Poètes and the monument to Molière in Pézenas.

Musée du Biterrois

Caserne St-Jacques, Rampe du 96ème, T04 67 36 81 61.
Nov-Mar Tue-Sun 0900-1200 and 1400-1700,
Apr-Jun, Sep-Oct Tue-Sun 0900-1200 and
1400-1800, Jul-Aug Tue-Sun 1000-1800. €2.70,
€1.90 concession.

This museum, dedicated to Béziers' history, houses
prehistoric, Greek and Roman finds; Romanesque
capitals and other sculpted bits from the city's
churches; and lovely ceramics. Other exhibits tell the
history of Béziers as a wine city: how it grew in leaps
and bounds thanks to the Canal du Midi, the founding
of Sète and later the railroad. Until the turn of the last
century, Béziers was the richest city in Languedoc, the
self-proclaimed 'World Capital of Wine' – at least until
the winemakers' revolt in 1907 (see History, page 35).

Eglise St Jacques

Rue St-Jacques

After leaving the Musée du Biterrois (see above),
stroll down Rue St-Jacques for a look at the **Arènes**,
or Roman Amphitheatre, which is now surrounded
by houses. It dates back to AD 80 and in its prime
could seat 15,000 spectators.

Just above the museum, on a garden belvedere
overlooking the plain of the Orb, you'll find the
12th-century Romanesque church of St Jacques,
noted for its beautiful polygonal apse decorated
with intricate stonework.

Oppidum d'Ensérune

Nissan-lez-Ensérune, T04 67 37 01 23, enserune.
monuments-nationaux.fr.
Apr-Sep daily 1000-1230 and 1400-1800,
May-Aug daily 1000-1900, Oct-Mar daily
0930-1230 and 1400-1730 (last admission 1 hr
before closing). €7, €4.50 young person (18-25),
under 18s free.

High on a hill, 10 km southwest of Béziers, this
Celto-Iberian settlement is fascinating. It was founded
in the sixth century BC, but by the first century AD
and the advent of the *Pax Romana* hilltop hunkering
made little sense and the site was abandoned.

There are archaeological remains here – walls,
terraces, and extensive underground storage silos
and amphoras (some scholars claim, in fact, that
amphoras were invented here by local potters) –
but also majestic views encompassing the Via
Domitia, the Canal du Midi and the astonishing
Etang de Montcady. This *étang*, a malarial swamp
drained in the 13th century, startlingly resembles a
giant pie chart in the landscape, sliced by drainage
canals. The **museum** has a superb collection of
pottery, weapons and imported goods from
across the Mediterranean.

Midi means midday but it also means the South;
the sunny region of long lunches and afternoon
naps, where this waterway winds languorously
under a cool canopy of plane trees, past vines and
villages. A World Heritage Site since 1996, its
240 km were completed in only 15 years (1666-
1681) by 12,000 workers, who moved seven million
tonnes of earth and built 130 bridges and 64 locks
to link the Bassin de Thau to Toulouse (and the
Atlantic via the Garonne river). Yet even more
extraordinary is the fact that the canal only came
about because of the vision, grit and resources
of one man – Pierre-Paul Riquet (1609-1680).

The Canal du Midi.

Riquet was born into a wealthy family of Béziers, with good enough connections to land him the much sought-after post of 'tax farmer' in Languedoc. The king told the 'farmer' how much he required and anything extra the farmer could wring out of the people he could keep. Riquet was good at his job and over 40 years acquired a fortune.

As he grew older, he became fascinated with the idea of a canal linking the Mediterranean and the Atlantic, especially as Spanish and English pirates were pouncing on French shipping going through the Straits of Gibraltar. A canal could cut a month from that dangerous journey. But where would the water come from, especially on the Mediterranean side? This had been the insurmountable obstacle to the ancient Romans, who had been the first to toy with the idea. After walking in the Black Mountains north of Carcassonne, Riquet came up with a brilliant solution: to capture the water here at the Atlantic-Mediterranean watershed through an ingenious system of underground channels and storage basins.

He presented his proposal to Louis XIV in 1660, but the king would only sign off on the 'Canal Royal des Deux Mers' once Riquet promised to pay for it; in return, his family would have the right to collect tolls in perpetuity. Riquet, then in his 60s, personally oversaw the works, solving problems as they arose; after a rectangular lock caved in, for instance, he changed the design to ovoid locks. He also planted hundreds of thousands of trees to hold in the soil along the banks.

Riquet died with just a mile to go on the project, and so in debt that his family had to give all the tolls to his creditors until 1724. His canal, however, was quickly recognized as the engineering feat of the century, the 'Eighth Wonder of the World'. It brought boom times to Toulouse and to the textile industries of Languedoc, now that they could easily transport their product to the North. Traffic peaked in 1856, the year before the Sète-Bordeaux rail line was completed, heralding its commercial doom.

Haut Languedoc & Minervois

Béziers is a good base for visiting two beautiful areas, beginning with the **Parc Régional du Haut Languedoc**. This encompasses the upper valley of the Orb, where the waters rush down in winter but in summer slow into rock pools – great places for a dip.

Your first likely stop is **Roquebrun**, a village rising picturesquely from the banks of the Orb, where a stone bridge spans a favourite swimming hole and the canoeing is safe for the whole family. Nicknamed 'Petit Nice' for its hot microclimate, Roquebrun has a Mediterranean Garden to prove it. On the second Sunday of February it holds a famous mimosa festival.

The most enchanting scenery is just to the north, above **Mons-la-Trivalle** in the extraordinary **Gorges d'Héric**, a deep dagger slash in the mountains where you can stroll under the cliffs and step off into the crystal rock pools among the boulders. From here, you can follow the Orb east to **Lamalou-les-Bains**, a belle époque spa town preserved in aspic, where Alexander Dumas Fils, Alphonse Daudet and the kings of Morocco and Spain once came to soak their aches and attend operettas in the bijou theatre.

Seven kilometres west of Mons-la-Tivalle, in a loop of the River Jaur, is **Olargues**. A lovely stone village, Olargues was first settled by the Visigoths and then rebuilt as a fortified town in the 13th century by the local barons, who also constructed its pride and joy, a magnificent triple-arched **Devil's Bridge**.

West of Béziers awaits the **Minervois**, another beautiful micro-region and one at the forefront of the Languedoc wine renaissance. Vineyards tidily stripe the pale land under rocky outcrops, and medieval villages are criss-crossed with rivers and the most verdant stretch of the Canal du Midi. Even if you aren't on a boat, visit the canal ports for a stroll, or cycle along the towpaths. If you want to swim, head north to lovely **Bize Minervois**, where there's a superb natural swimming pool in the River Cesse.

Named after the Roman goddess of wisdom, **Minerve**, the historic capital of the area, occupies a vertiginous promontory at the confluence of the Cesse and Brian. The **Musée Hurepel** (Rue des Martyrs, T04 68 91 12 26, Apr to mid-Jun 1030-1230 and 1400-1800, mid-Jun to mid-Oct 1000-1300 and 1400-1900, €3) tells the story of how, in 1210, Simon de Montfort catapulted boulders over the ravine onto the Cathars, and then burned 180 *parfaits* at the stake.

To the west, in the foothills of the Montagne Noire, medieval **Caunes Minervois** is built around the golden stone **Abbaye de St-Pierre et St-Paul** (T04 68 78 09 44, Sep-Jun 1000-1200 and 1400-1700, Jul-Aug 1000-1900, €4.50). Only the crypt has survived from its foundation in 780, while the rest dates from the 11th and 12th centuries. Note the marble altars: just north of Caunes they quarry red and green marble, used in the Grand Trianon at Versailles and the Paris Opéra.

The best and most unusual church, however, is the heptagonal 12th- to 13th-century Romanesque **St-Marie** in **Rieux-Minervois**. As far as we know, this is the only seven-sided church anywhere, built around seven central columns, reflecting the verse in Proverbs 1:9 on the seven pillars of Divine Wisdom. The intricate capitals are by the Master of Cabestany; the complicated vaulted roof extends to a 14-sided exterior, although its shape has been obscured by later chapels.

Boating on the Canal du Midi

Just as the last goods were transported in 1979, a new role for the Canal du Midi sprang up – that of a holiday destination. The idea that people might like to spend a slow holiday in a canal boat puttering along at 5 kph is British, and even today most of the operators who hire out barges are from the UK. The clients, however, hail from all corners of the globe. The boats come in all sizes, from a basic two-person model to luxurious barges worthy of Cleopatra. Firms also rent out bicycles so visitors can peddle off to nearby shops, restaurants and picnic spots. No previous experience is required, but note that once you go, you may be hooked.

The canal has some extraordinary features. One of Riquet's biggest headaches was lifting and lowering the barges 25 m from sea level to the river Orb by Béziers. He responded to the challenge by constructing a marvel: a 312-m 'stairway' of nine locks, the **Ecluse de Fonsérannes**. Yet the Orb often flooded and disrupted traffic, so in 1858 the 240-m **Pont-canal de l'Orb** was built over the river and the lock system was shortened to only five locks.

After Fonsérannes, the canal flows through another of Riquet's marvels near Ensérune: the world's first canal tunnel, the 170-m **Tunnel de Malpas**. This is part of a 53-km pound – the longest lock-free stretch on any French canal – offering a very pleasant 106-km return trip, a classic idyll passing through the pretty ports of **Capestang**, **Venentec-en-Minervois**, **Le Somail** (with its grocery barge and famous bookshop) and **Homps**.

Trips on the Canal du Midi can last anywhere from a couple of hours for a day outing to a week or more. Boats generally depart on Saturday afternoons from 1600-1800. The longer trips will take you down **Canal de la Robine** (see page 218) to Narbonne (see page 214) and Port-la-Nouvelle (via Le Somail), or along the **Canal du**

Rhône Sète to Beaucaire (see page 91) via the Bassin de Thau. It's not all daydreaming though, as there's a fair amount of work involved when going through the locks. It's recommended that two or more couples share a boat (and hence the work), to make for a more relaxing holiday. Locks all have keepers and are open September-June daily 0800-1230 and 1330-1730, July-August daily 0800-1230 and 1330-1900. Expect the occasional queue in summer but if you get peckish while you wait, many lock keepers sell local delicacies.

When you hire a boat, arrive with basic provisions (and gardening gloves to prevent rope blisters) so you don't have to race around shopping on your first day.

Low season prices for a week start at €600-700 for a four-berth boat. On top of the rental fee, allow around €120 per week for diesel as well as a damage waiver (around €100), €40 a week for bike rentals, and €25 for a map guide (essential for finding water points to refill tanks, stock-up on groceries, etc). For details of operators, see Activities & tours, page 191.

Sleeping

Montpellier & around

Baudon de Mauny €€€€

1 rue de la Carbonnerie, T04 67 02 21 77, baudondemauny.com.
Map: Montpellier, B3, p148.
This extremely stylish B&B occupies an 18th-century *hôtel particulier* in the heart of Montpellier. In the same family for seven generations, the decor is a charming mix of old (including high ceilings, decorative stuccoes and an elegant stone staircase) and 21st-century design. There's Wi-Fi, a library and honesty bar with wines and spirits.

Le Jardin des Sens €€€€

11 av St-Lazare, just north of the centre, near the No 2 tram line, T04 99 58 38 38, jardindessens.com.
Map: Montpellier, D1, p148.
Although it presents an opaque façade, inside is a chic world full of contemporary art and colour. Clean lines dominate the decor of the 12 rooms, and there's a cosy living room and 11-m rooftop swimming pool. It is also attached to one of Montpellier's finest restaurants (see Eating, page 183).

Hôtel d'Aragon €€€

10 rue Baudin, T04 67 10 70 00, hotel-aragon.fr.
Map: Montpellier, C5, p148.
This newly renovated boutique hotel is only a few minutes' walk from the Place de la Comédie. The 12 air-conditioned rooms, each named after a famous author, are equipped with flat-screen satellite TVs and Wi-Fi. The stair to the upper two floors is a bit narrow, but the staff are very helpful with the bags. Breakfast, full of fresh goodies, is served in the glass-roofed veranda.

New Hotel du Midi €€€

22 bd Victor Hugo, T04 67 92 69 61, new-hotel.com/Midi.
Map: Montpellier, B5, p148.
By the Opéra Comédie, this palatial belle époque institution was 'new' two centuries ago, and had its last facelift in 2006. In spite of the busy location, the 44 rooms done up in chocolate, pistachio and raspberry tones are perfectly soundproofed. Discounts are available in the nearby parking garage.

Hôtel des Arts €€

6 bd Victor Hugo, T04 67 58 69 20, hotel-des-arts.fr.
Map: Montpellier, B5, p148.
A simple but welcoming little hotel just off the Place de la Comédie. It offers en suite rooms in spring colours, all equipped with soundproofing, air conditioning, Wi-Fi and TV. There are also family rooms, which can sleep up to five. Prices are among the lowest in central Montpellier.

Hôtel Le Guilhem €€

18 rue Jean-Jacques Rousseau, T04 67 52 90 90, leguilhem.com.
Map: Montpellier, A3, p148.
Near the Faculté de Médecine and leafy Place de la Canorgue, Le Guilhem has 36 air-Canorgue, Le Guilhem has 36 air-conditioned, peaceful rooms in a 16th-century house with a delightful garden. Note that standard doubles are in this price range, but others are more expensive. Children under 10 sharing their parents' room stay for free.

Hôtel du Parc €€

8 rue Achille Bégé, T04 67 41 16 49, hotelduparc-montpellier.com.
Map: Montpellier, A1, p148.
A favourite with romantics, this 18th-century *hôtel particulier* (a short stroll north of the historic centre) was the home of Count Vivier de Châtelard, and still has an aristocratic feel about it. There are 19 spacious air-conditioned rooms off a beautiful spiral stair. Breakfast is served on the sunny terrace and there's a free car park and Wi-Fi.

Villa Juliette €€

6 chemin de la Faissine, Pézenas, T04 67 35 25 38, villajuliette.com.
Overlooking Sans Souci Park and only a three-minute walk from the centre of Pézenas, this charming B&B in a 19th-century villa is a quiet little oasis in a Mediterranean garden with a curvaceous pool. There are five en suite rooms, and one room sleeps four to six people. If weather permits, breakfast is served in the garden.

Hôtel des Etuves €

24 rue des Etuves, T0 467 607 819,
hoteldesetuves.fr.
Map: Montpellier, B5, p148.
On a peaceful pedestrian lane,
100 m from Place de la Comédie,
this reliable budget choice has
been in the same family for three
generations. The 15 rooms are en
suite and the continental
breakfast is a bargain at €5.

Hôtel le Mistral €

25 rue Boussairolles, T04 67 58
45 25, hotel-le-mistral.com.
Map: Montpellier, C5, p148.
This little hotel, within easy
walking distance of the train
station, has been recently
refurbished and is a good choice
in a city where bargains are few
and far between. Many rooms
have a little balcony, and all
come with flat-screen TVs and
Wi-Fi. Parking is available nearby
for €10 a day.

La Dordîne €

9 rue des Litanies, Pézenas,
T04 67 90 34 81, ladordine.com.
This B&B in the heart of Pézenas
is a medieval house with five
simple but attractive rooms (ask
for the 'Picpoul', with its views
over the countryside). The young
owners love wine and food and
this is evident from the wine
cellar, where you can go for a
tasting, and from the superb
breakfast of home-made cakes,
breads, brioches, jams, fresh
fruits and yoghurts.

Self-catering

Appart'City Montpellier l'Orangerie

29 bd Berthelot, T04 67 34 27 00,
appartcity.com/appart-hotel-montpellier.
Map: Montpellier, A7, p148.
This new apartment hotel is on
a quiet street south of the centre,
but it's only 150 m from a No 2
tram stop. Each of the 147
studios and apartments comes
with a kitchenette and
comfortable sofa bed. Extra
services include underground
parking, laundry, buffet breakfast
and broadband. Two days
minimum stay; rates begin at
€75 a night for two people.

Château Résidence de Bionne

1225 rue de Bionne, T04 67 45 20
93, chateau-bionne.com.
Map: Montpellier, A7, p148.
Once the country home of the
governor of Languedoc, this
early 18th-century house has
now been converted into 29
elegant suites with kitchenettes,
TVs and internet access. Set in a
beautiful mature park, it's a
favourite with wedding parties.
The grounds include an 11-hole
golf course, a pool and a fine
restaurant, Le Grand Arbre.
From €120 a night for two.

Hôtel le Guilaume d'Orange €€

2 av Guilaume d'Orange,
St-Guilhem-le-Désert, T04 67 57
24 53, guilhaumedorange.com.
Book early and bag one of the 10
delightful spacious rooms in this
stylish hotel built of old stone.
The decor of each is well thought
out, with light natural tones and
a mix of antiques. Owner Aurore
is very helpful and also runs an
excellent restaurant shaded by
ancient plane trees.

Hotel Les Norias €€

254 av des Deux Ponts, Cazilhac,
Ganges, T04 67 73 55 90,
les-norias.fr.
Peace and quiet is guaranteed at
this ivy-covered former silk mill.
With 11 rooms, it is set in a lush
park on the banks of the Hérault
and there's even a private beach
for dips in the river.

Hôtel Méditerranée €€€

277 allée du Vaccarès, La Grande-
Motte, T04 67 56 53 38,
hotellemediterranee.com.
If you belong to the half of
humanity that adores La
Grande-Motte, this 40-room
hotel is the place to stay. The
building, set in a pretty
Mediterranean garden 200 m
from the beach, dates from 1960s
but has recently been handed
over to local artists who have
frescoed and decorated the
rooms with imagination, colour
and panache. The pool, hamman
and restaurant-bar are added
bonuses.

Listings

Le Grand Hôtel €€€
17 quai de Tassigny, Sète, T04 67 74 71 77, legrandhotelsete.com.
Classy and centrally located, this hotel is full of the 19th-century charm of the bourgeoisie and there's a wonderful iron and glass patio by the lobby. Near the bottom of this price range, it offers airy, pastel, air-conditioned rooms with Wi-Fi. There's a huge breakfast buffet for €10 and use of a garage for €9.

Hôtel Venezia €
Les Jardins de la Mer, 20 La Corniche de Neuburg, Sète, T04 67 51 39 38, hotel-sete.com.
This hotel, run by friendly Christophe and his parents, is only 50 m from the beach. It offers 18 en suite rooms that can sleep up to four, each with a balcony. There's also free parking.

Béziers & around

Château d'Agel €€€
1 rue de la Fontaine, Agel (10 km from Minerve), T04 68 91 21 38, chateaudagel.fr.
This medieval château, high over the Cesse, was first recorded in the year 1100, and rebuilt after it was burnt in 1210 by the troops of Simon de Montfort. Beautifully restored over the decades by the current owners, the Ecals, it sits amid a pretty park and vineyard and offers four atmospheric suites with lofty ceilings, all superbly furnished with antiques (two of the suites sleep up to four people).

Château de Lignan €€€
Place de l'Eglise, Lignan-sur-Orb, T04 67 37 91 47, chateaulignan.fr.
Only 10 minutes from Béziers, this ninth-century fortress was converted into a summer palace for the bishops of Béziers in the 17th century – note the episcopal crown on the basin. It's wonderfully peaceful, set in a beautiful 400-year-old park on the banks of the Orb. There are 49 airy classically decorated rooms (some sleeping four), all en suite with tubs, and a lovely pool, gourmet restaurant (open to non-guests) and a helicopter pad in case you need it.

Château de Raissac €€€
Rte de Lignan, Béziers, T04 67 49 17 60, raissac.com.
This 19th-century château is set in a wooded park, with a 17th-century wine cellar. It's been in owner Jean Viennet's family since 1828; he's a painter/winegrower and his Norwegian wife Christine is an extraordinary *trompe l'oeil* ceramicist, who offers classes. The large period rooms with old-fashioned bathrooms are delightful and there are delicious *table d'hôte* dinners from the garden available, as well as cooking courses.

Hôtel des Poètes €€-€
80 allées Paul Riquet, Béziers, T04 67 76 38 66, hoteldespoetes.net.
Overlooking the Parc des Poètes, this hotel has stylish modern rooms that sleep up to four. All are en suite and equipped with TVs and Wi-Fi. Breakfast is a delight in the sunny breakfast room, and they'll even loan you a bike to explore the Canal du Midi, which is only a few minutes away.

Self-catering
Gîte Bastide Les Aliberts
Minerve, T04 68 91 81 72, aliberts. com.
On a hill near Minerve, this utterly tranquil 12th- to 13th-century *bastide* surrounded by vines has been beautifully restored by owners Monique and Pascal Bourgogne, and encompasses the five gîtes (sleeping between four and eight people). There's an exceptionally pretty pool, a hammam and a jacuzzi. Prices start at €600 a week in a gîte sleeping four; weekend stays start at €230.

Eating & drinking

Montpellier & around

La Maison de la Lozère: Cellier-Morel €€€€

27 rue de l'Aiguillerie, T04 67 66 46 36, celliermorel.com.
Tue, Thu-Fri for lunch, Mon-Sat for dinner.
Map: Montpellier, B4, p148.

Eric Cellier and Pierre Morel captain this elegant restaurant in a 17th-century townhouse, where politicians take visiting VIPs, dining either under the pale stone vaults or in the plant-filled courtyard. The classy, inventive dishes on the frequently changing menu are served on undulating white plates; the desserts are unique (mint and ginger meringue) and over 550 wines fill the cellars. Fixed menus start at €38; be sure to book.

Oysters from Bassin de Thau.

Le Jardin des Sens €€€€

11 av St-Lazare, T04 99 58 38 38, jardindessens.com.
Tue and Thu-Sun for lunch, Mon-Sun for dinner.
Map: Montpellier, D1, p148.

Twins Jacques and Laurent Pourcel serve their magnificent, creative cuisine in a stunning glass dining room in a Mediterranean garden. The ever-changing menu is based on the finest locally sourced ingredients, and features such things as soufflée of courgette blossoms with prawn tails, or caramelized duckling with pan-fried foie gras and cherries. There's a special dessert menu for chocolate lovers and excellent regional wines. Lunch menu €50.

La Réserve Rimbaud €€€

820 av St-Maur, T04 67 72 52 53, reserve-rimbaud.com.
Tue-Fri for lunch and dinner, Sat for dinner.
Map: Montpellier, E2, p148.

In an idyllic setting on the Lez, this spot started out as a *guinguette* in 1835, and now boasts a fresh, contemporary look. Talented young chef Charles Fontès prepares regional delights such as delicious foie gras with date chutney, lamb from the Aveyron, and seafood *a la plancha*. Lunch menus start at €27; dinner, when it's at its most gorgeously romantic, is decidedly more at €45.

L'Entre Pots €€€

8 rue Louis Montagne, Pézenas, T04 67 90 00 00, entre-pots@orange.fr.
Mon-Wed for dinner, Thu-Sat for lunch and dinner.

The handsome, designer dining room is in a vaulted wine warehouse, and the main courses (scallop tempura, duck cooked in three different ways) couldn't be better. Add to that an excellent wine list, morish fruity desserts and lovely alfresco dining on the patio. Best to book. Lunch menus from €21.

Le Pré St-Jean €€€

18 av du Mal-Leclerc, Pézenas, T04 67 98 15 31, leprest.jean@wanadoo.fr.
Thu and Sun for lunch, Tue-Wed, Fri-Sat for lunch and dinner.

Chef Philippe Cagnoli is a master of delicate, *mijotée* sauces that bring out the finest in the local oysters, mushrooms and other treats in this casual, chic, sunny restaurant. Excellent affordable wine list, too. Menus from €25-50.

Tamarillos €€€

2 place du Marché aux Fleurs, T04 67 60 06 00, tamarillos.biz.
Daily for lunch and dinner.
Map: Montpellier, B4, p148.

After working with celebrity chef Guy Savoy, Philippe Chapon opened this restaurant drenched in colour. Appropriately for a cuisine that's based on fruit and flowers, it's in the city's old flower market. Think sea bass with a purée of herbs in a vanilla and lime sauce, a rose- and raspberry-flavoured cream dessert and gourmet coffees to finish. Plat du jour €15.

Le Ban des Gourmands €€

5 place Carnot, T04 67 65 00 85.
Tue-Fri for lunch and 1900-2300, Sat 1900-2300.
Map: Montpellier, C7, p148.
This is a local favourite, with a friendly, informal, bistro atmosphere and fresh, market cuisine prepared with a Mediterranean flair. Vegetable lovers will enjoy chef Jacques Delépine's take on the seasonal harvest and the roast asparagus with lonza is delicious. The day's catch is perfectly prepared, and the succulent meats are sourced from one of Montpellier's top butchers.

La Pause Mermoz €

890 av Jean Mermoz, T04 99 54 65 19.
Mon-Fri 1130-1430.
Map: Montpellier, E4, p148.
A friendly, informal self-service just north of Antigone, with an all-you-can-eat lunch buffet for €10.90. The food is made fresh every morning and there are salads, crudités, charcuterie, mussels and delicious desserts as well.

L'Assiette aux Fromages €

17 rue Gustave, T04 67 58 94 48, assietteauxfromages.free.fr.
Sep-Jul Mon-Fri for lunch and dinner, Sat for dinner.
Map: Montpellier, A4, p148.
The resolutely traditional decor, jovial informality and filling

portions make this restaurant a firm favourite with families and groups of friends. Specializing in different styles of cheese fondue, it's especially popular in the cooler months. They also do salads and duck dishes.

Le Dilemme €

12 rue Farges, T04 67 69 02 13.
Mon-Sun 1900-2400.
Map: Montpellier, C6, p148.
In the heart of Montpellier, Le Dilemme offers refined cuisine, a friendly ambiance and value for money. There's a wide range of choices – the 'dilemma' is deciding what to order. The foie gras with onion *confiture* is delectable, and (rare in France) the bread is home made. Set-price menus start at €14.

Cafés & bars

Cocco e Fragola

8 rue de la Loge, place Jean-Jaurès, T04 67 02 03 28, coccoefragola.com.
Mon-Fri and Sun 1200-2000, Sat 1200-2400.
Map: Montpellier, B4, p148.
Superb home-made Italian gelato, sorbets and smoothies, as well as fine Italian-style coffees, served in a luminous modern setting.

La Tavola da Pépé

8 rue de l'Université, T04 67 02 19 25.
Tue-Sat 1930-0200.
Map: Montpellier, B3, p148.
This lively tapas bar stays open until the wee hours. A wide range of authentic tapas and seafood *a la plancha* accompany a choice of cocktails and wines.

Le Circus

3 rue Collot, T04 67 60 42 05, cusspinlounge.com.
Open 1800-0100.
Map: Montpellier, B4, p148.
A trendy New York-style bar with a cool, colourful circus theme and reasonable prices. It's a favourite place to start or end an evening out.

Le Huit

8 rue de l'Aiguillerie, T06 60 80 91 17, myspace.com/lehuit.
Map: Montpellier, B4, p148.
Hip 20-somethings flock to this late-night bar for the cocktails and the music – alternative, pop, rock, funk, etc. Frequent live performances.

Morceau de la Lune

14 rue du Pila St-Gély, T04 67 52 80 59, restaurant-morceau-de-lune.fr.
Tue-Sat 1200-1400 and 1900-2300.
Map: Montpellier, C3, p148.
A romantic wine bar/restaurant on a pedestrian street near Place de la Comédie, Morceau de la Lune serves seasonal, contemporary dishes to go with its 200 different wines, mostly from Languedoc. Bottles range from €14-95; they also do wine-tasting evenings.

Inland from Montpellier

Les Muscardins €€€€

19 rte des Cévennes, St-Martin-de-Londres, T04 67 55 70 28, les-muscardins.fr.
Wed-Sun for lunch and dinner.

Founded by chef Georges Rousset and now run by his son, Thierry, Les Muscardins draws gourmet pilgrims up from Montpellier to feast on succulent Aubrac beef and shallots, with a parsnip purée and *ravioli à la truffe blanche d'Alba*. This and other more exotic avant-garde dishes are matched by a superb wine cellar. Be sure to book.

La Cour €€€
Mas de Baumes, Ferrières-les-Verreries, T04 66 80 88 80, oustaldebaumes. com.
Open for lunch and 1730-2130.
Located east of St-Bauzille-de-Putois, this is a delightful haven of peace and quiet in an old stone farm, with views of the Pic St Loup. Chef Eric Tapié varies his menu according to season: in autumn try the mouth-watering risotto with cèpes, and pigeon with figs and pan-fried foie gras. Vegetarians are well catered for as well. Menus from €29, and they have lovely rooms so you don't have to drive home.

Restaurant de Lauzan €€€
3 bd de l'Esplanade, Gignac (south of St-Guilhem-le-Désert), T04 67 57 50 83, restaurant-delauzun.com.
Tue-Fri for lunch and dinner, Sat for dinner, Sun for lunch.
Young Mattheiu de Lauzun prepares gorgeous dishes on the palette of black and white plates in this modern, no-nonsense shrine to food. Try the slow-cooked pork, the seafood marinated in lime juice or his

own version of Sète's *bourride*. The *cave* is first rate, too, with a good choice of wines by the glass (€4). A €21 *formule* is served weekdays.

Le Mas de Coulet €€
Rte de Montpellier, Brissac (2.5 km south of St-Bauzille-de-Putois), T04 67 83 72 43, masdecoulet.com.
Oct-Mar Fri for dinner, Sat for lunch and dinner, Sun for lunch, Apr-Jun and Sep Thu-Sat for lunch and dinner, Sun-Tue for lunch, Jul-Aug daily for lunch and dinner.
In a peaceful rural setting, this restaurant serves hearty simple dishes such as onion tart, grilled lamb chops and delicious *salades composées* with duck, plus some you don't see often such as *joues de porc à l'ancienne* (pork cheeks). Set menus from €18-32. They also have pretty rooms (€€) and gîtes with a pool.

Coastal Hérault

Chez Philippe €€
20 rue de Suffren, Marseillan, T04 67 01 70 62.
Mid-Feb to May and Sep to mid-Nov Wed-Sun for lunch and dinner, Jun-Aug Tue-Sun for lunch and dinner.
The pretty setting under the pines near the Bassin de Thau, the menu full of finesse and with succulent seafood that changes every month, and the good list of Languedoc wines are the secrets behind Chez Philippe's

success. Try the seafood and garden vegetable combinations; they also serve delicious duck. Lunch menu €19.

Le Caquelon €€
13 chemin de l'Etang, Mèze, T04 67 74 63 81, restaurant-meze.com.
Open for lunch and dinner.
This is a cheerful restaurant with a big summer terrace right on the Bassin de Thau. The menu changes three times a year and specializes in regional seafood – the oysters gratinées are delicious.

Le Place €€
2 place de la Marine, Agde, T04 67 94 77 03.
Daily for lunch, Thu-Tue for dinner.
A traditional little restaurant with a bar, offering a single constantly changing €25 menu with five choices for entrée, main course and dessert. There's live piano music on Friday nights.

Les Demoiselles Dupuy €€
4 quai Maximin Licciardi, Sète, T04 67 74 03 46.
Open 1200-2300.
This wonderful bistro-cum-oyster shack with a terrace is a bit out of the way by the port, but it's well worth seeking out for some of the freshest oysters and seafood in Sète. Owner Gilles Dupuy was an artist who started farming oysters in Bouzigues and his son now sends in fresh supplies daily. Save room at the end for the home-made chocolate cake.

Listings

Ambassade €€€€
22 bd de Verdun, T04 67 76 06 24, restaurant-lambassade.com.
Tue-Sat for lunch and dinner.
In a 19th-century hotel opposite Béziers' train station, this *soignée* restaurant is famous for its creative Mediterranean dishes, with influences from Spain, Italy and North Africa. Set menus start at €29, but for a really special occasion indulge in chef Patrick Olry's extraordinary lobster-based *menu homard bleu* for an eye-watering €105.

Octopus €€€€
12 rue Boïeldieu, T04 67 49 90 00, restaurant-octopus.com.
Tue-Sat for lunch and 1730-2200.
Since it opened in 2005, the Octopus' young trio of owners have made waves with their contemporary, original cuisine (layers of foie gras and sardines with figs and almonds, fragrant spiced lamb with a Roquefort soufflé). Two of the four dining rooms open on to a pretty patio. Menus range from €30-72; a two-course lunch is €21.

En Bonne Compagnie €€
6 quai des Negociants, Homps, T04 68 91 23 16, in-good-company.com.
Mon for dinner, Tue-Sat for lunch and dinner.
Right on the Canal du Midi, this friendly restaurant run by Valerie and Craig serves meaty (lamb noisette stuffed with leaks on a bed of minted peas) and vegetarian (roast vegetables stacked with mozzarella in pesto coulis) dishes, rounded off with the house speciality: banana toffee vodka soufflé. Three-course lunch menus start at €15.50.

La Raffinerie €€
14 av Joseph Lazare, T04 67 76 07 12, la-raffinerie.com.
Tue-Fri for lunch and dinner, Sat for dinner.
With a terrace by the Canal du Midi, this fashionable restaurant occupies the former sulphur refinery in the old wine warehouse district. The dishes are as refined as the name, with a menu that changes seasonally – summer choices could include tuna carpaccio, tournedos of duck with stir-fried vegetables and a berry sauce, followed by a dreamy *pot au chocolat* with preserved orange.

Relais Chantovent €€
Minerve, T04 68 91 14 18, relaischantovent-minerve.fr.
Mon for dinner, Tue and Sun for lunch, Thu-Sat for lunch and dinner.
Choose between the arty dining room and the lovely summer terrace overlooking the Gorge de Bram, and feast on the Chantovent's delicious seasonal dishes. Menus range from €19-45 (one is based on duck, another on fresh herbs); the desserts are works of art. Reservations recommended.

Le P'tit Sémard €
13 bis place Pierre Semard, T04 67 80 31 04, leptitsemard-beziers.com.
Tue-Sun 0900-2400.
This popular and friendly bistro opposite the Halles serves excellent *cuisine de marché* classics, such as paella, moules frites and a rich, creamy mousse au chocolat. There are plenty of tables outside for prime people-watching, too.

Le P'tit Sémard.

Entertainment

Montpellier & around

Cinema

Cinéma Gaumont Comédie
10 place de la Comédie, T08 92 69 66 96, gaumontpathe.com.
A central, eight-screen complex showing new releases.

Clubs

JAM (Jazz Action Montpellier)
100 rue Ferdinand de Lessps, T04 67 58 30 30, lejam.com.
Montpellier's jazz club is a local institution and puts on several concerts a week from October to July. It's south of the centre, off Avenue Près d'Arènes.

La Dune
Rte des Plages, La Grande-Motte, T04 67 56 43 43, la-dune-montpellier.com.
Sep-Jun Thu-Sat 2300-0600, Jul-Aug daily 2300-0600.
Huge Ibiza-style venue that draws in clubbers from across the south of France.

La Villa Rouge
Rte Palavas, Lattes, take the Montpellier Sud exit off the A9, T04 67 06 52 15.
Wed-Sun from 0100.
Massive gay/straight techno club.

Le Cargo
5 rue du Grand St-Jean, T04 67 29 96 85, cargo-montpellier.fr.
Sep-Jun Tue-Thu 2000-0200, Fri-Sat 2000-0500.

Music bar/disco aimed at the university set, with plenty of salsa and merengue on Tuesdays. Free entry weekdays, on weekends it's free until midnight.

Le Rockstore
20 rue de Verdun, T04 67 06 80 00, rockstore.fr.
A red Cadillac pierces the façade of central Montpellier's rock temple, founded in 1986 and still going strong. There are frequent concerts, discos, DJs, etc. Performances usually start at 2200.

Gay & lesbian

Café de la Mer
5 place du Marché aux Fleurs, T04 67 60 79 65.
Montpellier's first gay bar with its big sunny terrace is an institution. It's a great place to meet up and find out what's on in the city.

Le Men's
26 rue de Candolle, T04 67 66 21 95.
Sep-Jun daily 1800-0100, Jul-Aug daily Sun 1800-0200.
Montpellier has a lively gay scene, and this glamorous tapas restaurant, bar and club spread out over five rooms with DJs from across France is a favourite rendezvous.

Music & theatre

Corum
Esplanade Charles de Gaulle, T04 67 61 67 61, enjoy-montpellier.com.
This contemporary conference centre also houses the Berlioz Opera, famed for its cutting-edge acoustics.

Le Zénith Sud
Domaine de Grammont, Montpellier Est exit off the A9, T04 67 64 50 00, enjoy-montpellier.com.
Modelled on Le Zénith in Paris, this is the venue for big names on tour (Arctic Monkeys, Sting, and the likes).

Opéra Comédie
Place Molière, T04 67 60 19 99, opera-montpellier.com.
Classic repertory performed by the Opéra National Montpellier Languedoc-Roussillon.

Opéra Comédie, Montpellier.

Shopping

The Ecusson is full of boutiques and fascinating little shops. Rue de la Loge is the high street, but side streets such as Rue St-Guilhem and Rue de l'Ancien Courrier are also full of treasures. The medieval lanes around St-Anne are the place to look for quirky shops and antiques.

Arts & antiques
Boutique 110 Volts
24 rue de la Mediterranée, T06 81 95 86 13, 110volts.net.
Mon-Fri 1000-1230 and 1500-1900.
Fun shop selling household items and accessories from the 1950s-1970s.

Clothing & accessories
Boutique Patricia Orssaud
16 rue de l'Argenterie, T04 67 66 04 47.
Mon 1430-1900, Tue-Sat 1000-1900.
Elegant clothes and shoes for women by French and Italian designers.

Diplodocus
1 rue Valedeau, T04 67 02 72 50.
Mon 1400-1900, Tue-Sat 1000-1900.
Women's clothing, aimed at the over 30s, with an emphasis on soft, natural fabrics from silk to cashmere.

Erbe
8 rue de la Loge, T04 99 63 23 27.
Mon 1400-1900, Tue-Fri 1000-1915, Sat 0930-1930.
Stylish, mostly Italian and Spanish shoes for men and women.

Food & drink
La Maison Régionale des Vins
34 rue St-Guilhem, T04 67 60 40 41.
Mon 1000-2000, Tue-Sat 0930-2000.
Excellent range of Languedocien wines and spirits and everything that goes with them.

Les Halles Castellane
Rue de la Loge, T04 67 66 29 92.
Mon-Sat 0730-1930, Sun 0700-1400.
Montpellier's wonderful covered market.

Pinto
14 rue de l'Argenterie, T04 67 60 57 65.
Mon 1430-1900, Tue-Sat 0845-1230 and 1430-1900.
For over 50 years Pinto has been selling both world and regional products, including Montpellier's 17th-century *Délice des Trois Grâces* dark chocolate with a touch of ginger and spice.

Puig Valero
5 bis place Laissac, T04 67 58 02 38.
Tue-Sat 0700-1300 and 1600-1930.
Perfect *fromages*; a must for any cheese lover.

Music
Comptoir du Disque
4 place Pétrarque, T04 67 60 91 71.
Mon 1400-1900, Tue-Sat 1100-1300 and 1400-1700.
Extraordinary selection of over 150,000 vinyl records of all genres.

Toys
Pomme de Reinette
35 rue de l'Aiguillerie, T04 67 60 52 78.
Mon 1400-1900, Tue-Fri 1000-1230 and 1400-1900, Sat 1000-1900.
A fascinating labyrinth filled with vintage toys and museum pieces, as well as all kinds of games, music boxes, models and much, much more.

Food & drink
Pâtisserie Alary
5 rue St-Jean, T04 67 98 21 39.
Tue-Sun 0800-1230 and 1430-1930.
Come here to buy Pézenas' sweet/savoury speciality, *petits pâtés de Pézenas*. The recipe was given to the town as a gift in the 18th century by the Indian Viceroy Lord Clive, who brought his chef along on holiday.

Petits pâtés de Pézenas.

Pick of the picnic spots

The indoor markets in Montpellier, Sète and Béziers are packed with picnic fixings. There are pretty spots along the River Hérault, the tables near the Devil's bridge by St-Guilhem-le-Désert (see page 161), or down in the meadow in Navacelles, near the banks of by the River Vis (see page 162); or overlooking the Cirque de Navacelles from the information centre on D130. Any spot in the dappled shade along the Canal du Midi is lovely (see page 174). Or, if you want to stay by the sea, buy some of France's finest oysters, a bottle of AOC Picpoul de Pinet and feast on the beach at Bouzigues (see page 167).

Inland from Montpellier

Food & drink
Mas de Daumas Gassac
D32, Aniane (south of St-Guilhem), T04 67 57 88 45, daumas-gassac.com.
Sep-Jun Mon-Sat 1000-1200 and 1400-1800, Jul-Aug daily 0930-1830.
One of the most famous vineyards in Languedoc, owned by Aimé Guibert who featured in the film *Mondovino*. The wines are organic and the grapes hand-picked. They also sell olive oil and vinegar.

Béziers & around

Books
Librairie Ancienne du Somail
28 allée de la Glacière, Le Somail, T04 68 46 21 64, le-trouve-tout-du-livre.fr.
Dec-Mar Wed-Mon 1430-1830, Apr-Jun and Sep-Nov Wed-Mon 1000-1200 and 1430-1830, Jul-Aug daily 1000-1200 and 1430-1830.
A truly remarkable, quality second-hand bookshop in a former wine cave. It relocated here from Paris in 1980 and offers a wide selection of books in English.

Food & drink
L'Oulibo
Hameau de Cabezac, Bize Minervois, T04 68 41 88 88, loulibo.com.
Mon-Fri 0800-1200 and 1400-1900, Sat 0900-1200 and 1400-1900, Sun 1000-1200 and 1400-1900. Free guided tours in Jul and Aug.
Cooperative specializing in Lucques de Bize olive oil, which is on sale here. Also stocks capers, tapenades, soaps, shower gels and other local products.

Activities & tours

Day walks

❶ **La Boucle de Navacelles** The famous cirque and waterfalls; 5½ hours. Park near St-Maurice de Navacelles.

❷ **Cirque de l'Infernet** Fairly easy, stunning walk with cliffs and viewpoints; 3½ hours. Start from St-Guilhem-le-Désert.

❸ **Roc de la Vigne** Beautiful walk over the hills of the garrigue; 4½ hours. Park near the dam 1.2 km from St-Guilhem-le-Désert.

❹ **Cirque de Mourèze** Rocky chaos and views from the summit of Liausson; 3½ hours. Park at Mourèze (north of Béziers). Rather difficult.

❺ **Gorges d'Héric** With rock pools for bathing along the way; three hours. Park at Mons-la-Trivalle.

Montpellier & around

Children

La Forêt d'Acrobates
Base de Bessilles, Motagnac, T06 07 13 43 80, loisirs-foret.com.
Some 90 activities, including Tarzan jumps and zip wires, in the forest that once belonged to the Abbaye de Valmagne. From ages three and up.

Golf

Golf de Coulondres
72 rue des Erables, St-Gély-du-Fesc, T04 67 84 13 75, coulondres. com.
Five minutes north of Montpellier, a beautiful piney 18-hole par 73 course. Also a nine-hole compact course.

Golf de Montpellier Massane
Baillargues, T04 67 87 87 87, massane.com.
Resort complex with an undulating 18-hole par 72 course, a nine-hole pitch and putt course and a spa for non golfers.

Ice skating

Vegapolis
Quartier Odysseum, T04 99 52 26 00, vert-marine.com.
France's first ice-skating rink devoted to fun, complete with disco music and lights. You can rent skates as well.

Water sports

Piscine Olympique d'Antigone
195 av Jacques Cartier, T04 67 15 63 00, montpellier-agglo.com.
Montpellier's biggest indoor pool. It's near both tram lines.

Inland from Montpellier

Canoeing

Canoe Rapido
Rue St-Benôit d'Aniane, St-Guilhem-le-Désert, T04 67 55 75 75, st-guilhem-le-desert.com/canoe-rapido.html.
Canoe or kayak 12 km down the gorge of the Hérault.

Canoesud
Laroque and St-Bauzille-de-Putois, T04 67 73 39 58, canoesud.com.
Canoesud has two bases for paddling down the Hérault. Trips run from 25 March to 15 October and last from one to 48 hours

(they provide tents for longer trips). During the summer, they also do descents by moonlight on Tuesdays.

Golf

Fontcaude
Rte de Lodève (direction Millau), Juvignac, T04 67 03 34 30, montpellierresort.com.
Near St-Guilhem-le-Désert, an 18-hole par 72 course, plus a nine-hole par 29 'executive course' in the *garrigue*.

Coastal Hérault

Boat trips

Sète Croisières
Quai du Général-Durand, Sète, T04 67 46 00 46, sete-croisieres. com.
Choose between three different cruises: red for sea cruises (departs from Pont de la Savonnerie); yellow with glass bottoms for the Bassins de Thau

and Bouzigues and the shellfish parks (departs from the Quai de la Résistance); and blue for visits of Sète's canals (Quai Durand).

Diving
Abyss Plongée
21 place du Globe-Le Pharo, Le Cap d'Agde, T04 67 01 50 54 (low season T06 21 97 16 10), abyssplongee.com.
Underwater lava flows make for good diving around Cap d'Agde: learn how, go out on dives or just fill up your tanks here.

Golf
Golf du Cap D'Agde
4 av des Alizées, Le Cap d'Agde, T04 67 26 54 40, golf.ville-agde.fr.
Flat 18-hole par 72 course and a nine-hole compact course, with water obstacles.

La Grande-Motte Golf Club
Av du Golf, La Grande-Motte, T04 67 56 05 00, ot-lagrandemotte.fr/golf.htm.
Designed by Robert Trent Jones Sr, this 42-hole complex is the biggest in Languedoc-Roussillon and includes the international 'Flamants Roses' course.

Water sports
Aqualand
Cap d'Agde, T04 67 26 85 94, aqualand.fr.
Water park, offering thrills and spills. Ideal for about ages 10 and up.

Parc Aquatique Le Grand Bleu
La plaine des jeux, La Grande-Motte, T04 67 56 28 23, ot-lagrandemotte.fr/parc-aquatique.php.
Several indoor pools, slides, saunas, etc. Outdoor water park in summer.

Wellbeing
Balnéocap
88 chemin de Notre Dame à St Martin, Le Cap d'Agde, T04 67 21 20 59, balneocap.com.
Opened in 2009, this state-of-the-art spa features the latest treatments and a bilingual staff, all in a cool Zen setting.

Thalasso Mediterranée
La Grande-Motte, T04 67 29 13 13, thalasso-grandemotte.com.
The biggest thalassotherapy spa in Languedoc, devoted to sun, sea and relaxation. It offers a wide selection of treatments.

Béziers & around

Boat trips on Canal du Midi
Ad' Navis
La Maison du Canal, 80 Grand Rue, Servian, T04 67 90 95 51, adnavis.com.
Hotel barges and rental boats (sleeping two to 12), based in Agde and Carcassonne.

Belle du Midi
Chemin des Patiasses, Le Somail, T04 68 93 53 94, belledumidicruises.com.
Weekly rentals sleeping four to six, and a day boat.

Croisieres du Midi
35 quai des Tonneliers, Homps, T04 68 91 33 00, croisieres-du-midi.com.
Two-hour cruises with commentary and boat hire for a half or full day.

Minervois Cruisers
38 chemin des Patiasses, Le Somail, T04 68 46 28 52, minervoiscruisers.com.
English narrow boats and wide- beam barges; sleep from two to 10.

Canoeing
Grandeur Nature
Chemin de Laroque, Roquebrun, T04 67 89 52 90, canoe-france.com.
The Orb is one of the friskiest rivers in Languedoc, but accessible to all. Tours from one to three days (37 km) are available.

Cycling
Mellow Velos
3 place de l'Eglise, Paraza, T04 68 43 38 21, mellowvelos.com.
Hire road, racing and mountain bikes on the Canal du Midi; they'll also deliver and meet you at the airport.

Golf
Golf de St-Thomas
Rte de Bessan, Béziers, T04 67 39 03 09, golfsaintthomas.com.
Eighteen-hole par 72 course in the *garrigue*, with low hills, bunkers and water.

Contents

Carcassonne.

Introduction

What to see in...

...one day
Start early in the day to beat the crowds in Carcassonne's Cité, and visit the Château Comtal and Ramparts and Basilique St-Nazaire. Have lunch in Narbonne, and afterwards take a look at its cathedral and museums. Cultural duties done, head over to Gruissan Plage for a late afternoon on the beach.

...a weekend or more
After Carcassonne and Narbonne, drive into the rugged Corbières to visit the Cathar castles, the vineyards and Rennes-le-Château (if you're curious to see what all the fuss is about). When you need even bigger thrills, stop at Quillan and go whitewater rafting down the Aude.

Now that heresy no longer brings down armies, the Aude proudly bills itself 'Le Pays Cathare'. Carcassonne, the city with the fairytale citadel, is the capital, while just to the south, in the rugged Corbières, rocky spurs are crowned with vertiginous castles where the last of the Cathars sought refuge from Simon de Montfort. Equally unorthodox Rennes-le-Château is here as well – not a place the tourist board actively promotes, but a must-see for fans of *Holy Blood, Holy Grail* and *The Da Vinci Code*.

And there's more. Down by the Mediterranean, Narbonne, the capital of Roman Languedoc, became the religious centre of the region in the Middle Ages. It has for a stunning centrepiece a towering Gothic complex, including the cathedral and episcopal palace; the latter is now home to two excellent museums. The once-powerful abbey of Fontfroide is a short drive away, as are long sandy beaches, and at Sigean you can visit the elephants, lions and giraffes wandering freely in the immense African Reserve. The Aude has a long stretch of the idyllic Canal du Midi, but most of all it has wine: Corbières, part of Minervois (which it shares with Hérault), bubbly Blanquette de Limoux, Fitou and Le Clape.

Abbaye de Fontfroide.

Carcassonne & around

The Aude's capital has three distinct parts. Down by the river there's the modern city that surrounds the tight-knit medieval 'new town', the Bastide St Louis; at the top is the outrageously picturesque prize, the Cité of Carcassonne. In a tiara of witch-hatted towers, the Cité is the perfect storybook citadel and since 1997 it has been a World Heritage Site.

Dame Carcas.

Essentials

❶ Getting around

By car There are huge pay car parks outside the Porte Narbonne of the Cité, and from mid-June to mid-September shuttle buses (€1.29) run every 25 minutes between the lower town and the Cité. **Taxi** For a taxi, call T04 68 71 50 50.

By bicycle Hire a bike at Evasion2Roues, 85 allée d'Iéna, T04 68 11 90 40, evasion2roues.eu. Tuesday-Thursday 0900-1200 and 1400-1900, Friday 0900-1900, Saturday 0900-1800.

❷ Bus station The bus station is on Boulevard Varsovie; service to some towns is provided by Kéolis, 2 boulevard Paul Sabatier, T04 68 25 13 74, and Tessier, Le Pont Rouge, T04 68 25 85 45. For regional bus travel, see page 275.

❀ Train station The gare is at Port du Canal du Midi. For regional rail travel, see page 274.

❸ ATM Banque Populaire, Rue du Comte Roger up in the Cité; Société Générale, 6 place Carnot.

❹ Hospital Centre Hospitalier Antoine Gayraud, Route de St-Hilaire, T04 68 24 24 24.

❺ Pharmacy Barbacane, 110 rue Barbacane; Roux Barnet, 10 rue Courtejaire.

❍ Post office 40 rue Jean Bringer, T04 68 11 71 13.

❶ Tourist information 28 rue de Verdun, T04 68 10 24 30, carcassonne-tourisme.com. September-June Monday-Saturday 0900-1800, Sunday 0900-1300; July-August daily 0900-1900. There's another office just inside the Porte Narbonnaise.

Cité de Carcassonne

Built at a strategic bend in the Aude, the site has been occupied since the eighth century BC. The Gauls, Romans, Visigoths, Arabs and Franks were here, followed in the 11th century by the Trencavels – the Viscounts of Carcassonne, Albi, Béziers and Nîmes, powerful allies of the Counts of Toulouse.

When Innocent III declared the Albigensian Crusade, the young Viscount Raymond-Roger Trencavel gallantly offered to shelter all the 'persecuted people' of the south. The Roman walls were still good enough to keep the Crusaders at bay for two weeks, so they resorted to trickery, luring Trencavel outside the walls and throwing him in prison. Soon after, he was found dead – poisoned, it was rumoured. Blame fell on Simon de Montfort, who declared himself count of all his lands, which his son later ceded to the French crown.

Louis XI (St Louis) and his son Philippe III made Carcassonne the seat of French power in Languedoc, building the greatest and most impregnable citadel in Europe. Never attacked, it became obsolete with the Treaty of the Pyrenees in 1659 and slowly fell into ruin, and there were moves to quarry its stone for new buildings in the Ville Basse. Novelist Prosper Mérimée, Inspector-General of Historic Monuments, raised the alarm, and in 1853 Eugène Viollet-le-Duc, restorer of Notre-Dame in Paris, came to the rescue and rebuilt it as it should have looked all along.

Porte Narbonnaise & Les Lices

Map: Carcassonne, E6, p198.

The Cité has four gates, but only the Porte Narbonnaise was (and still is) accessible by road. As powerful as it looks, with its two portcullises and towers, it is militarily the weakest point in the defences. Between the two curtains of walls (the outer ones were built by Louis IX, the inner ones

Tip...

Expect heaving crowds in summer (the Cité is the most popular destination in France after Paris and Mont St-Michel); get there early if you can.

Around the region

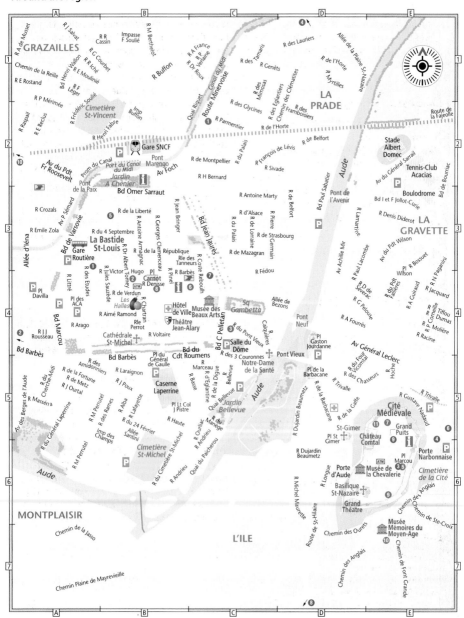

date back to Roman times) runs a broad open space, Les Lices, where the knights would train and hold their jousts. You can walk around the walls or take a guided tour in one of the horse-drawn carriages by the gate.

Château Comtal & ramparts

1 rue Viollet-le-Duc, T04 68 11 70 70, carcassonne. monuments-nationaux.fr.
Apr-Sep daily 0930-1830, Oct-Mar daily 0930-1700. €8, €5 young person (18-25), under 18s and EU citizens under 26 free. Guided tours of various lengths €7.50-12.50. Note that the ticket office closes 30 mins before the castle. Map: Carcassonne, E5-6, opposite.

This castle was built on Roman foundations by the Trencavels. The impressive outer walls and barbican had to be added when it became residence of the French seneschal, to protect him from the angry populace. Today, it houses models, sculptures and inscriptions dating back to Roman times, Merovingian tombs and 14th-century alabasters and altarpieces salvaged from destroyed churches in the countryside. There's a special exhibition on the restoration, including Viollet-le-Duc's drawings, plans and photos, paintings of what the Cité looked like before he arrived and audiovisuals and interactive displays. You can walk around most of the 3 km of walls with their 52 towers, and either hire an audio guide or join one of the free 45-minute guided tours in French.

Near the château, a little square has a massive well called the **Grand Puits**, the largest of the Cité's 22 wells. Legend has it that the Visigoths hid the Treasure of Solomon here when they heard Attila the Hun was coming; if anyone ever found it, they're not telling.

Carcassonne listings

● Sleeping

1 **42 Rue Victor Hugo** *42 rue Victor Hugo* **A3**
2 **Balladins** *3 alleé Gilles de Roberval* **A4** (off map)
3 **Hôtel de la Cité** *Place Auguste-Pierre Pont* **E6**
4 **Hôtel du Château** *2 rue Camille St-Saens* **E5**
5 **Hôtel la Bastide** *81 rue de la Liberté* **B3**
6 **Hôtel Montmorency** *9 rue Camille St-Saens* **E5**
7 **La Maison Coste** *40 rue Coste Reboulh* **C4**
8 **Le Domaine d'Auriac** *Route de St-Hilaire* **D7** (off map)
9 **Le Grand Puits** *8 place du Grand Puits* **E6**
10 **Les Gîtes de Cabardès** *7 rue des Jardins, Ventenac-Cabardès* 2A (off map)

● Eating & drinking

1 **Aux Berges du Canal** *48 route Minervoise* **C2**
2 **Café Saillan** *31 rue du Dr Tomey* **B4**
3 **Carpe Diem** *29 rue du Pont Vieux* **C4**
4 **Château de Saint-Martin** *Hameau de Montredon* **D1** (off map)
5 **La Barbacane** *Place Auguste-Pierre Pont* **E6**
6 **La Cantine de Robert** *Place de Lattre de Tassigny* **B4**
7 **La Cotte de Maille** *2 rue St Jean* **E5**
8 **La Roulotte** *6 rue Denisse* **B4**
9 **Le Bar à Vins** *6 rue du Pló* **E6**
10 **Le Parc Franck Putelat** *Chemin des Anglais* **E7**
11 **Le Saint Jean** *1 place St Jean* **E5**

Basilique St-Nazaire

Place de l'Eglise.
Apr-Sep Mon-Sat 0900-1145 and 1345-1800, Sun 0900-1045 and 1400-1700, Oct-Mar Mon-Sat 0900-1145 and 1345-1700, Sun 0900-1045 and 1400-1630.
Map: Carcassonne, D6, opposite.

Pope Urban V was visiting Carcassonne when he ordered the construction of this church in 1096. It started off Romanesque, until the northerners moved in and made it into a tall Gothic hybrid with a pair of enormous rose windows and projecting gargoyles. The organ is the biggest in the south of France. A plaque marks the tomb of Simon de Montfort, who was killed in 1218 while besieging Toulouse, but his relatives transferred his body to a safer resting spot in the north in 1224.

Around the region

Musée Mémoires du Moyen-Age

Chemin des Anglais, T04 68 71 08 65.
Daily 1000-1900, closed at Christmas. €5, €3 child.
Map: Carcassonne, E7, p198.

This is fun for the kids – models, videos and son et lumière evoke the Middle Ages and medieval siege machinery.

Musée de la Chevalerie

2 Porte d'Aude, T04 68 72 75 51, musee-chevalerie. com.
Mar-Dec 1000-1300 and 1500-1900. €6, €4 child, €2 extra for the guided tour (in French) at 1030 and 1530.
Map: Carcassonne, E6, p198.

Gilles Alessandri is an enthusiastic expert on derring-do (he often consults on films). His collection of weapons, armour, coins and more dates from the fifth to the 15th centuries. The adjacent boutique sells replica costumes, armour, tapestries…everything you need, in fact, to make your own film.

The Cité has 120 inhabitants; the other 45,400 Carcassonnais live and work in the lower city. Its slightly claustrophobic core is the Bastide St-Louis, a medieval 'new town' founded by St Louis in 1247, after the inhabitants (who used to live just outside the walls of the Cité) tried to help the son of Raymond-Roger Trencavel recapture his castle. Louis knocked their houses down and moved them here. Like all *bastides*, the streets were laid out in a grid around a square – in this case, pretty **Place Carnot**. The square has a marble Fontaine de Neptune (1770) and a market that takes place on Tuesday, Thursday and Saturday mornings. In winter part of the square is iced over for skaters.

Le Pont Vieux

Map: Carcassonne, D5, p198.

Built in the 14th century, this bridge, carried on twelve arches, is still in business; its tiny Gothic chapel of Notre Dame de la Santé (1538) is all that remains of a medieval hospital.

The Cathars

The ancient Gnostics were the first to conclude that the world, so full of trouble, could not possibly have been created by the Good (God), but was a creation of Evil (Satan). It followed that the right thing to do was to have as little as possible to do with it, and to seek the good through purity. This dualistic philosophy with a Christian slant re-emerged with the ninth-century Bogomils in Bulgaria before spreading to Languedoc, where its followers became known as Cathars.

The Cathars, or 'Good Christians' as they were called, wanted to live according to the Bible, without buildings, tithes, priests or swearing oaths. They were vegans, as they believed in reincarnation; money was easily loaned, unrestricted by Catholic rules against usury; sins, being unavoidable, were easily forgiven, and disputes were settled by mediation. Men and women were equal, but non-procreative sex was preferred, so as not to bring more people into the Evil World. The spiritually inclined could take a sacrament called the consolament and become a *parfait* or *parfaite*, and lead an ascetic life of work and prayer.

Cathar ideas resonated across all social classes in Languedoc. The great lords, the Count of Toulouse and Viscount of Carcassonne, sympathized with and protected their Cathar subjects. In 1206, Dominic de Guzmán founded the Dominican Order in Toulouse to convert the Cathars. Only a few listened.

Although the Albigensian Crusade ended with the capture of Montségur (1244) and 220 Cathars burned at the stake, some did take refuge in the castles south of Carcassonne and held out until 1255. The Inquisition, founded in Toulouse in 1229, would spend decades destroying the last remnants of the heresy, until the last Cathar was burned in Villerouge-Termenès in 1321.

The Siege of Carcassonne (1209), Jean-Paul Laurens (1858-1921).

Musée des Beaux-Arts

1 rue de Verdun, T04 68 77 73 70.
Tue-Sat 1000-1200 and 1400-1800. Free.
Map: Carcassonne, C4, p189.

This museum of mostly French works from the 17th to 20th centuries has works by Rigaud, Corot, Chardin (a charming still-life, *The Kitchen Table*), Courbet, local painter Jacques Gamelin and a collection of ceramics.

Five of the best

Books about the Cathars

❶ *The Cathars in The Languedoc* (2000), Malcolm Barber.

❷ *The Perfect Heresy: The Revolutionary Life and Death of the Medieval Cathars* (2001), Stephen O'Shea.

❸ *The Other God: Dualist Religions from Antiquity to the Cathar Heresy* (2000), Yuri Stoyanov.

❹ *The Cathars and the Albigensian Crusade* (1997), Michael Costen.

❺ *The Song of the Cathar Wars: A contemporary history of the Albigensian Crusade* (1996), William of Tudela (translation by J Shirley).

Around Carcassonne

Châteaux de Lastours

Lastours, 16 km north of Carcassonne, T04 68 77 56 02.
Feb, Mar, mid-Nov to Dec Sat-Sun and national holidays 1000-1700, Apr-Jun and Sep daily 1000-1800, Jul-Aug daily 0900-2000, Oct to mid-Nov daily 1000-1700. €5, €2 child.

There are actually four castles spread out dramatically across a ridge in the Cabardès, a ruggedly austere area of ancient iron and gold mines. The lords of the oldest castles, Cabaret, Surdespine and Quertinheux, were Cathars and famous patrons of the arts, and stood up to Simon de Montfort's attack in 1211. Cabaret later became the centre of a Cathar resistance movement until finally surrendering in 1229. In 1240, the king rebuilt the castles and added the fourth, the Tour Régine. The visit includes ruins of the medieval village of Cabaret and views from the **Belvedere de Montfermier**.

South of Carcassonne

From Carcassonne the D118 follows the Aude up into a relatively sleepy but pretty corner of Languedoc to **Limoux**, an attractive town on the river, famous for its sparkling Blanquette de Limoux wine and for its equally effervescent winter festival, the Fécos. It's a long, narrow town that was once enclosed in ramparts, with a 14th-century bridge, the **Pont Neuf**, and a lovely arcaded **Place de la République** and fountain in the shadow of the Gothic steeple of **St Martin**.

Besides tasting the local bubbly, visit the **Musée Petiet** on the Promenade du Tivoli (T04 68 31 85 03, Sep-Jun Mon-Fri 0900-1200 and 1400-1800,

Limoux.

Sat-Sun 1000-1200 and 1400-1700, Jul-Aug daily 0900-1900) next to Limoux's tourist office. This is in the atmospheric late 19th-century home and *atelier* of the Petiet family of artists, one of whom, Marie (1854-1893), painted intimate domestic scenes (*Les Blanchisseuses*, 1882). Her works are the star attractions, along with landscapes by the Aude's own pointillist, Achille Laugé.

Just north of Limoux, off the D118, the **Jardin aux Plantes parfumées la Bouichère** (T04 68 31 49 94, labouichere.com, May-early Oct Wed-Sun 1200-1800, mid-Jun to mid-Aug Wed-Sun 1000-1800, €6, €3 child) was planted 20 years ago by Gabrielle and Pierre Gerber. They created a 2-ha oasis with 2500 fragrant trees, plants and flowers, made all the more striking for the sprawl that has grown around them. Parrots and a pair of donkeys call it home.

Although they hate to admit it in France's great champagne cellars, the truth is that their world-famous bubbly is the copycat. The first fizzy wine was invented here in 1531, when a wine-making monk at the **Abbaye de St-Hilaire** accidentally discovered the technique for making it fizz – a method known as Blanquette Méthode Ancestrale, made solely of *mauzac* and bottled during the waning moon of March. The abbey (12 km northeast of Limoux, T04 68 69 62 76, Apr-Jun, Sep-Oct daily 1000-1200 and 1400-1800, Jul-Aug

Limoux festival.

daily 1000-1900, Nov-Mar 1000-1200 and 1400-1700, closed Christmas holidays, €4, €3 concession) has a magnificent 12th-century sarcophagus depicting the life of St Sernin of Toulouse by the Master of Cabestany, and a charming 14th-century cloister and Capitulary with a 16th-century painted ceiling. In the refectory, don't miss the lectern hollowed out of a pillar, so the dining monks could listen to a reader without seeing him.

South of Limoux, **Alet-les-Bains** is a pretty medieval hamlet snoozing alongside the Aude, with a thermal pool and free mineral water from the public taps, which is said to be good for the digestion. It's hard to believe, but its **Abbaye Notre-Dame d'Alet** (mid-Feb to Dec Mon-Sat 1000-1200 and 1430-1800, €3) was once the seat of a powerful bishop, who expanded a Carolingian abbey church into a cathedral in 1318. The Protestants left it a picturesque ruin.

The Razès

This is one of the most interesting historical regions in the Aude, or at least the one that, since the 17th century, has been the most investigated, scrutinized and scoured for secrets and treasures. If nothing else, they've found a lot of dinosaur bones.

Ste-Marie Magdalene, Rennes-le-Château.

High on its hill, with commanding views over the Razès, tiny Rennes-le-Château has long been the vortex of Languedocien weirdness. Was Jesus really buried here after coming to France with his wife Mary Magdalene and raising a family? Did the Visigoths come here to hide the Ark of the Covenant? Did three Cathars escape from Monségur and bring a 'secret' here? Over 100,000 visitors come every year to see what it's all about.

Ste-Marie Magdalene

Rue de l'Eglise.
Nov-Apr daily 1000-1300 and 1400-1715, Mid-May-Jun to Sep-Dec daily 1000-1815, Jul to mid-Sep daily 1000-1915.

This church, which is on the same spot as a Visigothic chapel, was remodelled over seven years by the Abbé Saunière, the central figure in Rennes-le-Château's mysteries, and it is certainly odd. *Terribilis est locus iste* (this is a terrible place) reads the inscription over the door, and a leering demon supports the holy water stoup. The confessional is strangely located near the door – does it hide the secret entrance to the crypt? There are statues of Mary and Jesus, each holding a baby Jesus, fuelling speculation of possible twins. The Stations of the Cross run anti-clockwise.

Domaine de l'Abbé Saunière: Boutique du Presbytère

Rue de l'Eglise, T04 68 31 38 85, rennes-le-chateau.fr.
Nov-Apr daily 1000-1300 and 1400-1715, May-Jun, Mid-Sep-Dec daily 1000-1815; Jul to mid-Sep daily 1000-1915. €4.50, €3.20 concession.

The village now owns Saunière's Villa Bethenia, which he never lived in. The visit takes in the much-studied pillar with the upside down cross of St Peter, believed to be Visigothic; the mysterious 'Dalle des Chevaliers', once part of the Carolingian

altar chancel; the altar balustrade where Saunière may have found the clue that led him to his mysterious wealth; as well as the oratory, orangerie and picturesque Tour Magdala, Saunière's library and office.

Dinosauria

Espéraza, T04 68 74 26 88/T04 68 74 02 08, dinosauria.org.
Jul-Aug daily 1000-1900, Feb-Jun, Sep-Nov half-term and Christmas school holidays daily 1030-1230 and 1330-1730. €7, €5 student/child (6-12), €20 family of 4, under 6s free. Visits to the digs Jul-Aug Mon-Sat €2.50, €1.50 child.

This corner of Languedoc isn't only famous for mysteries. France's first dinosaur museum opened in 1992 in Espéraza, and was soon so full that an extension was added to house the fossils and reconstructed skeletons of 35 different dinosaurs found in nearby Campagne-sur-Aude. In July and August you can watch them bring new fossils to light, in the biggest palaeontology dig in Europe.

Musée de la Chapellerie

2 av de la Gare, Espéraza, T04 68 74 00 75, museedelachapellerie.fr.
Sep-Jun daily 1030-1230 and 1330-1730, Jul-Aug 1000-1900 daily. Free.

Before dinosaurs, Espéraza was best known for its hats. Up until the early 1950s, 14 factories employed 3000 people, making the area the second-biggest maker of wool felt hats in the world. Today, only one factory survives and it's in nearby Couiza. Learn how hats are made here, from sheep to fedora; there's a hat boutique as well.

Tip…

In July and August Rennes is closed to vehicles; leave your car in one of the car parks along the road up the hill.

The mystery of Rennes-le-Château

It all began in the 17th century, when a local shepherd found a cache of gold and then died without saying where. Suddenly, some very powerful people became interested in the Razès, among them Nicolas Poussin who painted the *Shepherds of Arcadia* with the inscription "Et in Arcadia ego" and Rennes in the background. The last lady of the Razès, the Dame de Blanchefort died in 1781. Her tombstone in Rennes-le-Château's cemetery read "Et in Arcadia ego".

The village declined until the 1890s, when its parish priest Bérenger Saunière received a 1000 franc donation to restore the church. Soon, he and his housekeeper Marie Dénarnaud were seen digging in the cemetery around the Dame de Blanchefort's tomb (which he defaced) and he asked the Louvre for a copy of Poussin's painting. He then began spending money – the equivalent of €2.5 million – building the Villa Bethania and the Tour Magdala, constructing a new road and bringing in running water.

Where did the money come from? Many believe that during his restoration work on Ste-Marie Magdalene, Saunière discovered something in the altar – a clue, a treasure map or knowledge that enabled him to blackmail the Vatican. He was suspended from the priesthood when he refused to explain his wealth to the diocese. The priest who heard Saunière's deathbed confession in 1917 refused to administer the last rites. When Marie Dénarnaud sold the Villa Bethania in 1946, she promised to tell the new owner the secret before she died – only she had a fit and died speechless, in 1953.

A local newspaper wrote about Saunière in 1956, inspiring journalist Gérard de Sède's 1966 novel *L'Or de Rennes*. This in turn inspired Pierre Plantard and Phillippe de Chérisey to plant forged documents on a secret organization they called the 'Priory of Sion' in the Bibliothèque Nationale in Paris. Michael Baigent, Richard Leigh and Henry Lincoln's Holy Blood Holy Grail followed in 1982, beginning an esoteric industry popularized by *The Da Vinci Code*.

Corbières & Cathar castles

The Corbières is a stunning, if sparsely populated region striped with vines between wild rocks tufted with Mediterranean scrub and castles balanced on vertiginous ridges. The Gauls who refused to get along with the Romans were the first to hide here. It later became the front line between the Visigoths and the Saracens, but it was most famous during the Albigenisan Crusade, when its castles, built in the 10th and 11th centuries by the Counts of Besalú in Catalonia, provided last refuges for the Cathars.

These days, the Corbières is synonymous with wine. It's nothing new, as the soil here isn't good for much else, but since the 1980s the wine has improved in leaps and bounds, as switched-on *vignerons* have learned to maximize the mosaic of soils, exposures and microclimates. Much of the wine is produced in village cooperatives, and quite a few of these are open for visits; Bizanet and Douzens are the main centres.

Château de Quéribus.

These count, if nothing else, as some of the most strikingly picturesque castles ever built. Their masters were Cathars, and after their demise, when the Treaty of Corbeil (1258) set the border between France and Aragon, the castles guarded the front lines as the 'five sons of Carcassonne'. Like Carcassonne, they lost their raison d'être when the Treaty of the Pyrenees moved the border to the Pyrenees, and fell into ruin. But what ruins.

Tip...

Wear good non-slip shoes (not flip-flops), and bring water and a hat in the summer.

Château de Termes & around

Termes, T04 68 70 09 20, chateau-termes.com. Mar, Nov to mid-Dec Sat-Sun and school national holidays (or phone ahead) 1000-1700, Apr-Jun, Sep-Oct daily 1000-1800, Jul-Aug daily 1000-1930. €3.50, €1.50 child.

The Termenès is the wildest corner of the Corbières, and its castle stands in a strategic spot high over the River Sou. Its lord was the elderly Viscount Raymond, the brother of the Cathar *parfait* Benoît de Termes, who famously debated religion with St Dominic at the Colloquy of Montréal in 1207.

In 1210, after conquering Carcassonne, Minerve and Béziers, Simon de Montfort dragged his catapults here. The siege was a stalemate for three

Above: Château de Termes. Opposite: Château d'Aguilar.

months, until the castle's water supply turned stagnant. Afflicted with dysentery, the defenders fled one night through a secret passage, but Viscount Raymond was hauled off to prison in Carcassonne where he died.

His son Olivier de Termes became one of France's greatest knights, and after trying to retake Carcassonne for the Trencavels, he submitted to the king and was chosen as a leader of the Seventh Crusade. In gratitude St Louis returned the Termenès to his family. He brought about the final peaceful surrender of Cathar Quéribus, accompanied Louis to Tunis on his ill-fated Eighth Crusade and died in Jerusalem in 1274.

Unlike the other Cathar castles, Termes was blown up by royal order in the 17th century, so only the outer walls and a few ruins remain, but the views into the ravines are spectacular.

For a more complete castle, head east to 13th-century **Villerouge-Termenès**, where the very last Cathar *parfait* Guilhem Bélibaste was burned at the stake in 1321. Learn more about him and life in the 14th century from the fascinating audiovisual tour in English (T04 68 70 09 11, Mar Sat-Sun 1000-1700, Apr-Jun, Sep to mid-Oct Mon-Fri 1000-1300 and 1400-1800, Sat-Sun 1000-1800, Jul-Aug daily 1000-1930, mid-Oct to mid-Dec Sat-Sun and national holidays 1000-1700 – 1 Nov 1000-1300 and 1400-1700 – €6, €2 young person/child 6-15).

Five of the best

Views

❶ **Château de Quéribus**

❷ **Château de Peyrepertuse**

❸ **Rennes-le-Château**

❹ **Château de Termes**

❺ **The Pont Vieux** Carcassonne

Château d'Aguilar

Tuchan, T04 68 45 51 00.
Apr to mid-Jun 1030-1730, mid-Jun to Sep 1000-1900, Oct-Nov 1100-1700. €3.50, €1.50 young person/child (10-15), under 10s free.

Although its name means 'eagle', the 13th-century castle of Aguilar, set on a relatively low outcrop amid a sea of vines, is the tamest looking of the Cathar castles. A possession of Termes, captured by Simon de Montfort in 1210, it was sold by Olivier de Termes to fund the Abbaye de Fontfroide. The French maintained a garrison here, although it was constantly threatened and finally abandoned in 1561 after Charles V captured it for Spain.

What the author says

I had the advantage of rather foggy conditions, even in June, when I visited the Cathar castles. If I could have actually seen them, I might have had second thoughts about whether I had the puff to make the trek. It's no wonder most of them have never been attacked.

Like the Cité of Carcassonne, these castles are places that tease the imagination; perhaps more so, because no Viollet-le-Duc ever fixed them up. Nor are they equipped with more than the most rudimentary safety features, hand or guard rails. I would think twice and maybe thrice about bringing young children. However, the lack of modern intrusions makes the old stones and ruins all the more evocative, lost in tendrils of mist.

There were a number of other visitors when I was there. A young couple at Peyrepertuse, perched on a wall, had a hand-held device playing medieval songs, spirited ones full of verve and rhythm that seemed vaguely Middle Eastern. "They're the songs of the troubadours in Occitan, from the court of Eleanor of Aquitaine", they told me.

I listened with them. Along with the ruins around us, these songs of mystical and carnal love are the most tangible survivors we have of the days when greater Languedoc – the entire south of France – was the most sophisticated region in Europe. The extraordinary Eleanor (I looked her up later) died in 1204, so never had to see the destruction of the great civilization she helped to create. Occitan, after all, was her first language, and her son Richard the Lionheart's, too. It was so closely associated with the great poetry of the day that even Dante considered writing the *Divine Comedy* in Occitan before opting for Tuscan vernacular.

The music was full of life and passion, and I couldn't help thinking how unutterably poignant it must have been to be holed up in one of these castles, knowing that you were among the last torchbearers of a brilliant civilization that was being ruthlessly destroyed at your feet. Yet, even after nearly eight centuries, the memory of that civilization swells hearts in Languedoc, along with its seductively strange belief in *paratge* (an 'ethereal substance' in the universe, that included elements of chivalry, honour, gentility, natural balance, cosmic order and joy).

Our daydreams were interrupted by a deep, rumbling boom of thunder. Off went the music as we scattered and slid down towards the car park. Be warned: Peyrepertuse is slippery when wet.

I remember reading somewhere that no matter how hard we try we can never know what the past, even the recent past of our parents, was truly like. So, imagining what *paratge,* or the sculpted capitals at Serrabonne, or the mysterious seven-sided church at Rieux Minervois meant to their creators is well nigh impossible. But there are places where it's fascinating to try, and these last lonesome refuges of the Cathars are some of them.

Château de Peyrepertuse

*Duilhac-sous-Peyrepertuse, T04 68 45 40 55,
chateau-peyrepertuse.com.*
Feb-Mar, Nov-Dec daily 1000-1700, Apr-May, Oct
daily 1000-1830, Jun and Sep daily 0900-1900,
Jul-Aug daily 0900-2030. €7.50, €3 young
person/child (6-15), audio guides €4. Visits are
suspended during stormy weather. Check the
website for special events.

Peyrepertuse ('pierced rock') is a breathtaking
sight, teetering on a narrow 780-m precipice. Its
walls encompass the same area as the Cité de
Carcassonne but it's in such an impossible position
that no one has ever attacked it.

The walls actually protect two castles. The
lower one, begun in the ninth century by the
Count of Besalú, belonged to Guillaume de
Peyrepertuse. He gave it up in 1240, after the son of
Roger Raymond Trencavel failed in his attempt to
re-take Carcassonne. You can explore the triangular
courtyard, the old keep, the curtain walls, the
chapel of Ste Marie and the medieval latrines. The
second, higher castle, was added by Louis XI and
was built around the Donjon de St Jordi atop a
steep stone stair.

Ruins of Château de Peyrepertuse.

Château de Quéribus & around

Cucugnan, T04 68 45 03 69.
Feb 1000-1730, Mar 1000-1800, Apr-Jun and Sep
0930-1900, Jul-Aug 0900-2000, Oct 1000-1830,
Nov-Dec 1000-1700. €5, €3 young person/child (6-15).

Nine kilometres southeast of Peyrepertuse (and
in easy signalling distance) the vertigo-defying
Quéribus castle seems to grow organically from its
pinnacle, with views from the top terrace (728 m)
that stretch from the sea to the Pyrenees. Its lord,
Pierre de Cucugnan, was a fierce protector of the
Cathars and his castle turned out to be their very
last bastion before they finally surrendered to
Olivier de Termes in 1255, 11 years after Montségur.
It's one of the most intact of the castles: the keep,
defended by three outer walls, still has a
flamboyant Gothic hall.

A long way below is **Cucugnan** and its
windmill, a village famous in literature. Alphonse
Daudet's tale, *Le Curé de Cucugnan* (in his *Lettres de
Mon Moulin*) recounts a fire-eating sermon given
by the village priest after he dreamed of a visit to
Heaven and Hell in search of his parishioners. From
May to October there's a free audiovisual *And if the
story of Cucugnan was told to me* in the little Theatre
Achille Mir (the name of the local author of the
original tale in Occitan), which is on Place du
Plantane (T04 68 45 09 09). The village **church**
houses a rare statue of the Pregnant Virgin, who
also bizarrely holds the baby Jesus in her arms.

Just west of Quéribus and Peyrepertuse, and
north of St-Paul de Fenouillet, you can drive along
the narrow windy road under the sheer cliffs and
overhanging rock of the **Gorge de Galamus**, and
perhaps spot its rare Bonelli eagles.

Tip...

Buy a **Pays de Cathars passport** for €3, and get a
€1 discount and free child entry to 19 sites in the
Aude. It's available at all participating sites or see
payscathare.org.

Château de Puilaurens

Puilaurens, T04 68 20 65 26.
Feb, Apr, Oct to mid-Nov daily 1000-1700, Mar Sat-Sun 1000-1700, May daily 1000-1800, Jun and Sep daily 1000-1900, Jul-Aug daily 0900-2000. €4, €2 young person/child (6-15).

Built on a 700-m rocky outcrop, this castle was a 10th-century outpost of St Michel de Cuxa before it came under the Counts of Besalú and the kings of Aragon. Guillaume de Peyrepertuse arrived here after surrendering his own castle, followed by other *parfaits*, including some from Monségur, came here and defended Puilaurens under the last great Cathar military commander, Chabert de Barbaira. No one is quite sure what happened but

by around 1250 history says that Puilaurens was under royal control as the southernmost citadel of France; Louis IX strengthened and garrisoned it with the largest number of troops. Spain attacked it on numerous occasions and captured it in 1635, shortly before having to give it back after the Treaty of the Pyrenees.

Much of what survives was built after 1250: the two curtain walls and four round towers defended the keep. The southwestern Tour de Dame Blanche recalls Blanche of Bourbon, who spent time at Puilaurens before she was murdered by her husband Pedro the Cruel of Castile; her ghost is said to be seen occasionally strolling across the wall. The tower has a rare relic, a built-in 'speaking tube' allowing communication between floors.

Narbonne

Founded in 118 BC, Narbo Martius was Rome's first successful colony and the ancient capital of Languedoc, then known as Gallia Narbonensis. Yet, only bits from Roman times have survived. Instead, its startling centrepiece was left by its 12th- to 14th-century viscounts, who gave it a stupendous if abbreviated Gothic cathedral and archbishop's palace. Narbonne is a likeable little city, and when you need a break from all the history, the leafy quays of Canal de la Robine are never far.

Cathédrale St-Just-et-St Pasteur.

Essentials

❶ **Getting around** It's usually easy to find street parking just outside the compact historic centre. Otherwise, park at the Parking Relais du Parc des Sports (follow the Canal de la Robine to avenue de la Mer) and catch the free shuttle (Mon-Sat 0740-1250 and 1325-1925). City bus No 8 goes to Gruissan Plage-Narbonne Plage-St-Pierre-la Mer; for schedules, T04 68 90 18.

❷ **Bus station** Avenue Carnot, next door to the train station. For regional bus travel, see page 275.

❸ **Train station** Avenue Carnot. For regional train travel, see page 274.

❹ **ATM** BNP-Paribas 50 rue Jean Jaurès; Société Générale, 3 cours République.

❺ **Hospital** Centre Hospitalier de Narbonne, boulevard du Docteur Lacroix, T04 68 42 60 00.

❻ **Pharmacy** Des Halles, 13 boulevard du Docteur Ferroul, T04 68 32 01 67; Pont des Marchands, 7 rue Pont des Marchands, T04 68 32 00 75.

❼ **Post office** 19 boulevard Gambetta, T04 68 65 87 00.

❽ **Tourist information office** 31 rue Jean Jaurès, T04 68 65 15 60, narbonne-tourisme.com. Mid-September to March Monday-Saturday 1000-1230 and 1330-1800, Sunday and national holidays 1000-1700; April to mid-September daily 0900-1900.

Cathédrale St-Just-et-St Pasteur

Rue Armand Gautier, T04 68 32 09 52.
Oct-Jun daily 0900-1200 and 1400-1800, Jul-Sep daily 1000-1900. Trésor de la Cathédrale Oct-Mar daily 1400-1700, Apr-Jun daily 1400-1800, Jul-Sep Mon-Sat 1100-1800, Sun 1400-1800. €2.20. Map: Narbonne, p216.

Begun in 1272 by Pope Clement IV, a former archbishop of Narbonne, this Cathedral was designed to rival the soaring Gothic masterpieces of the Ile de France. It would have succeeded, too, had the city fathers not got with cold feet in 1340 when it came to demolishing part of the town wall. So the cathedral project came to an abrupt end, leaving a splendid choir and transept – and a blank wall where the nave should have been. From the Cour St-Eutrope, you can see signs of the architects' unfulfilled ambition – the walls, truncated pillars and flying buttresses.

Inside, the church's stumpiness makes the 130-ft **choir** seem even higher than it is. There's an enormous organ in a madly ornate wooden case that took a century to complete, beautiful stained glass from the 13th and 14th centuries, sumptuous tombs of archbishops and knights and a 14th-century polychrome stone *Déposition*. In 1981, the cathedral's 14th-century Gothic **retable**, broken and hidden during a remodelling in 1732, was rediscovered and has now been restored. It has some 200 figures, including vivid scenes of Purgatory, Hell and Limbo. The **treasury**, entered by way of the right ambulatory chapel, has a remarkable pair of 16th-century Flemish tapestries: one on the seven days of the *Creation*, the other an *Allegory on Prosperity and Adversity*. It is also home to beautiful gold and silver work, crystal cases, ivories and illuminated manuscripts.

The monumental but worn 14th- and 15th-century **cloisters** link the cathedral to the Palais des Archevêques by way of the **Passage de l'Ancre**.

Tip...

Save money with a Billet global. For €5.20 you can see the Horreum, Archaeology, Art and History and Lapidary museums; for €7.50 it also includes the Donjon, Cathedral Treasure and Charles Trénet's birthplace.

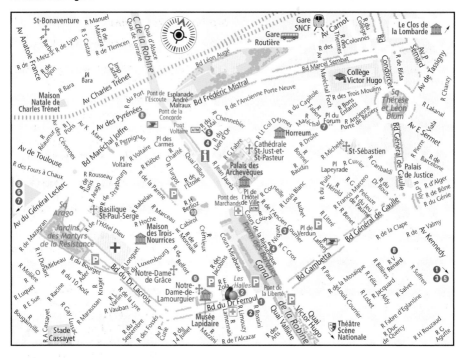

Place de l'Hôtel-de-Ville.

Place de l'Hôtel-de-Ville & Palais des Archevêques

Map: Narbonne, above.

This big square is the busiest in Narbonne, and has been since the city's foundation. A slice of pavement has been cut away to reveal a section of **Via Domitia**. Looming over all is the **Palais des Archevêques**, an ecclesiastical fortress residence that in size and importance is surpassed in France only by the Papal Palace in Avignon. There are actually two palaces: the 'old' palace from the 12th century on the right, and the 'new' palace from the 14th century on the left, with a façade restored by Viollet-le-Duc. The complex is now home to Narbonne's Mairie (note the relief over the door, recalling the city's early maritime vocation) and its two most important museums.

Narbonne listings

❶ Sleeping

1 Château L'Hospitalet *Route de Narbonne-Plage (D168)* (off map)
2 Hôtel de France *6 rue Rossini*
3 Hôtel de la Clape *4 rue des Fleurs, Narbonne Plage* (off map)
4 Hôtel de Paris *2 rue du Lion d'Or*
5 Hôtel La Résidence *6 rue 1er Mai*
6 Jardins de St Benoît *Route de Talairan, St Laurent de La Cabrerisse* (off map)
7 La Demeure de Roquelongue *53 av de Narbonne, St-André-de-Roquelongue* (off map)
8 Le Régent *13 rue Suffren*

❶ Eating & drinking

1 Brasserie Co *1 bd du Docteur Ferroul*
2 Chez Bébelle *Les Halles, bd du Docteur Ferroul*
3 Cocodélices *30 rue de l'Ancien-Courrier*
4 En Face *27 Cours de la République*
5 L'Air Marin *Bd Méditerranée, Narbonne Plage* (off map)
6 La Table de Saint-Crescent *68 av du Général Leclerc*
7 Le Chillout *7 place du Forum*
8 Le Petit Comptoir *4 bd Maréchal Joffre*
9 Les Cuisiniers Cavistes *1 place Lamourguier*
10 Les Ramblas *Place des Quatre-Fontaines*

Musée Archéologique

Palais des Archevêques, Place de l'Hôtel-de-Ville, T04 68 90 30 54.
Apr-Sep 0930-1215 and 1400-1800, Oct-Mar Tue-Sun 1000-1200 and 1400-1700. €3.70.
Map: Narbonne, opposite.

France's third most important archaeological collection outside Paris, Narbonne's museum has a rich pre-Roman collection of Bronze Age swords and Greek ceramics, as well as finds from the Gallo-Roman city. The museum's best-known treasures are the extremely rare, well-preserved frescoes that once adorned the homes of the smart set in the Clos de la Lombarde. Also look out for milestones from the Via Domitia, statues, sarcophagi and artefacts relating to daily life and the ancient port.

Musée d'Art et d'Histoire

Palais des Archevêques, Place de l'Hôtel-de-Ville, T04 68 90 30 54.
Apr-Sep daily 0930-1215 and 1400-1800, Oct-Mar Tue-Sun 1000-1200 and 1400-1700. €3.70.
Map: Narbonne, opposite.

This museum occupies the princely 17th- and 18th-century apartments of the archbishop of Narbonne, once the most powerful prelates in the South of France. The **Salle des Audiences** has a portrait of the last archbishop, Dillon, who also served as President of the Estates of Languedoc and did much to help Narbonne before the Revolution forced him into exile in London. In 2006 his tomb was exhumed at St Pancras during work on the Eurostar station, and in 2009 his remains were interred in Narbonne cathedral (except for his porcelain dentures, which are in the Museum of London).

Earlier archbishops not only lived like princes but hosted them: both Louis XIII and Louis XIV stayed in the **Chambre du Roi**, with a Roman mosaic floor and frescoed ceiling. In art, episcopal taste tended towards the Italians and the academic: in the **Grande Galérie** and **Oratoire** are paintings by Salvator Rosa, Canaletto, Rosalba Carriera, Ribera and other followers of Caravaggio, Breughel, and best of all, *Le Sacre de Roi David*, by Veronese. The **Salle des Faïences** houses 18th-century pharmacy jars and enamels from leading French centres (Moustiers, Sèvres, Montpellier). Lastly, the museum has a compelling **Orientalist Gallery**, housing a collection of 19th-century paintings on North African and Middle Eastern themes, some realistic, some imaginary, and displayed in rooms designed with motifs from the Great Mosque of Córdoba and a Moroccan Palace.

Tip...

On Tuesdays from July to mid-September, the tourist office offers 90-minute tours of Roman Narbonne, in English (€6.50, €4.20 concession, under 10s free).

Around the region

Donjon Gilles Aycelin

Place de l'Hôtel de Ville, access through the Mairie.
Oct-Jun 0900-1200 and 1400-1800, Jul-Sep daily
1000-1800. €2.20.
Map: Narbonne, p216.

The 13th-century Archbishop Gilles Aycelin built
this 41-m tower just to show he was in charge;
there are great views over the city from the top.

Horreum

7 rue Rouget de Lisle.
Apr-Sep daily 0930-1215 and 1400-1800, Oct-Mar
Tue-Sun 1000-1200 and 1400-1700. €3.70.
Map: Narbonne, p216.

The ancient geographer Strabo called *Narbo
Martius* the 'greatest emporium' in the south of
France, and these long subterranean galleries (a
horreum is a granary) from the first century BC are
proof that he wasn't full of baloney. Hollowed out
in the form of a giant 'U', arms, grain, oil and wine
were stored here at a constant 12-14°C. Two of the
wings are open, equipped with a sound and light
evocation of Roman Narbo.

Canal de la Robine

Map: Narbonne, p216.

In Roman times, before the river silted up and
moved, ships could sail up the Aude to Narbonne.
With the success of the Canal du Midi, Narbonne
wanted a piece of the action, and in 1686 the
Aude's ancient bed was made into the Canal de la
Robine, reattaching the city to its long-lost river.
From there, goods were transported overland to
Le Somail until 1776, when the Canal de Jonction
provided a direct link to the Canal du Midi.

Today, the Canal de la Robine doubles as
Narbonne's favourite promenade. The southern
stretch is dominated by the beautiful **Halles** built
in 1905, not far from the **Pont des Marchands**,
Nabonne's 'Little Ponte Vecchio' – the only bridge
in France with buildings. Underneath are the
arches of the Roman bridge that carried the Via
Domitia over the Aude.

Horreum.

Canal de la Robine.

Basilique St Paul-Serge & around

Rue de l'Hôtel Dieu, T04 68 90 30 65.
Mon-Sat 0900-1200 and 1400-1800,
Sun 0900-1200.
Map: Narbonne, p216.

This handsome church of 1180, the third on this site, was one of the first in the south to be built in the new Gothic style. It stands over the tomb of St Paulus-Sergius, the first bishop of Narbonne. The interior, with its massive choir, vaults and arcades, is stunning; the holy water stoup has a little frog, which according to legend was petrified by an archbishop when it started to croak heresy during Mass. Ask to visit the **Paleochristian crypt** (AD 250), containing the oldest Christian sarcophagi in Gaul, in what was originally a shared pagan/Christian necropolis along the road to Bordeaux.

The adjacent hospital is built around the medieval incarnation, or **Hôtel Dieu**, which incorporates a fancy baroque chapel from 1782. Further along rue de l'Hôtel Dieu stands one of the finest Renaissance houses in Languedoc, known as the **Maison des Trois-Nourrices** (1558) (House of the Three Wet Nurses) after the busty caryatids around the windows.

Maison Natale de Charles Trénet

13 av Charles-Trénet, T04 68 90 30 66.
Apr-Sep Wed-Mon 1000-1200 and 1400-1800,
Oct-Mar Wed-Mon 1400-1800. €5.20.
Map: Narbonne, p216.

Singer and songwriter, Charles Trénet (1913-2001), nicknamed *le fou chantant* (the singing fool), donated his birthplace near the train station to the city on the condition that it *didn't* become a museum. Instead it has remained as it was, with its piano, old photos and furnishings. The sound system plays Trénet's biggest hits, including *Y a d'la joie!*, surely the happiest song ever recorded.

Notre-Dame-de-Lamourguier & Musée Lapidaire

Place Emile Digeon.
Apr-Sep daily 0930-1215 and 1400-1800, Oct-Mar Tue-Sun 1000-1200 and 1400-1700. €3.70.
Map: Narbonne, p216.

With nearly 2000 inscriptions, tombs, altars, stelae and sculptures, this 13th-century Benedictine church holds the second largest lapidary museum anywhere outside Rome. Most were incorporated into the city walls, and recovered when the walls were dismantled. Audiovisual images of ancient and medieval buildings put them in context.

Around the region

Le Clos de la Lombarde

Rue de Chanzy, T04 68 90 30 54.
Sep-Jun guided tours by appointment,
Jul-Aug daily 1000-1200 and 1500-1900.
Map: Narbonne, p216.

This cluster of six Roman houses along the Via
Domitia has been the focus of archaeological
excavations since 1974. The paintings it has
yielded are on display in the Archaeology Museum
(see above, page 217).

Around Narbonne

Abbaye de Fontfroide

*D 613, 12 km southwest of Narbonne, T04 68 45
11 08, fontfroide.com.*
Mid-Jul to Aug tours every 30 mins 1000-1800,
Mar to mid-Jul, Sep-Oct tours every 45 mins
1000-1215 and 1345-1730, Nov-Feb tours every
hour 1000-1200 and 1400-1600. Tours in French,
English audio guide provided. €9; €6 young
person (18-25), €2.50 child (8-18). In Jul-Aug
nocturnal visits at 2200 on certain days, with a
booking at the Table de Fontfroide restaurant
€15, €6 child (8-18).

Isolated amid the wooded hills, Fontfroide was the
most powerful Cistercian monastery in the south. It
was founded by the Viscount of Narbonne in 1093
and adopted Cistercian rule after being visited by
St Bernard in 1145. It rapidly grew in importance,
with fingers in many political pies and monks
and abbots who acted on an international stage:
Pierre de Castelnau, the Papal Legate who was
assassinated in Beaucaire, triggering the
Albigensian Crusade in 1209; another abbot was
Papal Legate in the trial against the Templars; and
Jacques Fournier was elected pope Benedict XII
in Avignon in 1317. At the abbey's peak, its
surrounding farms and vines supported a
community of 300. In 1348, the Black Death
killed all but 20 monks.

Fontfroide recovered, but like many Cistercian
houses it gradually became more worldly. In 1791
the last monks left, and the abbey managed the
rare feat of escaping the Revolution undamaged.
It even knew a brief revival from 1858-1908 when
it was home to a community from Sénaque.

The tour takes in courtyards worthy of palaces,
the large vaulted refectory and the elegant late
12th-century cloister, with its lace work of arches
set in arches. The majestic church, towering 20 m
at the crossing, was begun right after St Bernard's
visit, and has colourful stained-glass windows
added in the 1920s. Collages of older stained glass
collected from churches in northern France after
the First World War decorate the dormitories. The
rose garden has some 3000 bushes, including
many medieval varieties, and at least as many
butterflies.

Left: Abbaye de Fontfroide's courtyard.
Below: Fontfroide's stained glass.

St-Pierre-la-Mer.

Narbonne's coast

A big chunk of *garrigue*, the vine-covered **Montagne de La Clape**, separates Narbonne from the Aude's seaside playground.

St-Pierre-la-Mer & Narbonne Plage

Northernmost St-Pierre-la Mer has merged with Narbonne Plage, forming your basic beach resort. It does have something unique, however: there's an 800-m hike from the car park at St-Pierre, and hidden in the rocks is the turquoise freshwater pool known as **Gouffre de L'Oeil Doux**, under a sheer white cliff.

Gruissan Plage

Surrounded by flamingo-filled lagoons, Gruissan Plage has more character than those mentioned above. It has an old town that sweeps around a ruined tower, the **Tour de Barbarousse**. The tower was probably named after the Turkish pirate admiral, who in the 1540s was an ally of the French against Charles V. Gruissan is famous for its **Plage des Pilotis** – a wide beach backed by 1300 wooden cottages on stilts. The first were built in the 1850s when the craze for sea bathing took hold, back when the land flooded every winter. Many owners have since 'improved' them by cladding them in aluminium siding.

Sigean

The Réserve Africaine de Sigean

D 6009, Sigean, T04 68 48 20 20, reserveafricainesigean.fr.
Nov-Feb 0900-1600 (last admission), Apr-Sep 0900-1830 (last admission), other months vary by 30 mins. €25, €19 child (6-14).

In a sunny landscape of *garrigue* and lagoons, the Sigean reserve opened in 1974 and has grown into one of the most popular attractions in Languedoc. No longer strictly reserved for African animals, it currently hosts 3800 mammals, lizards and birds, many of them rare and endangered (white rhinoceros, Somali ass, Tibetan bears). They roam freely over 300 ha, in various parks. Allow at least three hours by car and foot.

Listings

Sleeping

Carcassonne & around

Hôtel de la Cité €€€€
Place Auguste-Pierre Pont, T04 68 71 98 71, hoteldelacite.com.
Map: Carcassonne, E6, p198.
In the heart of the Cité, these 40 sumptuous rooms and 21 suites in the former bishop's palace have hosted everyone from Queen Elizabeth to Walt Disney. Expect bags of medieval atmosphere and luxury amid oak beams, marble baths, spiral stairs, secret terraces, heated pool and gardens and a gorgeous library/bar. Kids under 16 can stay for free in their parents' room.

Le Domaine d'Auriac €€€€
Rte de St-Hilaire, T04 68 25 72 22, domaine-d-auriac.com.
Far from the crowds but only 7 km from Carcassonne airport, this manor house hotel has 24 rooms lavishly decorated in flowery patterns. The hotel sits on a 70-ha estate of woods and vines, with a large outdoor pool, tennis court, an 18-hole golf course and a fine restaurant serving traditional cuisine with tables by the roaring fire in winter, or alfresco in the garden in summer.

42 Rue Victor Hugo €€€
42 rue Victor Hugo, T09 77 52 44 36, 42ruevictorhugo.com.
Map: Carcassonne, A3, p198.
Just off Place Carnot in the Bastide St-Louis, this elegant B&B in an 18th-century *hôtel particulier* is perfect for couples. There are two apartments and a master bedroom, sleekly designed in shades of grey, all with superbly decadent showers and exquisite cotton sheets. Owner Peter is exceptionally helpful, knowledgeable and an excellent chef. Minimum stay is two nights, and there are special weekend offers.

Hôtel du Château €€€
2 rue Camille St-Saens, T04 68 11 38 38, hotel-du-chateau.net.
Map: Carcassonne, E5, p198.
This cushy little 16-room hotel is located just outside the Cité. Rooms are stylish and cosy, equipped with flat-screen TVs, air conditioning and CD players. The attractive grounds under the medieval walls offer a heated pool (Easter-November) and year-round jacuzzi. The hotel has no restaurant, but there's a bar and the breakfast (€10) is copious.

Hôtel la Bastide €€
81 rue de la Liberté, T04 68 71 96 89, hotel-bastide.fr.
Map: Carcassonne, B3, p198.
This pleasant 28-room hotel makes a nice change from the cookie-cutter chain hotels in the same price range. It doesn't have a restaurant, but it has everything else you need: friendly owners, air conditioning, flat-screen TVs, internet, breakfast (€6) and a private garage. Prices are at the bottom of this range.

Hôtel Montmorency €€
9 rue Camille St-Saens, T04 68 11 96 70, lemontmorency.com.
Map: Carcassonne, E5, p198.
Just a few minutes from the Cité, this stylish hotel offers 20 quiet, air-conditioned if rather small rooms. There's a garden patio, and guests can also make use of the pool and jacuzzi at the nearby Hôtel du Château, which has the same owners. Free parking, and computers in the lobby.

Hôtel de la Cité.

La Maison Coste €€
40 rue Coste Rebouhl, T04 68 77 12 15, maison-coste.com.
Map: Carcassonne, C4, p198.
The charming owners of this B&B, Manu and Michel, run an interior design boutique so everything in the three spacious rooms and two suites is in immaculate taste. There's a jacuzzi and a tea room but no TV or phones, so peace and quiet guaranteed. Price includes a hearty continental breakfast.

Balladins €
3 allée Gilles de Roberval, T04 68 71 99 50, etoilecarcassonne.fr.
Map: Carcassonne, A4, p198.
Although located by the airport in an industrial zone, this immaculate, modern, family-run hotel is very popular with budget travellers. Red, white and black prevail in the public rooms and 38 bedrooms, and there's a good restaurant, too.

Le Grand Puits €
8 place du Grand Puits, T04 68 25 16 67, legrandpuits.free.fr.
Map: Carcassonne, E6, p198.
Situated in the Cité, book early to stay in one of these three rooms with wood-beam ceilings. The blue room sleeps four and comes with a patio and kitchenette; the orange room sleeps five and has a kitchenette and beautiful views over the Montagne Noir; the yellow room sleeps two and has all you need to make your own continental breakfast.

Self-catering
Les Gîtes de Cabardès
7 rue des Jardins, Ventenac-Cabardès, T04 68 24 08 23, carcassonne-holidays.com.
On the edge of a village only 10 minutes from Carcassonne, these are three modern and very well-equipped gîtes that sleep up to six people and share a pool. A week in high season starts at €860 for two; the same owner has an apartment in Carcassonne for €500 a week.

The Razès

Château des Ducs de Joyeuse €€€
Allée du Château, Couiza, T04 68 74 23 50, chateau-des-ducs.com.
Mar to mid-Nov.
Built in the 16th century by the Lieutenant Governor of Languedoc, this handsome castle with its fat round towers has 23 spacious rooms and 12 junior suites that combine Renaissance touches (dark wood furniture, four-poster beds and fabrics) with modern comforts and luxurious bathrooms. There's a pool, or you can swim in the nearby Aude. Price includes buffet breakfast.

La Maison de Chapelier €
7 rue Elie Sermet, Espéraza, T04 68 74 22 49, esperaza.net.
This big bourgeoise mansion, built in 1923 by a hat maker, has five big rooms full of character and high ceilings, with much of the original decoration intact.

The house has three living rooms open to guests, and a shady park. There's even a pool and a sauna with a wooden deck for soaking up the sun. No credit cards.

Self-catering
Domaine de Mournac
Antugnac, T04 68 74 21 10, mournac.com.
Located 8 km northwest of Rennes-le-Château, this beautiful stone-built property set in 9 ha dates back to the 11th century and was long used as a post house. It has three very stylish B&B rooms (€90-110), a studio and gîte sleeping 10 (from €900 a week). The views from the terrace and pool seem to go on forever.

Corbières & Cathar castles

Ecluse du Soleil €
Sougraigne, T04 68 69 88 44, ecluseausoleil.com.
Peace and quiet is guaranteed in this hilltop hamlet 11 km south of Rennes-le-Château, with big views over the Pyrenees and en suite rooms spread among several stone houses. The owners know all about local activities, and there's tennis, a pool and restaurant serving tasty *cuisine de terroir*.

Listings

Château L'Hospitalet €€€
Hospitalet, rte de Narbonne-Plage (D168), T04 68 45 28 50, gerard-bertrand.com.
Map: Narbonne, p216.
Ten minutes south of Narbonne in the hills of La Clape, this recently refurbished wine château has 38 immaculate if slightly sterile rooms, each named after one of the wines. It's very peaceful, and there's a pool (or the beach, five minutes away) and a good restaurant called H. Guests are welcomed with a free bottle of wine.

La Demeure de Roquelongue €€€
53 av de Narbonne, St-André-de-Roquelongue, T04 68 45 63 57/ T06 98 87 11 44, demeure-de-roquelongue.com.
Map: Narbonne, p216.
This very stylish five-room B&B in a 19th-century townhouse has featured in a number of French design magazines. Located 12 km from Narbonne, it's close to the Canal du Midi and Corbières. Each room is named after a wind: Espan has a wonderful old-fashioned bathtub in an alcove resembling a mini-theatre; the Eole rooms sleeps four. There's a large garden and the price includes an excellent breakfast.

Hôtel de la Clape €€
4 rue des Fleurs, Narbonne Plage, T04 68 49 80 15, hoteldelaclape. com.
Map: Narbonne, p216.
This Logis de France, in a quiet area only 80 m from the beach, is equipped with a pool and makes an excellent choice for families, with rooms sleeping up to five. Rooms have air conditioning and many have balconies. The very welcoming hosts Corinne and Nicolas also have an excellent restaurant, with occasional jazz nights in summer.

Hôtel La Résidence €€
6 rue 1er Mai, T04 68 32 19 41, hotelresidence.fr.
Map: Narbonne, p216.
This is a charming reworking of an old 19th-century hotel and is situated in the heart of Narbonne. It offers 26 classic rooms in soft pastels, most with unusually large bathrooms. There's a private garage, an internet area and they offer light meals, as well as wine tastings.

Hôtel de France €
6 rue Rossini, T04 68 32 09 75.
Map: Narbonne, p216.
This charming 15-room hotel on a quiet street has air conditioning, firm mattresses, satellite TV and parking. The owner speaks English.

Hôtel de Paris €
2 rue du Lion d'Or, T04 68 32 08 68, hoteldeparis-narbonne.com.
Map: Narbonne, p216.
This old budget standby offers basic but adequate rooms. Parking nearby is fairly easy (it's a 10-minute walk from the station), and room prices vary by the amount of plumbing you choose – the cheapest have bathrooms in the hall. Nevertheless, all rooms are equipped with Wi-Fi.

Le Régent €
15 rue Suffren and 50 rue Mosaïque, T04 68 32 02 41, leregentnarbonne.com.
Map: Narbonne, p216.
Just south of the Boulevard Gambetta, this little 15-room hotel has recently been refurbished. All rooms are different, some have bathrooms and some have toilets down the hall, and some sleep five people. There are fine views over Narbonne from the roof terrace. There's a little garden; garden rooms Nos 16 and 17 are the nicest. Parking is easy, and they have a garage for bikes.

Jardins de St Benoît
Rte de Talairan, St-Laurent-de-la-Cabrerisse, T04 67 11 87 15, garrigaeresorts.com/st-benoit.
Map: Narbonne, p216.
Inland from Sigean, this riverside spa-resort consists of 171 traditional one- to five-bedroom village-style houses, each with a garden and terrace (larger ones have private pools). Adjacent is the 'real' village of St-Laurent, which has a restaurant, spa, babysitters, children's club and designated gardens for picking vegetables. Off-peak special offers start at €714 per week for a one-bedroom house.

Eating & drinking

Carcassonne & around

La Barbacane €€€€
Place Auguste-Pierre Pont, T04 68 71 98 71, hoteldelacite.com.
Thu-Mon for dinner.
Map: Carcassonne, E6, p198.
The Hotel de la Cité's (see Sleeping, page 222) restaurant offers fabulous dining in a hall where the viscounts would have felt at home. The food lives up to the setting; classics include Charolais beef with foie gras, and sole glazed in champagne. There are exquisite vegetarian options, home-made bread, and masterpieces prepared by the special pastry chef, including a modern take on crêpes Suzette. Reservations required. The hotel's brasserie, **Chez Saskia**, is excellent and less pricey.

Le Parc Franck Putelat €€€€
Chemin des Anglais, T04 68 71 80 80, leparcfranckputelat.com.
Tue-Sat for lunch and dinner.
Map: Carcassonne, E7, p198.
Young Franck Putelat, one of the stars in France's culinary firmament, runs this laid-back, quirky and stylish restaurant in a garden at the foot of the Cité. Menus feature a mix of classics (truffled Bresse chicken) and innovations (roast scallops with savoy cabbage, Morteau sausage and juniper) that have won him accolades from even the snootiest critics. Set-price weekday lunch with a glass of wine and coffee is €29, or let him follow his fancy for €95 a head. Book in advance.

Château de St-Martin €€€
Hameau de Montredon (3 km from Carcassonne) T04 68 71 09 53, chateausaintmartin.net.
Apr-Sep Thu-Tue for lunch and dinner, Oct-Mar Mon-Tue, Thu-Sat for lunch and dinner, Sun for lunch.
No one makes cassoulet better than chef Jean-Claude, and it can be slowly savoured either in the garden or in the atmospheric 12th-century tower. He also specializes in seafood. It may not be easy, but try to save a bit of room for the lovely desserts. Menus from €32-56.

Aux Berges du Canal €€
48 rte Minervoise, T04 68 26 60 15, pagesperso-orange.fr/auxbergesducanal.
Thu-Tue for lunch and dinner.
Map: Carcassonne, C2, p198.
On the banks of the Canal du Midi, this unpretentious little family-run restaurant offers a varied menu, including fish, beef and lamb dishes, as well as a cassoulet. Good value for money; menus start at €16.

La Cantine de Robert €€
Place de Lattre de Tassigny, T04 68 47 37 80, restaurantrobertrodriguez.com.
Mon-Tue 1200-1500 and 1900-2200, Wed 1200-1500, Thu-Sat 1200-1500 and 1900-2200.
Map: Carcassonne, B4, p198.
Robert Rodriguez's 1930s-style bistro is opposite his far pricier headquarters, L'Atelier. It offers an affordable chance to taste well-prepared southern French classics from *daube* to platters of cheese and charcuterie, all with a superb choice of wines. Book.

La Cotte de Maille €€
2 rue St-Jean, T04 68 72 36 24, cottedemailles.com.
Jul-Sep daily for lunch and dinner, Oct-Mar Fri-Wed for lunch and dinner.
Map: Carcassonne, E5, p198.
This candlelit restaurant offers a chance for total sensory medieval immersion. Chef Claudine serves medieval cuisine in filling portions, from the original cassoulet de Carcassonne cooked with lamb (instead of duck) and beef with salsify, to parsnips and Jerusalem artichokes and game dishes. All can be washed down with *hypocras* (spicy wine) or *moretum* (medieval sangria).

La Roulotte €
6 rue Denisse, T04 68 25 07 03.
Tue-Sat for lunch and dinner.
Map: Carcassonne, B4, p198.
This welcoming little restaurant (a *roulotte* is a gypsy caravan) off Place Carnot is great for a romantic evening, but also fine for kids – they even supply crayons. The furnishings come from antique shops and flea markets, and you can dine alfresco in good weather. The menu is small and changes according to the market, but the food is fresh and prepared with an exotic flair.

Listings

Le Saint Jean €
1 place St Jean, T04 68 47 42 43, le-saint-jean.fr.
Jun-Sep daily 0900-2200, Oct-May Wed-Mon 0900-2200.
Map: Carcassonne, E5, p198.

The terrace overlooking Viollet-le-Duc's pointy-roofed towers is an oasis of calm in the Cité, but that's not the only reason to stop here. The duck and cassoulet are tasty, and there are a selection of fresh *salades composées*, including the 'Visigoth' with four kinds of cheese. In July and August there's often live jazz or salsa, when the bar stays open late. They also do breakfast.

Cafés & bars

Café Saillan
31 rue du Dr Tomey, T04 68 71 39 96.
Open 0700-0200.
Map: Carcassonne, B4, p198.

In the same family for three generations, this extremely popular café has had an arty overhaul and stays open late; live music some weekends.

Carpe Diem
29 rue du Pont Vieux, T09 54 22 28 85, estelle-carpediem.eu.
Tue-Sun 1130-1530 and 1800-0200.
Map: Carcassonne, C4, p198.

Atmospheric wine/tapas bar near the bridge, often featuring live salsa, reggae, blues and gypsy music.

Le Bar à Vins
6 rue du Plô, T04 68 47 38 38.
Map: Carcassonne, B6, p198.

A large enclosed garden near St-Nazaire, away from the crowds. This is a favourite for an aperitif and offers good music and wines.

The Razès

La Cour des Ducs €€€
Allée du Château, Couiza, T04 68 74 23 50, chateau-des-ducs.com.
Mar to mid-Nov for dinner.

This elegant restaurant is the perfect setting for a feast; you can dine in the courtyard or in the stone-vaulted rooms of the Château des Ducs de Joyeuse. The food has a Provençal/Italian touch – mesclun salad, risotto, lamb cooked in the Niçoise style – and is accompanied by Corbières' finest wines.

Maison Gayda €€€
Brugairolles, T04 68 20 65 87, maisongayda.com.
Wed-Sat for lunch and 1900-2100, Sun for lunch and 1800-2000.

This high-tech vineyard, 10 minutes from Limoux, has a cutting-edge restaurant on top of the winery, with views in all directions. The menu features the likes of seared king prawns, red pepper and fresh coriander with Espelette jam, or roast suckling pig. Alternatively, enjoy a luxury barbecue in one of six private *paillotes* in the pines. Lunch menus €22, others start at €39.

Corbières & Cathar castles

Gilles Goujon €€€€
5 av de St-Victor, Fontjoncouse, T04 68 44 07 37, gilles-goujon.fr.
Mar-May, Oct-Dec Wed-Sat for lunch and dinner, Sun for lunch; Jun-Sep Mon for dinner, Tue-Sun for lunch and dinner.

Gilles Goujon, one of France's top chefs, draws gourmets to tiny Fontjoncouse east of Termes. His complex, creative, highly personal cuisine is constantly evolving, using only seasonal ingredients – in winter, for instance, wild hare (each cut of meat undergoes its own cooking method and is served with cocoa spaghetti and caramelized beetroot). Weekday lunch menu is €58. After your meal, you can choose to stay in Goujon's **Auberge du Vieux Puits** (aubergeduvieuxpuits.fr) around a Hollywood-style pool.

Tip...

Don't miss the chance to try the red wine of Cabardès, one of France's newest AOC areas (since 1998). All growers must plant 50% Atlantic varieties (Merlot, Cabernet Sauvignon and Franc, Cot and the local Fer Servadou) and 50% Mediterranean varieties (Syrah and Grenache); although how they blend the two is up to their own discretion.

Auberge du Vigneron €€
2 rue Achille-Mir, Cucugnan, T04 68 45 03 00, auberge-vigneron.com.
Mid-Mar to Jun, Sep to mid-Nov Tue-Sat for lunch and dinner, Sun for lunch, Jul-Aug daily for lunch, Mon-Sat for dinner.
Exploring Cathar castles is hungry work and this restaurant in a former wine cellar has a good choice of food – duck stewed with olives and mushrooms, bream and onion tarte, langoustines with asparagus. Menus start at €22.

Narbonne

L'Air Marin €€€
Bd Méditerranée, Narbonne Plage, T04 68 43 84 89, restaurantairmarin.com.
Map: Narbonne, p216.
This waterfront restaurant draws seafood lovers year round with its delicious and fresh cuisine. There are mussels prepared in 10 different ways, oysters, *bourride narbonnais*, *sarsuela* (Catalan-style seafood 'opera'), lobster, gambas and much more, including salads and meat courses. The weekday lunch menu is €15.

La Table de Saint-Crescent €€€
68 av du Général Leclerc, T04 68 41 37 37, la-table-saint-crescent. com.
Tue-Fri for lunch and dinner, Tue-Sat for dinner, Sun for lunch.

Map: Narbonne, p216.
Elegant dining in a former oratory. Lionel Giraud's cuisine is inventive, and includes such dishes as salmon *tartare* with grilled sesame and sea lettuce, red peppers in clam juice and preserved lemon emulsion, or the surreally named *Conception d'une volaille sphérique* in morel cream, with asparagus, soy risotto and the quintessence of parmesan in spaghetti. Desserts and wines are equally astonishing. The three-course weekday €25 lunch menu with a glass of wine is excellent value.

Brasserie Co €€
1 bd du Docteur Ferroul, T04 68 32 55 25.
Mon-Sat 0800-2400.
Map: Narbonne, p216.
This chic art-deco brasserie run by a charming *patronne* is near the market, and is where locals meet for a meal or just a coffee on the pavement terrace. The dishes are a real cut above typical brasserie fare, with the likes of *foie gras en millefeuille au caramel de figues*. The lunch *formule* is only €9 with a glass of wine dinner menus start at €15.

Le Petit Comptoir €€
4 bd Maréchal Joffre, T04 68 42 30 35, oternet.com/comptoir.
Tue-Sat for lunch and dinner.
Map: Narbonne, p216.
This resolutely retro restaurant – all dark wood and white linen – has become one of the trendiest in Narbonne. The menu changes every week, but oysters

and foie gras in various forms (and together) usually feature, along with classics such as fillet of beef en croûte and monkfish 'stitched' with anchovies, Gruissan style. Lunch menus start at €16.50, dinner €25.

Les Cuisiniers Cavistes €€
1 place Lamourguier, T04 68 65 04 43, cuisiniers-cavistes.com.
Tue-Sat for lunch and dinner. The shop is open Tue-Sat 0900-1900.
Map: Narbonne, p216.
This is an unusual restaurant/ wine bar/shop highlighting 52 of the finest wines of Languedoc, which you can buy or drink on the spot accompanied by a gourmet lunch. They also sell specialities such as truffles, sun-dried tomatoes and bread baked in a 100-year-old wood-fired oven.

Chez Bébelle €
1 bd du Docteur Ferroul, T06 85 40 09 01.
Open 0600-1400.
Map: Narbonne, p216.
Located in Narbonne's beautiful market, Les Halles, this is a great place for your morning meat fix: Bébelle was a rugby player and he makes great steaks.

En Face €
27 Cours de la République, T04 68 75 16 17.
Thu-Mon for lunch and dinner, Tue for lunch.
Map: Narbonne, p216.
This has a family atmosphere, red checked tablecloths and serves

regional favourites such as cassoulet and *bourride*. It's such a favourite for lunch that it's best to arrive at exactly noon.

Cafés & bars

Cocodélices
30 rue de l'Ancien-Courrier, T04 68 65 00 89.
May-Sep Tue-Sun 0900-1900, Oct-Apr Tue-Sat 0900-1900.
Map: Narbonne, p216.
Tea room/café serving delicious coffees, cappuccinos, teas and excellent cakes with home-made whipped cream.

Le Chillout
7 place du Forum, T04 68 65 58 83, lautrechillout.free.fr.
Oct-May Mon-Thu 0730-1900, Fri 0730-1900, Sat 1000-1900; open later in Jul and Aug.
Map: Narbonne, p216.
True to its name, with cushions on the floor, world music, 60 kinds of tea and Middle Eastern pastries for nibbling. They also have a cybercafé, a crafts boutique and offer inexpensive lunches.

Les Ramblas
Place des Quatres-Fontaines, T04 68 49 68 11.
Mon-Wed 0700-2200, Thu-Sat 0700-0200, Sun 1800-0200.
Map: Narbonne, p216.
Trendy bar for those in their 20s, especially popular after dark when everyone meets before going clubbing.

Entertainment

Carcassonne & around

Clubs

Black Bottom
Rte de Limoux, T04 68 47 37 11.
Thu-Sat 2200-0500.
Four kilometres south of Carcassonne, this is a classic disco of long standing.

La Bulle
115 rue Barbacane, T04 68 72 47 70, labulle-carcassonne.fr.
Wed-Sun 2200-0500.
The DJs keep a young crowd on their feet playing House and techno hits.

Le Conti
16 rue de l'Aigle-d'Or, T04 68 25 39 40.
Tue-Sun 2200-0500.
The after-hours bar and disco in the lower town, attracting a mostly 20-something crowd. They often put on Latin nights.

Festivals & events

Le Chevalier de la Foi
Les Lices de la Cité, ring the tourist office for times T04 68 10 24 30.
Every afternoon in Jul and Aug.
A bravura display of jousting, costumes and storytelling, in which Simon de Montfort's crew satisfyingly lose.

Narbonne

Clubs

Chakana Club
ZI Croix Sud, 300 m from the Narbonne Sud autoroute exit, chakana-club.fr.
Thu-Sun.
This huge Ibiza-style club attracts famous international DJs. It plays 1980s disco on the patio (heated and sheltered in winter) and House inside. Check their website for theme nights.

Dancing GM Palace
Centre Commercial Forum Sud, rte de Perpignan, T04 68 41 59 71.
Fri-Sat 2200-0500, Sun 1500-2000.
A retro disco that appeals to an older crowd, complete with a traditional Sunday 'tea dance'.

Le Botafogo
8 av des Pyrénées, T04 68 41 95 09, botafogo.fr.
Tue-Sun 2200-0200.
Music bar/restaurant/lounge with a Moroccan/Indonesian decor and DJs after dinner. Mainly popular with people in their 30s and 40s.

Theatre & cinema

Le Théâtre Scène Nationale
2 av Maître Hubert Mouly, T04 68 90 90 00, letheatre-narbonne. com.
New theatre with two auditoriums; one for plays, concerts and ballets and the other showing art movies.

Shopping

Carcassonne & around

Art

La Maison du Chevalier
56 rue Trivalle, T04 68 47 36 36, maisonduchevalier.com.
Apr-Sep Mon-Sat 1030-1200 and 1330-1830, Oct-Mar ring ahead.
On the road to the Cité, a sleek gallery of contemporary art, sculpture and photography.

Clothes & accessories

La Maison du Sud
15 rue Porte d'Aude, T04 68 47 10 06.
Open 1000-2000.
Most of the many souvenir shops in the Cité are much of a muchness – this one has a touch of class and sells handsome straw hats, soaps and cotton and linen shirts.

Lauranne de France
11 rue St Louis, T04 68 71 89 10.
Jul-Aug 0900-2130, Sep-Jun 0930-2000.
Handmade lace in all its forms.

Crafts

Le Vieux Lavoir/Coopérative Artisanale de la Cité
11 rue du Plô, T04 68 71 00 04.
Jul-Aug 1000-2000, shorter hours the rest of the year.
Items made by craft workers from across Languedoc.

Food & drink

Cabanel
72 allées d'Iéna, T04 68 25 02 58.
Mon-Sat 0800-1200 and 1400-1900.
Cabanel's distillery and boutique offers boozy treats you won't find elsewhere: herbal liqueurs, their own pastis, and a fifth-century aperitif called Micheline, as well as a wide choice of wines.

La Ferme
55 rue Verdun, T09 61 21 87 87.
Tue-Fri 0800-1230 and 1500-1930, Sat 0700-1300 and 1500-1930.
Upmarket food shop that stocks 6000 different products, ranging from fine artisinal cheeses and charcuterie to teas and coffees. There are also curiosities such as salt diamonds from the Himalayas.

Le Panier Gourmand
1 rue du Plô, T04 68 25 15 63.
Open 1030-2000.
Gourmet speciality shop in the Cité, selling goodies from across Languedoc.

Les Halles
Rue de Verdun/rue Aimé-Ramond.
Mon-Sat 0800-1300.
Historic U-shaped market near Place Carnot, which has recently been restored to its full glory.

Pick of the picnic spots

At Carcassonne, pick up goodies at Les Halles or La Ferme (see Shopping, above), then leave your car in the Cité car parks, walk along the Chemin des Anglais and find a spot with magical views over the walled city or try one of the tables by the Lac de la Cavayère. Alternatively, fill your basket at Narbonne's Halles (see Shopping, page 228) and picnic by the Abbaye de Fontfroide (see page 220) or in a pretty spot on the Canal de la Robine (see page 218).

Fresh apricots.

Listings

Housewares
Esprit de Sel
*10 rue de la République,
T04 68 72 03 01.*
Tue-Sat 1000-1230 and
1400-1900.
A trove of traditional and
designer furnishings and goods
for the home and garden. Also
sells soaps and beauty products.

Maison Coste
*40 rue Coste Rebouhl,
T04 68 77 12 15, maison-coste.com.*
Mon-Fri 1400-1900, Sat
1000-1900.
A lovely boutique selling items
for the home, including scented
balls of *terre d'Anduze*.

Crafts
Des Bouts du Monde
*6 rue Benjamin-Crémieux, T04 68
90 78 86, blog.
desboutsdumonde.fr.*
Jul-Aug Mon-Sat 0900-1900,
Sep-Jun Tue-Sat 0930-1230 and
1400-1900.
Fair-trade, ecologically sound
crafts, foods, music and clothes
from the Arctic circle to Africa.

Food & drink
La Ferme Narbonnaise
*21-23 rue Droite, T04 68 49 57 01,
epicerie-fine.lafermenarbonnaise.
fr.*
Mon 1100-1300 and 1430-1900,
Tue-Sat 0900-1300 and
1430-1900.
Gourmet delicacies ranging from
farm cheeses to olive oils, caviars,

rillettes de sardines and
champagne.

Les Halles
1 bd du Docteur Ferroul.
Open 0600-1400.
Narbonne's beautiful market
built in 1905 has 70 stands
offering the finest regional
produce. On Thursdays and
Sundays, stalls extend outside
along the canal, selling clothes,
flowers, etc.

Tendance & Gourmandise
*2 rue Raspail, Cours Mirabeau,
T04 68 91 43 92, tendance-
gourmandise.com.*
Mon 1400-1900, Tue-Sat
1000-1900.
Personalized sugar-coated
almonds and chocolates and
23 flavours of macaroons, plus
teas, coffees, foie gras and other
goodies.

Activities & tours

Boat trips
Lou Gabaret & Hélios
*27 rue des Trois Courronnes, T04
68 71 61 26, carcassonne-
croisiere.com.*
Ninety-minute trips on the Canal
du Midi, departing from the car
park near the train station.

Children
02 Aventure
*Lac de la Cavayère, 7 km
southeast of Carcassonne, T04 68
25 33 83, 02aventure.spaces.live.
com.*
The Lac de la Cavayère is great
for swimming but if you want
more thrills, spend a couple of
hours hanging from the trees
and swinging like Tarzan from
the branches.

Golf

Golf de Carcassonne

Rte de St-Hilaire, T04 68 72 57 30, golf-de-carcassonne.com.

Handsome 18-hole par 71 course with views of the Black Mountains and Pyrenees.

The Razès

Esoteric

Enigma Tours

5 Grand' Rue, Rennes-le-Château, T04 68 74 34 47, enigmatours.net.

Spend a week trying to work out what's going on in Rennes-le-Château.

Rafting

Pyrenees Outdoor

St-Martin-Lys (south of Quillan), T06 19 36 16 47, pyrenees-outdoor-sports.com.

Whitewater rafting, hydrospeed (body boarding) and canyoning down the Aude in the Gorge de St Georges and also in the Défilé de la Pierre-Lys. They also hire out mountain bikes.

Rodeo Raft

3 quartier de la Condamine, Belvianes (south of Quillan), T04 68 20 98 86, rodeoraft.com.

Guided inflatable rafting trips, 'canoe hot-dog', hydrospeed and canyoning down the Aude.

Wellbeing

Rennes-les-Bains

T04 68 74 71 00, renneslesbains. org.

Village spa offering jacuzzi, hamman, massages and an outdoor hot-water pool suitable for the whole family. €4.50, €2 child (3-12).

Wine classes

Vinécole

Domaine de Gayda, Chemin de Moscou, Brugairolles, T04 68 31 64 14, vinecole.com.

Just north of Limoux, this wine school specializing in Languedoc-Roussillon offers 'intelligent' wine-tasting, classes and seminars in English.

Narbonne

Birdwatching

Station orinthologique de Gruissan

Rte de Tournebelle, T04 68 49 12 12, gruissan-mediterranee.com.

Some 200 migratory species have been sighted here; in summer, spring and autumn naturalists offer free birdwatching walks (ring ahead for times).

Boat trips

Les Coches d'Eau du Patrimoine

Cours Mirabeau, T04 68 90 63 98, cpie-narbonnais.org.

Jul to mid-Sep.

See Narbonne from canal level or sail down to the Mediterranean on the Canal de la Robine to the nature reserve of Ile Ste-Lucie.

Promenades en Bateau

Promenade des Barques, T06 03 75 36 98.

Mid-Jun to mid-Sep 1100-1900.

Hire a little electric boat for an hour or two on the Canal de la Robine.

Children

Espace Liberté

Rte de Perpignan, T04 68 42 17 89, espaceliberte.com.

Good for rainy days: a family-oriented leisure centre with pools, bowling alley and ice skating rink.

Walking

Le Sentier Cathar

Starting in Port-La-Nouvelle, this 12-stage 250-km path of the Cathars takes in the most beautiful scenery of the Corbières and Cathar sites and ends in Foix in the Pyrenees, passing through Montségur. Carcassonne-based Areobus Haute-Vallée (T04 68 20 15 54, aerobus-hautevallee.com) can provide baggage forwarding. Organize room and board with UK-based World Walks (T+44 (0)1242-254353, worldwalks.com) or the Paris-based Sentiers de France (T01 45 69 86 46, sentiersdefrance.com).

Contents

Roussillon

Tour Madeloc, Côte Vermeille.

Introduction

Although Roussillon (Pyrénées-Orientales) has been part of France ever since the 1659 Treaty of the Pyrenees, many locals prefer to think of their home as northern Catalonia, especially now that the Schengen accords have made passports and customs obsolete. Catalan language classes are encouraged, street signs have been changed, and the red and yellow Catalan stripes flap from flagpoles. People dance the *sardane;* seafood comes *a la plancha*.

It all adds a nice cultural fizz to Languedoc. Catalonia's sacred mountain, the Pic du Canigou, dominates the plains of eastern Roussillon like a benevolent spirit, guarding this lush land of vines, orchards and market gardens, and endless sandy beaches. To the south, the mood changes on the Côte Vermeille, the jagged northern extension of the Costa Brava, much favoured by artists and anchovies. Two valleys, the Conflent and the Vallespir, link to the Pyrenees and offer stunning scenery and a vast range of outdoor activities, plus the chance of a spectacular narrow-gauge train ride. Some of France's greatest Romanesque monuments are here, Renaissance castles (built by Spain, to keep out the French), fortress towns (built by the French, to keep out the Spanish) and the lively capital of Perpignan.

Le Castillet, Perpignan.

What to see in...

...one day

In the morning visit Roussillon's capital, Perpignan, its cathedral, Castellet and Palace of the kings of Majorca, then take the N114 south to little Elne for its superb Romanesque cloister. Afterwards, carry on down to lovely, colour-drenched Collioure for anchovy snacks and an afternoon by the sea.

...a weekend or more

After Collioure, head south to visit the rest of the Côte Vermeille, before driving inland to the arty town of Céret and its Museum of Modern Art. The next day, cut across to the Têt Valley to see the Romanesque marvel of St Michel-de-Cuxa at Prades, before continuing to Villefranche-de-Conflent for a breathtaking on the Petit Train Jaune. And if you have time, you could do much worse than spending a couple of days walking in the sunny meadows of the Cerdagne.

Perpignan

Perpignan has a convivial medieval core, ringed by elegant boulevards. It's home to a cosmopolitan population – Catalan and French but also Romany and North Africans – who add an exotic buzz that may tempt you to linger after doing the sights. Winning the French national rugby title in 2009 (for the first time in 50 years) has put a bounce in Perpignan's step, as has the promise in the new TGV lines that will make 'southern' Catalonia more accessible than ever; you can zip to Figueres, and they promise Barcelona in 2012.

Cathédrale St-Jean.

Palais des Rois de Majorque

Rue des Archers, T04 68 34 48 29.
Oct-May 0900-1700, Jun-Sep 1000-1800. €4, €2 concession/young person (12-18), under 12s free. Map: Perpignan, p238.

This, the oldest royal palace on French soil, was begun when the Kingdom of Mallorca was established in 1276 by Jaume I the Conqueror, king of Aragon, for his second son Jaume II. The new kingdom included the Balearic Islands, Roussillon and Montpellier, and only lasted until 1349 when Montpellier was sold to the king of France and Roussillon was re-absorbed by Barcelona. Yet the three kings of Mallorca lived here in style, with an exotic menagerie in the moat and gardens described as a 'Paradise'. From the 16th century onwards, it was used as a military citadel – the sturdy outer walls were built by Philippe II.

Bits of decoration recall its former glory, notably in the Cour d'Honneur and in the central Donjon, which houses two flamboyant chapels. The upper one, for the royal family, has a lovely Romanesque portal, a vaulted ceiling and Kufic inscription that announces in Arabic that "Only God is God", a lasting witness to the syncretism of the ephemeral Mallorcan court. The tower offers commanding views over Perpignan.

Le Castillet: Casa Pairal Musée des Arts et Traditions Populaires

Place de Verdun, T04 68 35 42 05.
Oct-Apr Wed-Mon 1100-1730, May-Sep 1000-1830. €4, €2 student, under 18s free. Map: Perpignan, p238.

This crenellated red-brick symbol of Perpignan, with its gate and two fat towers, was built around 1368 by the king of Aragon to reinforce the palace's defences from the north. Under the French it became a prison, and today stands as a last vestige of the city walls. Inside, exhibits are arranged as in a Casa Pairal (paternal home), with an excellent ethnographic collection, gathered together by a local pharmacist: there's a traditional kitchen from an old farmhouse and surprising items like wicker helmets for toddlers just learning to walk. In the section on religious traditions, you'll find the *goigs*, religious poems in Catalan engraved on wood, that people would commission to cure illness or celebrate major events.

At the end, there's a striking 17th-century popular sculpture of the Last Supper, and a village confraternity's 'Cross of Insults' similar to the one in St-Jacques (see page 240).

Essentials

❶ **Getting around** The historic centre of Perpignan is compact and surrounded by parking garages. City bus 1 (ctpmperpignan.com) goes to the nearest beach, Canet-Plage. Route 66 (route66000.free.fr) provides transport between Perpignan and Canet's clubs on Saturday nights from 2330-0600.

❷ **Bus station** Avenue du Général-Leclerc (T04 68 35 29 02); serves much of the department. For schedules, see cg66.fr/routes_transports/transports/bus. For regional bus travel, see page 275.

❸ **Train station** Place Salvador Dalí, just west of the historic centre. For regional rail travel, see page 274.

❹ **ATM** Banque Populaire du Sud, 4 rue Cloche d'Or; Société Générale, 33 quai Vauban.

❺ **Hospital** 20 avenue du Languedoc, T04 68 61 66 33.

❻ **Pharmacy** Ollet, 3 rue Argenterie, T04 68 34 20 72; Vauban, 23 quai Vauban, T04 68 34 44 24.

❼ **Post office** 15 place Fontaine Neuve, T04 68 35 66 63.

❽ **Tourist information** Palais des Congrès, Place Armand Lanoux, T04 68 66 30 30, perpignantourisme. com. Mid-June to mid-September Monday-Saturday 0900-1900, Sunday and national holidays 1000-1600, mid-September to mid-June Monday-Saturday 0900-1800, Sunday and national holidays 1000-1300.

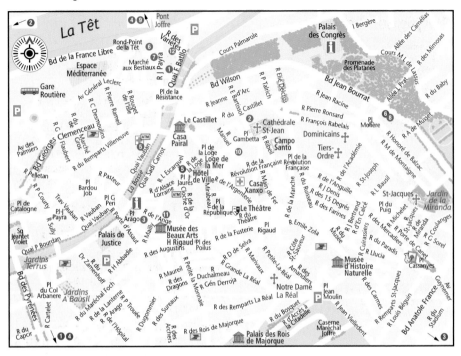

Place de la Loge

Map: Perpignan, above.

This narrow square paved in pink marble was the hub of old Perpignan, all streets converging here in front of the striking 14th-century Gothic **Loge de Mer**. This was the stock exchange and seat of the Consolat de Mer (a branch of Barcelona's famous maritime council); today it's a restaurant. Look up to see the sailing ship weathervane sticking out of the corner.

    Next door, the 13th-century **Hôtel de Ville** has its distinctive symbol as well: three bronze arms sticking out of the wall, symbolizing the three estates of the nobility, the bourgeois and the guilds. Duck inside to the patio to see the elaborately sculpted beams and Aristide Maillol's sculpture, *La*

Méditerranée. To its right, the 15th-century **Palais de la Députation** is a masterpiece of Catalan Renaissance civil architecture.

Cathédrale St-Jean

Place Gambetta, T04 68 51 33 72.
Open 0730-1830.
Map: Perpignan, above.

Catalan Gothic is notable for width rather than the verticals of northern Gothic, and this is no exception. Planned as a church with three naves in 1324, St-Jean was daringly reworked in 1433 by architect Guillem Sagrera (builder of the cathedral in Palma de Mallorca) into a single nave supported by immense piers. The exterior wears an attractive pattern of brick and river

Perpignan listings

Sleeping

1 **Bastide Le Petit Clos** *Catalunya 34 rue de Sitges* (off map)
2 **Château La Tour Apollinaire** *15 rue Guillaume Apollinaire* (off map)
3 **Domaine du Mas Boluix** *Chemin du Pou de les Colobres* (off map)
4 **Hôtel Aragon** *17 av Gilbert Brutus* (off map)
5 **Hôtel de la Loge** *1 rue des Fabriques Nabot*
6 **Park Hotel** *18 bd Jean Bourrat*

Eating & drinking

1 **Al Perp'inyà** *9 quai Batllo*
2 **Bistrot St-Jean** *1 rue Cité Bartissol*
3 **Brasserie L'Aragó** *1 place Aragó*
4 **Café de la Loge** *38 Av Xavier-Llobères, Salses-le-Château* (off map)
5 **Espi** *43 bis quai Vauban*
6 **Konfusius** *7 rue Alphonse Simon*
7 **La Galinette** *23 rue Jean Payra*
8 **Le Chap'** *1 bd Jean Bourrat*
9 **Le Rocher des Pirates** *Rue Georges Méliès, Rivesaltes* (off map)
10 **Les Trois Soeurs** *Place Gambetta*
11 **Paradis Fouillis** *17 rue de l'Ange*
12 **Spaghetteria al Dente** *1 place des Variétés*

---

stones; the white marble porch is all that survives of a more elaborate entrance of 1631. The city is especially proud of the rare 19th-century four-octave carillon in the bell tower.

Elegant 16th- to 18th-century Catalan retables fill the interior and there's a medieval baptismal font bearing a Latin inscription: "The wave of the sacred fountain smothers the hiss of the guilty Snake". The sculpted Moor's head under the superb late 15th-century organ case once had an articulated jaw that could be manipulated by the organist to stick out its tongue or vomit sweets for the children. A leather-covered door on the right aisle leads to the **Chapelle du Dévôt Christ**, with its strikingly realistic, painful figure of crucified Christ sculpted in Cologne in 1307. His head droops towards his chest and according to legend, the world will end when it actually touches.

Campo Santo

Behind the Cathedral.
Oct-Mar Tue-Sun 1100-1700, Apr-Sep
Tue-Sun 1200-1900, closed Jul-Aug.
Map: Perpignan, opposite.

For centuries the Perpignais buried their dead in the white marble Campo Santo (1300-1330), the only surviving enclosed cloister cemetery in France. Amid the arcades, each wealthy and bourgeois family had its own Gothic niche, or *enfeu*, while the poor were buried in the centre. After the Revolution the Campo Santo was closed down and after undergoing several other uses, it's now the perfect venue for summer concerts.

Musée des Beaux Arts Hyacinthe Rigaud

16 rue de l'Ange, T04 68 35 43 40.
Oct-Apr Wed-Mon 1100-1730, May-Sep
Wed-Mon 1200-1900. €4, under 18s free,
1st Sun of each month free.
Map: Perpignan, opposite.

Located since 1979 in the Hôtel Lazerme, this museum is named after Louis XIV's Perpignan-born portrait painter, Hyacinthe Rigaud (1659-1743). Among key early works there's a meticulous *Retable de la Trinité* (1489), showing a fanciful view of Perpignan with the Loge de Mer by the sea, and the 17th-century triptych of *St Vincent Ferrer*. From the 20th century, there are works by Maillol and Picasso, and powerful works on Spanish Civil War exiles by Catalan-American artist Pierre Daura.

The most remarkable works, however, are by Hyacinthe himself. He was much more than your run-of-the-mill Versailles sycophant, evident especially in his self-portraits with their knowing look and five o'clock shadow. Then there's the sumptuous exhibitionist *Portrait of Cardinal Bouillon* (1709), portraying all his pomp and honours: from his cash box (he had been Grand Almoner of France) and cardinal's biretta to the golden hammer showing that he had been in charge of opening the Holy Door at St Peter's for the 1700 Jubilee. His expression is jovial, amid stormy

Five of the best

Romanesque churches

❶ Saint-Michel-de-Cuxa, page 252

❷ Cathédrale Sainte-Eulalie-et-Sainte-Julie d'Elne, page 245

❸ Le Prieuré de Serrabonne, page 251

❹ Abbaye Saint-Martin de Canigou, page 254

❺ Saint-Martin-de-Fenollar, page 259

St-Jacques.

weather and two gesturing children (one representing his younger self, the other his nephew). Because Rigaud showed his squint, however, the cardinal refused to pay for the picture, so Rigaud refused to return the golden hammer.

St-Jacques & around

Rue de la Miranda, T04 68 34 74 62.
Generally open around services, Tue-Thu 1030-1200 and 1800-1900, Fri 1800-1900, Sat 1030-1130, Sun 1100-1200.
Map: Perpignan, p238.

Founded around 1245 by Jaume I the Conqueror, St-Jacques stands on Puig des Lépreux (Lepers' Hill), on top of the city's Jewish quarter. It's the local hotbed of Catholic tradition, and one of the very few churches in France that celebrates Mass in Latin (OK'd by the Pope in 2007). Inside the 14th-century marble portal, a lavish Catalan interior awaits. Note the 'Cross of Insults' with symbols of all the afflictions suffered by Christ, and a Pregnant Virgin – similar to the one in Cucugnan. The Confraternity of the Holy Blood (*de la Sanch*) was founded here in 1416 by St Vincent Ferrer, the self-styled 'Angel of the Apocalypse', to give comfort to condemned prisoners; on Good Friday they don black and red hoods and robes and go on a procession through Perpignan, bearing the *misteri* (symbols and statues of the Passion), silent except for the sound of tambourines and mournful *goigs*.

The **Quartier St-Jacques** is currently Perpignan's colourful and piquant Romany and North African quarter, and a good place to find a kebab or a tagine. There's been some friction over the years, and it's best to stay away after dark, but during the day it's lively and authentic, full of mums, kids and laundry and the Gypsy Kings (who are really Catalan, too).

Musée d'Histoire Naturelle

12 rue Fontaine-Neuve, T04 68 66 33 68.
Mon-Fri 1000-1700. €2.
Map: Perpignan, p238.

Founded in 1770 as a cabinet of curiosities, this museum in the 18th-century Hôtel Cagarriga has handsomely displayed exhibits on the flora, fauna and geology of the Pyrenees and south of France, as well as a room dedicated to Egypt. The mummy was donated in 1847 by Ibrahim Pasha, after he took the cure at Vernet-les-Bains.

Casa Xanxo

8 rue de la Main de Fer, T04 68 51 09 72.
Oct-Mar Tue-Sun 1100-1730, Apr-Sep
Tue-Sun 1200-1900. Free.
Map: Perpignan, p238.

This elegant residence of 1507 (pronounced 'Sancho') is one of the few left from the period in Perpignan. Built by parvenu cloth merchant Bernat Xanxo (his and his wife's portraits decorate one of the doors), its façade is notable for its fascinating narrow stone frieze representing the Seven Deadly Sins, apparently as a warning to passers-by. The house has an enormous dining room on the first floor, where they entertained, and a sumptuous red marble fireplace, but unfortunately little else has survived. On the first floor there's a 3D model of Perpignan in 1686, with its fortifications planned by Vauban for Louis XIV; the rest of the building is used for exhibitions.

Gare de Perpignan

Av Charles de Gaulle.
Map: Perpignan, p238.

Perpignan's train station is a handsome but unexceptional building, at least in the eye of the average beholder. But by any measure, Salvador Dalí was not average. While sitting at the station one day he had "an example of a cosmogonic ecstasy" and stated "I had a precise vision of the constitution of the Universe." Later, on 19 September 1963, while he was riding past the station in a taxi: "It all became clear in a flash: there, right before me, was the centre of the universe."

Dalí, who lived just south of the border in Cadaquès, was no stranger to Perpignan's *gare*, as he used to send his canvases from there, and claimed that his very best inspirations came while sitting in the waiting room. He painted his taxi vision, the *Mystique de la gare de Perpignan* (Museum Ludwig, Cologne) in 1965, a work now recalled by the station's luminous column topped by a laser beam.

As this is Dalí, the story gets even stranger. After the death of his beloved wife Gala in 1982, he spent a lot of time hallucinating from drugs and dehydration. During these moments he often saw the French mathematician René Thom, the founder of catastrophe theory, who convinced him that Europe would soon vanish, or be 'abducted', beginning in a spot near Salses. This was the subject of Dalí's strange 1983 drawing, the *Topological Abduction of Europe – Homage to René Thom.*

A new Dalí business centre is in the works by the new TGV station.

Tip...

Save money in Roussillon by picking up a free **Pass inter-sites** of the Réseau Culturel Terre Catalan, available at all participating sites. Discounts begin after your first visit.

Around the region

Centre de Sculpture Romane Maître de Cabestany

Parc Guilhem, Cabestany, T04 68 08 15 31, maitre-de-cabestany.com.
Oct-Apr Tue-Sun 1000-1230 and 1330-1800, Mar-Sep Tue-Sun 1000-1230 and 1330-1830. €3, €1 young person (12-18).

Cabestany is now a suburb of Perpignan, but in art it's been synonymous with a brilliant 12th-century sculptor known as the Master of Cabestany ever since the tympanum of the church of **Notre Dame des Anges** was rediscovered during restoration work in 1930. Currently displayed in the transept of the church, the tympanum's originality and masterful style created a sensation. Subsequent studies found that the same hand was behind some 121 surviving capitals, tombs and other works around Languedoc, Catalonia and even Tuscany. The centre has casts of over 60 of the sculptor's works and explores just who this master might have been.

Forteresse de Salses

Salses-le-Château, T04 68 38 60 13, salses.monuments-nationaux.fr.
Jun-Sep 0930-1900, Oct-May 1000-1215 and 1400-1700. Last tour 1 hr before closing. €7, €4.50 concession, under 18s free.

This late 15th-century Renaissance citadel built by Ferdinand and Isabella of Spain is the most visited sight in Roussillon. Originally, the Salses lagoon came further inland, so the fortress occupied a narrow strip of land between the water and mountains, along the same road used by Hannibal and his elephants in 218 BC.

The French had long coveted Roussillon and had taken an older fort on this site, so Ferdinand ordered Aragon's top military architect, Ramiro López, to build a stronger state-of-the-art defence. López came up with an immense 110- by 90-m

stone and red-brick bunker, capable of holding 1500 men. It lay low as a defence against the artillery of the day, and was surrounded by dry moats that held stables for 300 horses. The surrounding walls were 10-12-m thick. If the enemy breeched them and survived the rows of canon facing the inner courtyard, a whole range of defences and tricks were in store in the confusion of corridors. Although the life of the typical soldier would have been grim, officers enjoyed some surprising perks, such as indoor toilets, central heating and hot baths. The bill for the final product was said to be 20% of Aragon's annual budget.

For all that, the French captured it twice, in 1639 and 1640 (both times Spain managed to grab it back), before it became redundant with the Treaty of the Pyrenees in 1659. Louis XIV's own military genius Vauban wanted to demolish it (from jealousy, perhaps?), but to save the expense it was allowed to stand and be used for storage. In 1886, it was declared a *Monument Historique*.

Musée de Préhistoire

Av Léon-Jean Grégory, T04 68 29 07 76, tautavel.com.
Jan-Mar, Oct-Dec 1000-1230 and 1400-1700, Apr-Jun, Sep 1000-1230 and 1400-1800, Jul-Aug 1000-1900. €8, €4 child (7-14).

Northwest of Perpignan, where the Corbières meet the foothills of the Pyrenees, pre-Neanderthal *Homo erectus* made their home in an enormous karstic cave in 690,000-300,000 BC. Fossils of these nomadic hunters were first discovered in 1971, and since then over 100 have come to light. They hadn't yet discovered fire, so Tautavel Man and Woman ate their deer, rhinoceri and bison *tartare*.

Forteresse de Salses.

Côte du Roussillon

Although the main attractions here are endless sandy beaches and shimmering lagoons, all prettily framed by the distant Pic du Canigou, there's art mingled among this stretch of fun-in-the-sun.

Canet-en-Roussillon.

Le Barcarès & Canet-en-Roussillon

Roussillon's coast runs straight as a die north to south, lined by wide sands where the population of Perpignan pours out to bake every August. The northernmost beach, Le Barcarès, was a traditional fishing village until 1967, when its promoter bought a 1930s steamship, the *Paquebot Lydia*, and ran it into the shore for an instant landmark. It's still there, and currently houses a casino. Further south is Canet-en-Roussillon, Perpignan's favourite, backed by a modern resort and the **Aquarium de Canet-en-Roussillon** (Bd de la Jetée, T04 68 80 49 64, Sep-Jun 1000-1200 and 1400-1800, Jul-Aug 1000-2000, €6, €4 child) with 54 tanks of sea- and freshwater fish, including a prehistoric coelacanthe.

Etang de Canet

A road and bike path head south across a long spit of wild sand dunes, dividing the sea from the bird-filled Etang de Canet; in late summer some 2000 flamingos call it home. A traditional reed hut fishing village was reconstructed on its banks, and from June to September it is home to an exhibit and shop. Park wardens offer guided tours.

St-Cyprien Plage

St-Cyprien Plage at the south end of the lagoon prides itself on being rather artier than Canet. Once the home of painter François Desnoyer (d 1972), it has the **Collection François Desnoyer** (Rue Emile Zola, T04 68 21 06 96), with 19th- and 20th-century art (Boudin, Modigliani, Utrillo, Marquet), and the **Collection d'Art Contemporain** (Place de la République, T04 68 21 32 07), which annually features exhibitions by four major contemporary artists. The two collections share a website and the same opening hours (collectionsdesaintcyprien. com, Jul-Aug 1000-1200 and 1500-1900, Sep-Jun Wed-Mon 1000-1200 and 1400-1800, €6, €4 concession, under 12s free).

Cathédrale d'Elne

T04 68 22 70 90, ot-elne.fr.
Nov-Mar 0930-1145 and 1400-1645, Apr-May 0930-1745, Jun-Sep 0930-1845, Oct 0930-1215 and 1400-1745. €5.

On a hill overlooking St-Cyprien, Elne is an ancient Iberian settlement that in 568 became the seat of an archbishop. It dwindled after the honour moved to Perpignan in 1603, but the memory of its glory days survive in this austere, fortified 11th-century cathedral dedicated to saints Eulalie and Julie.

The cloister, one of the finest and best preserved in France, steals the show. Each of the four galleries of capitals and columns were sculpted in 50-year intervals (the south is rugged, 12th-century Romanesque and the other three sides are elegant Gothic), often repeating the same subjects – mermaids, dragons, flora and Old Testament scenes. Your admission ticket includes the **Musée Terrus** (Rue Porte-Balaguer), dedicated to the watercolour painter born in Elne in 1857.

Maison d'Art Roman de St-André

St-André, T04 68 89 04 85, saint-andre66.fr.
Mid-Mar to mid-Jun, mid-Sep to mid-Nov Tue-Sat 1000-1200 and 1500-1800; mid-Jun to mid-Sep Tue-Sun 1000-1200 and 1430-1900. €2, €1 concession.

South of Elne, St-André is named after its large Romanesque church dating back to 1161 and with a good section of pre-Romanesque masonry and carvings around the window and door. The nearby 'House of Romanesque Art' is dedicated specifically to Catalan art, with capitals from St André's cloister, and originals and casts of works from the great Benedictine abbeys in the area.

In the next village, **St-Génis-des-Fontaines**, the white marble church lintel has the oldest dated Romanesque carving, of Christ in a mandorla with owl-like angels and saints (1019).

Côte Vermeille

After campsite-lined Argelès-sur-Mer, the beeline coast of Roussillon goes a bit crazy. Called the 'Vermillion Coast' for its reddish rocks, it tumbles into picturesque cliffs and coves under vine-clad hills. There are beaches, but the stars of the show are the colourful fishing ports; the Côte Vermeille is the northern extension not only of the Costa Brava, but also the 'Anchovy Coast' stretching north of L'Escala. Back when Roussillon's other beaches were malarial swamps, Collioure was the port of Perpignan, and it wasn't so long ago that smuggling over the border was a major economic activity. Today, the mainstay is tourism, wine and fishing.

This almost indecently picturesque fishing village is the one everyone falls in love with. In 1905, when Henri Matisse arrived with his friend André Derain for a summer of painting, he declared, "In all of France there is no sky as blue as the one above Collioure". This was before creating works that so shocked the art world they were labelled as the products of wild beasts, or Fauves.

With its pretty church and castle directly on the sea and the colourful houses and narrow lanes of the Quartier du Mouré, Collioure gets so crowded in summer that it can literally be elbow-to-elbow. Come in the low season if you can, or take the bus – parking is a nightmare.

Notre Dames des Anges

Vieux Port.
Open 0900-1200 and 1400-1800.

Rebuilt after 1670, with its bell tower crowned by a pink dome (originally it was a light house), Collioure's 17th-century parish church was a favourite subject of the Fauves. Inside, the walls are lined with baroque retables by Catalan master Josep Sunyer, including a wildly lavish three-storey altarpiece glittering in the penumbra. The rich treasure contains more art – a 16th-century reliquary, paintings and religious items. The Spanish poet Antonio Machado (1875-1939), who fled the Spanish Civil War and died in Collioure, is buried here. Every February he is honoured with a poetry competition.

Le Château Royal

Vieux Port, T04 68 82 06 43.
Oct-May 0900-1700, Jun and Sep 1000-1800, Jul-Aug 1000-1900. €4, under 12s free.

Standing on Roman and Visigoth foundations, this castle was built by the kings of Mallorca as a summer residence (1276-1344). In 1670, Vauban, charged by Louis XIV to improve the town's defences, did so in a way that shows the absurdity

Notre Dames des Anges.

of war is nothing new: he demolished all of Collioure to expand the fortress. It housed a French garrison for many years, and in 1939 was used to hold 1000 refugees from the Spanish Civil War. All the original furnishings are long gone, but you can wander through the rooms and there are often special exhibitions.

Espace Fauve

Quai de l'Amirauté, T04 68 98 07 16.
Jun-Sep 0930-1230 and 1500-1900, Oct-May Tue-Fri 1000-1200 and 1500-1800, Sat-Sun 1500-1800.

Paul Signac 'discovered' Collioure, followed in 1905 by Matisse and Derain, and together they produced 242 works that changed the history of art. It wasn't only the colour, liberated from reality that made jaws drop when Matisse showed his paintings in Paris, but brushstrokes that made a statement in themselves. Vlaminck, Picasso, Braque and Dufy would follow them in turn. Although none of their art remains in Collioure, the *Chemin des Fauves* displays replicas of twenty works on the various spots were the artists planted their easels. Pick up a map here; on Thursdays in July and August they run guided Fauve tours at 1000 (€6).

Musée de l'Art Moderne

Villa Pams, Rte de Port Vendres, T04 68 82 10 19.
Sep-Jun Wed-Mon 1000-1200 and 1400-1800;
Jul-Aug daily 1000-1200 and 1400-1800.

This collection in the villa of a former senator was founded in 1930. While it doesn't have any of the famous Fauves, you will find works by the likes of Cocteau, Joan Brosses, Baloffi and Henri Martin.

Port-Vendres & around

Port-Vendres

South of Collioure, Port-Vendres is nothing less than the ancient Port of Venus (*Portus veneris*). Its lacks Collioure's upfront charm but has the biggest fishing fleet in the area and it bags more anchovies (and sardines). It is home to an obelisk dedicated to Louis XVI, who had great plans to develop the port before losing his head, and an **art walk** dedicated to Charles Rennie Mackintosh. In his last two years (1925-1926), Mackintosh gave up working in three-dimension to paint watercolours here. Guided walks run on Thursday mornings at 1000 and can be booked at the tourist office (T04 68 82 07 54, in French and English, €5).

Paulilles Bay

There are three pretty beaches 3 km south in Paulilles Bay (where Nobel once had a dynamite factory) backed by rose-tinted rocks, with lifeguards in July and August. The bay marks the beginning of the **Réserve Naturelle Marine de Cerbère-Banyuls**, France's oldest marine reserve.

Banyuls-sur-Mer

Further south, Banyuls-sur-Mer is an attractive, laid-back resort town with a big beach, and plenty of palms and plane trees. Its hinterland, the steep rolling Monts-Albères, produces sweet AOC Banyuls, first made by the Knights Templars in the 12th century.

Aquarium

Av du Fonautlé, T04 68 88 73 39, aquarium.
obs-banyuls.fr.
Sep-Jun 0900-1200 and 1400-1830, Jul-Aug
0900-1300 and 1400-2100. €4.60, €2.30 child
(6-12).

The aquarium of the Observatoire Océanologique Laboratoire Arago, founded in 1885, is the oldest on the French Mediterranean. It displays local flora and fauna (that you can touch as well as look at).

Musée Maillol

Le Métairie, Vallée de la Roume, T04 68 88 57 11,
musee-maillol.com.
Oct-Apr Wed-Mon 1000-1200 and 1600-1900,
closed national holidays, May-Sep daily
1000-1200 and 1600-1900. €3.50, €2.50 young
person/child (7-18).

After Rodin, Aristide Malliol (1861-1944) is probably the best-known French sculptor of the early 20th century. His chief form of expression was the female spirit of the Mediterranean: a well-rounded nude. Maillol was born in Banyuls and spent his last decade in this peaceful house, before dying in a car accident aged 83. His tomb is here, under a copy of *La Méditerranée*, and the house holds a collection of his works and drawings set up by his model and companion Dina Vierny.

Port-Vendres.

Conflent & the Cerdagne

The River Têt is the main artery of Roussillon, and its valley, the Conflent, is as varied and full of interest as any in the Pyrenees. It offers the chance to climb the Pic du Canigou and ride the Petit Train Jaune into the high plateau of the Cerdagne.

Ille-sur-Têt.

Ille-sur-Têt (pronounced 'Eeya'), 25 km west of Perpignan, is the first large town you come to, with an intricate medieval core and a rare geological treat.

Les Orgues

North of Ille-sur-Têt on the D21, T04 68 84 13 13. Nov-Jan 1400-1700, Feb-Mar 1000-1230 and 1400-1730, Apr-Aug 0930-2000, Sep 1000-1830, Oct 1000-1230 and 1400-1800. €3.50, under 10s free. Last tickets 45 mins before closing. The site's a 30-min walk from the car park.

This is where Mother Nature, over the past five million years, sculpted the clay away to leave spectacular walls of tall chimneys and organ pipes in a natural amphitheatre, like an abandoned dream city.

Hospici d'Illa

Hospice de St-Jacques, Ille-sur-Têt, T04 68 84 83 96. Feb to mid-Jun, Oct-Nov Wed-Mon 1400-1800, mid-Jun to Sep Mon-Fri 1000-1200 and 1400-1900, Sat-Sun 1400-1900, closed Dec-Jan. €3.50, €2.50 concession, under 13s free.

Illa's 17th-century hospice houses a fine collection of sacred art from the Romanesque (notably, detached 12th-century frescoes from Casesnoves) to the baroque.

Le Prieuré de Serrabonne

South of Ille-sur-Têt, Boule-d'Amont, T04 68 84 09 30. Open 1000-1800. €1.50.

It's a long winding road south of Ille-sur-Têt but the remote little Priory of Serrabonne (the 'Good Mountain'), founded in the 12th century, is worth the drive. Its dark schist façade is austere but rose-coloured wonders, sculpted from the local marble, wait inside. There's a cloister gallery decorated with four pairs of columns and marble capitals and an even more elaborate tribune,

Les Orgues, Ille-sur-Têt.

resembling an interior cloister, decorated with a medieval bestiary, monsters, symbols of the Evangelists, St Michael and the dragon, and a worried-looking fellow blowing a horn.

Although it was a refuge of the famous Catalan cellist, Casals, after the Spanish Civil War and has proudly held the Pau Casals Chamber Music Festival since 1951, Prades has an alternative buzz. The main vortex is the Place de la République, where the church of **St-Pierre** contains a wonderful over-the-top baroque *retable* (1699) by Josep Sunyer. There's also a small **Musée Pau Casals** (next to the tourist office, 4 rue Victor Hugo, T04 68 05 41 02, Apr-Sep Mon-Fri 0900-1200 and 1400-1800, Oct-Mar 0900-1200 and 1400-1700).

Eus, 5 km northeast, is strikingly piled on its hill, crowned by a 17th-century church built into the walls of a medieval castle. **Moltig-les-Bains**, 7 km north of Prades, is a sweet little spa amid the forests, famous since Roman times for skin treatments. A couple of kilometres further up, **Mosset** takes pride in being 'the world's smallest ski resort' (it has three runs); it also has a pine tree growing out of its bell tower.

St-Michel-de-Cuxa.

What the locals say

One of the reasons we came to Prades was the climate; you've probably heard mention of the 300 sunshine days a year, and it hasn't let us down. Best of all, there's plenty to do on all those sunny days. Walk around the magnificent **Lac des Bouillouses** and its myriad little lakes, where you might spot a marmot, lizard or eagle. Or trek down the **Caranca Gorge**, over tiny suspension bridges and gantries bolted to the walls; afterwards take a relaxing hot soak in the outdoor pools at **St-Thomas-les-Bains** (see Activities & tours, page 269), while gazing up at the mountains all around. In the evening, head to **Catllar**, a village just north of Prades, and sit in the church square at La Casa de l'Olivier for delicious tapas in a perfect setting.

Nick Wilcock owns the Villa Lafabrègue in Prades.

St-Michel-de-Cuxa

3 km south of Prades, T04 68 96 15 35, cuxa.org. Oct-Apr 0930-1150 and 1400-1700, May-Sep 0930-1150 and 1400-1800. €4, under 12s free.

With its tower rising 40 m above the orchards, St-Michel-de-Cuxa was one of the most important religious houses in Catalonia, founded in 840 and placed under the protection of Wilifred the Hairy, the first Count of Barcelona. By 978 it was important enough for Doge Pietro Orseolo to come all the way from Venice to retire and die here 'in the odour of sanctity', and it reached its peak of prominence in 1008 when the brilliant multi-lingual Oliba, like Wilifred a descendant of the Counts of Cerdagne, became abbot. By then much of the abbey's building was completed except for its chief glory, the cloister, with its superb capitals sculpted from the local pink marble in the 12th century.

The monks left during the Revolution and over the years the monastery decayed; one of the bell towers collapsed in 1829 and the cloister capitals were sold off to collectors (most were re-used in a bathing house in Prades). In 1913 the remaining dozen capitals were sold to the Cloisters Museum in New York City, mobilizing the locals at long last to protect and reinstall the remaining ones.

The oldest section of the abbey is the slightly uncanny 11th-century circular crypt with a central column known as the 'Crèche' or nativity scene, which is unique in medieval architecture. The nave is remarkable for its rounded Visigothic arches, and the half a cloister that remains in situ is delightful, its columns decorated with imaginary beings, lions and monsters.

Since 1965, St-Michel has been home to a small community of Benedictines from Montserrat who make sheep cheeses (on sale in the shop) and tend the **iris garden**, which explodes into colour in late May/early June.

Squeezed in its long, narrow walls between the river and road, Villefranche was founded in 1092 by Count Guillaume-Raymond de Cerdagne. He granted it tax advantages in order to attract settlers to defend this strategic neck of the valley, and also built the church of **St-Jacques** with its ornate pink marble portal. In the 1680s, the great engineer Vauban doubled the height of the walls and in 2008 UNESCO included Villefranche in its list of Vauban World Heritage Sites. Its vocation these days is tourism and its two long narrow streets, which are filled with boutiques, can seem like a mini-Carcassonne in season.

Les Remparts

32 bis rue St-Jean, T04 68 96 22 96, villefranchedeconflent.com.
Mar-May, Dec-Jan 1400-1700; Jun-Sep 1000-1900; Feb and Oct-Nov 1030-1200 and 1400-1700. €4, €3 concession, under 12s free.

You can retrace the steps of the guards patrolling Vauban's walls and bastions; many of the walkways are covered because of the danger of attacks from the mountains. Note the inward-facing loopholes – a precaution after the Catalan revolt in the 'Conspiracy of Villefranche' (1674).

Château-Fort Libéria

T04 68 96 34 01, fort-liberia.com.
Jul-Aug 0900-2000, May-Jun 1000-1900, Sep-Apr 1000-1800. €5.50, €4.60 young person (11-18), €2.80 child (5-10). Visit with shuttle €8, €4.10 young person/child (under 19).

Vauban added this fort in 1681 to defend the heights, and Napoleon III modernized its fortifications. It is linked to Villefranche by a path and a '1000-step' (actually 734) subterranean staircase (if you don't want to use the shuttle bus). The fort has grand views, cannons and prisons. Eight women accused of poisoning and witchcraft in Versailles were detained here at the time of Louis XIV; one spent 44 years chained to the wall.

Tip...

There aren't many roads up here: if you'd rather not backtrack down the Conflent, head north of Formiguères on the scenic mountain D118 into the Corbières.

La Cova Bastera

N11, opposite Villefranche's public gardens, T04 68 05 20 20, www3grottes.com.
Jun, Sep 1400-1700, Jul-Aug 1100-1900. €6.

The smallest of Villefranche's caves, this was used by the rebels before Vauban incorporated it into the defences, building a casemate gallery to defend the road. There's no guided tour, but a film and models tell the history of Villefranche – starting with scale models of dinosaurs and cave men.

Villefranche-de-Conflent.

Around the region

Grotte des Grandes Canalettes

Rte de Vernet, 300 m from Villefranche, T04 68 05 20 20, grotte-grandes-canalettes.com.
Apr-Jun daily 1000-1800, Jul-Aug daily 1000-1930 (1900 son et lumière), Sep-Nov daily 1000-1730, Dec-Mar Sat-Sun 1100-1700, French school holidays 1100-1700. €8, discounts for visits to 2 or more caves.

Discovered in the 1980s, the Grandes Canalettes is known as the subterranean Versailles of Roussillon. It boasts spectacular formations, including a magical white chamber; 'Angkor Wat'; a ceiling of eccentric formations; a bottomless pit; a subterranean lake and more.

Grotte des Canalettes

Rte de Vernet, near the Grandes Canalettes, www3grottes.com.
Jul-Aug visits on the hour 1100-1800. €8.

Discovered in 1951, this family-run stalactite cave has draperies and pretty formations, although if you only have time for one, the Grandes Canalettes is admittedly more spectacular.

Notre Dame de Corneilla-de-Conflent

On the road to Vernet-les-Bains, T04 68 95 77 59.
Jun-Sep Mon-Sat 1000-1300 and 1500-1800. €2.50.

This 11th-century priory has a red marble tympanum of the Virgin in Majesty and is full of art: there's a white marble retable from 1345, beautiful polychrome statues, a 15th-century Déposition and a gorgeous carved walnut wardrobe from the 14th century.

Tip...

The tourist office at Vernet-les-Bains (2 rue de la Chapelle, T04 68 05 55 35, vernet-les-bains.fr) has a brochure in English on the several routes to the summit of Le Canigou, most of which involve a night in a mountain gîte. Whenever you go, check the weather before setting out.

Vernet-les-Bains & around

Further up the road from Notre Dame de Corneilla-de-Conflent is this charming little spa town. It attracted a following of well-to-do Brits in the 1800s and included Rudyard Kipling among its regular visitors. The British gave their name to a beautiful waterfall, the **Cascade des Anglais**, which is a three-hour hike from town and back.

Le Pic du Canigou

At 2784 m it's not the tallest, but the Pic du Canigou, the national symbol and *Montanya Regalada* (fortunate mountain) of the Catalans, stands out as prominently as Mount Fiji. The first recorded climber, King Pere III of Aragon in 1285, found a dragon at the top and some believe it shelters the Holy Grail. On 23 June, the eve of St John's Day (the Festa Major), a flame lit on Canigou at midnight is conveyed down by torches and a relay of runners to light 30,000 bonfires all across French and Spanish Catalonia.

Reaching the summit of the Pic du Canigou isn't difficult. The ideal time is September, when the skies are usually clear. You can drive up in a jeep as far as the Chalet des Cortalets (T04 68 96 36 19, open early Jun-early Oct), but you'll need to set off before 0800, when the road closes to private vehicles. Alternatively, take a jeep taxi from Prades or Vernet-les-Bains (€24-25, based on six passengers); contact Garage Villacèque (T04 68 95 51 14), Tauringa (T04 68 05 63 06) or Jean-Paul Bouzan (T04 68 05 99 89). From the chalet, it takes about two hours to reach the top. Bring sturdy shoes, a pullover, a windcheater (it can get very gusty up there), water, sun block and binoculars.

Abbaye Saint-Martin de Canigou

Casteil, above Vernet-les-Bains, T04 68 05 50 03, stmartinducanigou.org.
Guided tours Jun-Sep daily 1000, 1100 (not on Sun), 1200, 1400, 1500, 1600 and 1700, Oct-May Tue-Sun 1000, 1100 (Sun 1200), 1400, 1500, 1600, closed Jan. If you can't walk, you can arrange a

lift with a 4WD through Garage Cullel, T04 68 05 64 61.

It's a steep 30- to 45-minute walk from the car park (bring water and a hat), but St-Martin's setting under the Pic du Canigou couldn't be more stunning, isolated amid the mountains and forests. Founded in 1009 by Giufré, the Count of Cerdagne and brother of the famous Catalan churchman Oliba, the last five monks left in 1768, and St-Martin gradually became a picturesque ruin. In 1902 it was purchased by the bishop of Perpignan and gradually restored, and since 1988 it's been home to a community of Béatitudes (men and women) devoted to prayer.

Mont-Louis & Le Capcir

Guarding the pass into the Cerdagne, Mont-Louis (1580 m) is the highest fortified town in France and one of the few built from scratch by Vauban, in 1679. Named after Louis XIV, it has few of the tourist trappings of Villefranche-de-Conflent, and in fact still houses a garrison and commando training centre in its citadel.

The French army also financed its claim to fame with the 50 kW **Four Solaire** (T04 68 04 14 89, guided tours Sep-Jun 1000-1200 and 1400-1800,

Jul-Aug 1000-1230 and 1400-1900, €6), the first solar furnace in the world. It was built in 1949 under the supervision of its inventor Félix Trombe for high-temperature experiments in physics and chemistry. Most of these experiments now take place in the bigger model at Odeillo (see page 257).

Le Capcir, the pine-wooded plateau north of Mont-Louis, is a seductive detour, where tiny stone-built villages and glacier lakes were only linked by road to the outside world in the 19th century. The medieval kings of Mallorca used to come up to the atmospheric little capital **Formiguères** for their asthma. It's a favourite spot for winter sports (**Les Angles**), but also for the magnificent hiking around the sapphire lakes at **Lac des Bouillouses**.

Le Petit Train Jaune

In 2010, this jaunty, 62.5-km narrow-gauge cog railway celebrates the centenary of its beginnings. Designed to inject new life into Roussillon's mountain villages, the project of running a train up the wildest reaches of the Têt valley to the Cerdagne was so daunting it took until 1927 to complete, at a rate of less than 4 km of track per year. It's an engineering marvel and, unlike many heritage trains, is also a useful way to travel. It runs year round; summer is a lovely time to visit, when the journey is made in open-top cars (although the new cars, with big picture windows, have views that are nearly as grand).

Villefranche-Vernet-les-Bains is the base for the Little Yellow Train. From here, it makes a breathtakingly steep ascent, mostly on a narrow ledge carved into the side of the mountains that make it look like a toy; a couple of times it sails high over gorges on France's highest railway bridges. At the final station, **Latour-de-Carol** (three hours from Villefranche) you can either carry on to Toulouse or Barcelona, catch a bus to Andorra or do what most people do – catch the next train down.

The Cerdagne

At 1200 m, the high plateau of the Cerdagne occupies the bed of a prehistoric lake surrounded by high mountains and forests. Royal eagles circle high in soft blue skies over green meadows that are bathed in sunshine for 3000 hours a year; in winter the slopes become a popular playground. The 1659 Treaty of the Pyrenees divided the Cerdagne equally between Spain and France, but on both sides roots lie deep in Catalan culture: in the cuisine, language and in the little Romanesque chapels.

From Mont-Louis, the N116 swoops in grand loops down to the market town of **Saillagouse**, with its playful statues and murals in the main square. By-roads lead up to bijou hamlets: **Eyne**, where the valley is a nature reserve, filled with wild flowers in May and June; and **Llô**, at the base of the pretty Gorges de Sègre, which has a Romanesque church and hot springs that fill an outdoor pool and jacuzzi (T04 68 04 74 55, lesbainsde.llo.free.fr, Mon-Sat 1000-1930, €8.50). **Ste-Léocadie**, further

along, claims to have the highest vineyards in Europe. Tiny **Hix**, once the seat of the Catalan counts of Cerdagne, has a good Romanesque church from 1177, containing a superb statue of the Virgin; the Romanesque church at neighbouring **Caldégas** has frescoes of hunting scenes.

Bourg Madame sits on the busy frontier, sandwiched between Spain and **Llivia**. Llivia is an enclave of Spain 6 km from the rest of the country, an anomaly left over from the treaty of the Pyrenees that gave France 33 'villages' in the upper

Cerdagne – but not the 'town', a status little Llivia was proud to hold. In a ring of sprawl, Llivia's pretty medieval core surrounds a huge 16th-century church, **Nostra Senyora dels Angels**, containing a beautiful 13th-century statue of Christ (ask the sacristan to see it); and a **pharmacy** that opened in 1415, one of the oldest in the world and now part of the municipal museum.

To the west lies **Ur** with another fine church and tiny **Latour-de-Carol**, the end of the line on the Petit Train Jaune and legendary among trainspotters as the only place where three lines with three different gauges meet: the Petit Train Jaune's narrow gauge, standard European (French) gauge and Spain's wider RENFE gauge.

From here, the D618 circles back east, where you might be tempted into a side trip up to **Dorres**, for a hot soak at the open-air granite basins at the **Bains de Dorres** (T04 68 04 66 87, open 0830-2000, €4). The main D618 crosses the striking **Taragosse Chaos**, where the hills are strewn with boulders left behind by an ancient glacier. Amid the rock formations at Odeillo towers the strikingly incongruous glimmering concave mirror of the 1000 kW **Le Grand Four Solaire Odeillo-Héliodyssée** (T04 68 30 77 66, Sep-Jun 1000-1230 and 1400-1800, Jul-Aug 1000-1930, €6, €3.50 young person/child, under 8s free). Put into use in 1969, this solar furnace is the biggest in the world and is used for experiments and research – the fascinating tour explains all. Just above, brash and modern **Font-Romeu** and **Bolquère** are the biggest winter/summer sports resorts in the eastern Pyrenees, and a favourite destination for French athletes training to compete at high altitude.

The Vallespir

The River Tech flows down this wooded valley from the Spanish border to just north of Argèles-sur-Mer. Its medieval capital, up in the hills to the north, was **Castelnou** (a member of the 'Most beautiful villages in France' association), built in 990 around a lofty pentagonal castle of the Vicomte de Vallespir.

The current capital of Vallespir, Céret resembles an inland Collioure – a laid-back, quintessentially Mediterranean town of winding lanes set around a medieval core. There are buildings with leopard façades of dappled shade, pretty squares filled with cafés, and, *de rigueur,* a stunning bridge – the 14th-century Pont du Diable, with an arch spanning 45 m. Just like Collioure, Céret was discovered by artists in the early 20th century, this time by the Cubists. Céret is also proud of being France's cherry capital and, May to early June, when the roadside stands do a brisk business, is a luscious time to visit.

The River Tech flows through Céret.

Musée d'Art Moderne de Céret

8 bd du Maréchal-Joffre, T04 68 87 27 76, musee-ceret.com.
Mid-Jun to Sep daily 1000-1900 (at the tail end of Sep 1000-1800), Oct to mid-Apr Wed-Mon 1000-1800, Mid-Apr to mid-Jun daily 1000-1800. €8, €6 concession, under 12s free.

This museum was founded in 1950 when Matisse donated 14 of his sketches from Collioure, and Picasso contributed 53 works – mostly scenes of a corrida that he created in an intense five-day period. A good number of the other paintings, by Braque, Gris, Soutine, Marquet, Lhote, Kissling and Manolo, are of Céret itself. As in Collioure, plaques with copies of paintings in key locations tell where artist and easel stood.

Le Boulou & St-Martin-de-Fenollar

East of Céret, Le Boulou may be best known as the last stop in France on the *autoroute*, but Romanesque lovers will want to have a look at the marble lintel on its church, sculpted by the Master of Cabestany. Just south, near the hamlet of Maureillas-las-Illas, the chapel of **St-Martin-de-Fenollar** (T04 68 87 73 82, mid-Jun to mid-Sep daily 1030-1200 and 1530-1900, mid-Sep to mid-Apr Wed-Mon 1400-1700, €3, under 12s free) has rare 11th-century frescoes in the apse, painted by the monks of Arles-sur-Tech and studied by Braque and Picasso. They are colourful, primitive but heart-felt scenes showing the Nativity story, Christ in Majesty and the 24 Elders of the Apocalypse.

The medieval capital of the Vallespir, Arles-sur-Tech is an introspective old place; most of the tourist amenities in the area are concentrated in the old spa of Amélie-les-Bains, 4 km downriver.

Abbaye Ste-Marie

Entrance via the tourist office, T04 68 83 90 66.
Open 0900-1200 and 1400-1800. €3.20.

Ste-Marie was founded on the ruins of Roman baths in Amélie during the late eighth century. It was built by Sunifred, brother of Wilifred the Hairy, not long after Charlemagne conquered the area from the Moors, but it was relocated to Arles in the ninth century for safety reasons. It was famous for an unusual relic, which can still be seen today: an empty late-Roman sarcophagus known simply as **Ste Tombe**, which miraculously fills up with water from an unknown source.

Enter through the late 13th-century cloister into the massive Romanesque church that's so old it's aligned to the west, and corrected by a 'counter apse' in the east with a frescoed upper chapel dedicated to St Michael. In the 10th century, the chronicles tell how Arles was invaded by ape-like 'Simiots', and to counter them the abbot went to Rome for some proper relics. He brought back the bones of two obscure Persian martyrs, SS Abdon and Sennen, and installed them in cupboards high up in the pillars, which solved the Simiot problem; the 17th-century retable in the saints' chapel tells the story. Note the rare 18th-century Schmidt organ.

The tower-framed façade has an austere beauty, while tucked on the side is the famous Sainte Tombe. On 30 July, its 500 litres of pure water are siphoned out and distributed to the faithful.

Gorges de la Fou

RN9, T04 68 39 16 21.
Apr-Nov 1000-1800, Jul-Aug 0930-1830. €6.60, €3.40 child (5-12).

This Dante-esque crack in the limestone (deliciously translated in a brochure as 'the throats of the insane') is said to be the narrowest gorge in the world, so narrow that you can often touch both walls with your outstretched hands. A metal walkway wends through and visitors must wear hard hats.

Listings
Sleeping

Perpignan

Château La Tour Apollinaire €€€
15 rue Guillaume Apollinaire, T06 30 89 11 02, latourapollinaire. com.
Map: Perpignan, p238.
Only 10 minutes' walk from the centre, this boutique hotel is in a baronial mansion dating from the belle époque (the baron was a cousin of the French-Russian poet Apollinaire). It offers 11 very stylish rooms, and seven well-equipped one- to three-bedroom apartments with optional home cinema and a massive DVD library. The walled subtropical garden has 'Zen cascades' and a heated pool is open from April to October. Two-night minimum stay in high season.

Domaine du Mas Boluix €€
Chemin du Pou de les Colobres, T04 68 08 17 70, T06 21 26 25 61 (mob), domaine-de-boluix.com.
Map: Perpignan, p238.
Located southwest of Perpignan, this 18th-century farmhouse set amid vines and orchards isn't easy to find (see details on the website) but it's worth the trouble. There are four large air-conditioned, soundproofed rooms with private bathrooms and satellite TV, and a family suite sleeping four. Prices include breakfast and a visit to the vineyard with the friendly owner, Jean-Louis Ceilles.

Park Hotel €€
18 bd Jean Bourrat, T04 68 35 14 14, parkhotel-fr.com.
Map: Perpignan, p238.
A five-minute stroll from the centre, this traditional 67-room hotel is Perpignan's best-known lodging. Rooms vary in size, but are all well equipped and soundproofed. There's Wi-Fi and a parking garage, and you only have to go downstairs to dine at Le Chap'.

Hotel Aragon €
17 av Gilbert Brutus, T04 68 54 04 46, aragon-hotel.com.
Map: Perpignan, p238.
This welcoming little hotel on the edge of the centre, just off boulevard F Mercador, has 30 homey, immaculate en suite rooms with air conditioning Wi-Fi and satellite TV. The helpful owners speak English and there is parking for €6 a day. The €7 breakfast is good value.

Hotel de la Loge €
1 rue des Fabriques Nabot, T04 68 34 41 02, hoteldelaloge.fr.
Map: Perpignan, p238.
Located a stone's throw from the Place de la Loge (if you're driving, the République and Wilson garages are closest), this is a basic, good-value hotel with en suite rooms and air conditioning. Furnishings are charmingly old-fashioned and a bit faded, but comfortable.

Self-catering

Bastide Le Petit Clos
Catalunya, 34 rue de Sitges, T04 68 85 54 60, bastide-lepetitclos.com.
Map: Perpignan, p238
It's a bit hard to find, south of the centre off the D900, but it's very peaceful once you arrive. The two lodgings (sleeping eight and 14) in this 19th-century house combine traditional features such as wooden floors and tiles with luxury high-tech design. Non-smokers only. Prices start at €1290 per week

Côte Vermeille

Casa Pairal €€€
Impasse des Palmiers, Collioure, T04 68 82 05 81, en.hotel-casa-pairal.
Apr-early Nov.
This delightful 19th-century Catalan 'paternal mansion' in the heart of Collioure offers 27 traditionally designed rooms, each different and complete with air conditioning, flat-screen TV, minibar and Wi-Fi. There's a wonderful inner garden with a heated pool, a lavish buffet breakfast and parking – a rarity in Collioure.

Les Templiers €€€
12 quai de l'Amirauté, Collioure, T04 68 98 31 10, hotel-templiers. com.
Right in the centre, the Templiers was much frequented by artists in its day, and over the years it has accumulated walls of art.

Catalan golds and reds and painted furniture dominate the decor. Rooms at the front have views over the Vieux Port but can be a bit noisy in season, and there's a wonderful bar and a good, reasonably priced restaurant. Avoid the annex.

Auberge de la Roua €€
Chemin du Roua, Argèles-sur-Mer, T04 68 95 85 85. aubergeduroua.com.
Away from the coastal hubbub, this 17th-century stone Catalan *mas* is a relaxing place to stay. It has views of the mountains and is set in a pretty little garden with a pool. Rooms have recently had a facelift and there's free Wi-Fi, and an excellent (if expensive) restaurant. Note, it's best to study the map online before setting out to find it.

Hôtel des Elmes €€
Plage des Elmes, Banyuls-sur-Mer, T04 68 88 03 12, hotel-des-elmes.com.
Set in a narrow inlet with a sandy beach, this hotel offers 31 contemporary-styled rooms equipped with air conditioning and soundproofing. Some rooms are big enough to sleep an extra child. They also have a boat you can hire to explore the coast from Collioure down to Cadaquès in Spain.

Les Caranques €€
Rte de Port-Vendres, Collioure, T04 68 82 06 68, les-caranques. com.
The next best thing to staying in Collioure is looking at it, which you can do from this peaceful 22-room hotel perched on the seaside rocks a 10-minute walk from the centre. Rooms are fairly spartan, but are bright and clean and nearly all come with a terrace; No 31 has the best views. The hotel also has a little car park.

Conflent & the Cerdagne

Château de Riell €€€€
Moltig-les-Bains, T04 68 05 04 40, chateauderiell.com.
This 19th-century baroque folly is a magical oasis in the woods. The 19 stylish rooms (in the château or surrounding houses, some of which have private terraces) are richly decorated in shades of ochre. There's a spa (the waters are rich in freshwater plankton), a garden, a pool and an excellent restaurant open to non-guests; you can even sip your cocktails in the dungeon.

Listings

Hôtel Restaurant Planes €€
*Place de Cerdagne, Saillagouse,
T04 68 04 72 08, planotel.fr.*
For over a century the Planes
family has been running this inn
at one of the Cerdagne's main
crossroads. The 19 rooms are
nicely decorated and most have
views over the mountains. The
Planes also own the Planotel,
150 m away, which has a heated
covered pool and sauna that
guests can use. The restaurant is
excellent, and the *demi-pension*
option is good value.

Villa Lafabrègue €€
*15 av Louis Prat, Prades, T04 68
96 29 90, villafrench.com.*
English Kate and Nick Wilcock are
welcoming and knowledgeable
hosts, and their B&B in a
luxurious Florentine-style villa
(1870) makes a great base. Each
of the five rooms has its own
character and stunning
mountain views. There's Wi-Fi
and a sunny walled garden with
a pool, and the delicious
breakfast is included in the price.

Auberge La Chouette €
*2 rue de la Liberté, Font-Romeu,
T04 68 30 42 93, chouette.fr.*
An old stone inn by the church at
Odeillo, this has 14 basic en suite
rooms (sleeping up to four) for
old-fashioned mountain holiday
fun. Half-board mandatory; bring
your own towel.

Cal Xandera €
*49 rte de Font-Romeu (D618),
Angoustrine, T04 68 04 61 67,
calxandera.com.*
This cosy, family-run inn offers
simple rustic rooms in an
18th-century farmhouse with
grand views, not far from all the
activities at Font-Romeu. The
excellent restaurant serves
seasonal dishes (foie gras with
roast figs or pheasant terrine)
either on the terrace in summer
or by an open fire on cold
evenings; the prices are
reasonable.

Self-catering
Mas d'en Roca
*Los Masos, T04 68 05 25 59,
giteking.com.*
Just 3 km from Prades, this is
a stone barn converted by its
British owners into a very
attractive beam-ceilinged gîte
sleeping eight, plus an
apartment sleeping four. Prices
for four start at €275 per week.

La Mas Trilles €€€
*Le Pont de Reynes, Céret, T04 68
87 38 37, sicosa.com/mas.*
This traditional stone farmhouse
from 1631 has been restored by
its French and Hungarian owners
into a delicious 10-room hotel.
Set by the river in a pretty garden
with a heated pool, it has
well-appointed rooms (the ones
in the main house have the most
character). Most sleep up to four
and prices include breakfast.

Relais des Chartreuses €€
*106 av d'en Carbonner, Le
Boulou, T04 68 83 15 88,
relais-des-chartreuses.fr.*
There are 12 cosy rooms in this
17th-century Catalan *mas*
located between Céret and
Collioure. It's far enough away
from the crowds to offer a
peaceful stay and there's a
garden and a welcoming
outdoor pool. They have a family
room available, and there are a
range of special offers on their
website.

Hôtel des Arcades €
*1 place Picasso, Céret, T04 68 87
12 30, hotel-arcades-ceret.com.*
Over the years a score of artists
have checked into this spotless,
family-run hotel in the centre of
Céret, many of whom have left
paintings on the walls. There are
30 rooms; 22 are en suite (some
with air conditioning) and sleep
up to three people, whereas
eight have kitchenettes and are
rented out by the week.

Eating & drinking

Perpignan

La Galinette €€€€
23 rue Jean Payra, T04 68 35 00 90.
Tue-Sat for lunch and dinner.
Map: Perpignan, p238.
Chef and owner Christophe Comes is obsessed with vegetables, often seeking out rare varieties for his *potager*. In his cuisine, they share top billing with the seafood, his other great passion – try the saint-pierre (John Dory) *a la plancha* with the best carrots you've ever tasted. The bright dining room and white linen is smart, casual and fashionable, so be sure to book. Menus from €17-€50.

Le Chap' €€€€
18 bd Jean Bourrat, T04 68 35 14 14, parkhotel-fr.com.
Tue-Fri for lunch and dinner, Sat for dinner.
Map: Perpignan, p238.
The restaurant of the Park Hotel (see Sleeping, page 260) is sleek and elegant, and chef Alexandre Klimenko's food is elegant, too:

ravioli filled with snails and fresh goat's cheese in a sauce of nettles and quail's eggs, or fricassée of venison with baby spinach and upside down macaroni gratin in a Banyuls sauce. The wines of Roussillon hold pride of place; menus start at €30.

Bistrot St-Jean €€€
1 rue Cité Bartissol, T04 68 51 22 25, st-jean-le-bistrot.com.
Sep to mid-Jun Tue-Sat for lunch and dinner, mid-Jun to Aug daily for lunch and dinner.
Map: Perpignan, p238.
A pretty bistro with a terrace in the shadow of the cathedral, St-Jean offers a wide choice of *tartines* with a range of toppings on grilled *pain de campagne*; cheese lovers can feast on the special *Menu spécial fromages d'Auvergne* (€24). Finish with a classic *crème catalan*.

Al Perp'inyà €€
19 quai Batllo, T04 68 59 00 19
Tue-Sun for lunch and dinner.
Map: Perpignan, p238.
This friendly, laid-back restaurant near Le Castillet serves big

portions of well-prepared Catalan specialities. The desserts are excellent (the chocolate ones especially so) and the house wine is cheap and good. This is also one of the few places open on a Sunday. Weekday lunch menu with wine €13.90.

Konfusius €€
7 rue Alphonse Simon, T04 68 66 88 88.
Mon-Sat 1200-1500 and 1900-2200.
Map: Perpignan, p238.
When you need a change, head here for a bit of lemongrass, lime and coconut. This Thai restaurant, with an intimate decor set around a fishpond, ships ingredients from Thailand every week for delicious hot and tangy salads, soups and curries.

Brasserie L'Aragó €
1 place Aragó, T04 68 51 81 96.
Daily 0900-0200.
Map: Perpignan, p238.
The typical brasserie menu (mussels, grilled fish and steaks, pizza, pasta, salads) is nothing special, but the balcony and terrace are great for people-watching and soaking up the sun, or sitting out in the evening.

Café de la Loge €
38 av Xavier-Llobères, Salses-le-Château, T04 68 38 62 86.
Dec-Oct open for lunch.
Map: Perpignan, p238.
This café first opened its doors in 1825 and is still decorated with fancy 19th-century ceiling mouldings. Catalan dishes

Listings

dominate, including the house speciality, *rap y galtes* (monkfish sautéed with prawns and pork cheeks, *déglacé* with Rivesaltes and served with salsify).

Le Rocher des Pirates €
Rue Georges Méliès, just north of Perpignan, Rivesaltes, T04 68 57 15 84, lerocherdespirates.com.
Open for lunch and dinner.
Map: Perpignan, p238.
This family restaurant is disguised as a Caribbean pirates' den and serves pizza, pasta, salads, grilled meats and seafood *a la plancha*. Waiting staff are dressed as pirates, and on most evenings there are various animations (cannon fire, volcanic eruptions, etc).

Spaghetteria al Dente €
1 place Variétés, T04 68 61 11 47.
Mon-Sat 1200-1500 and 1900-2200.
Map: Perpignan, p238.
This Italian restaurant with Aldo tending the pots (and often popping out for a chat) offers a huge menu of pasta dishes – the sun-dried tomatoes, goat's cheese, basil and olive oil is delicious.

Cafés & bars
Espi
43 bis quai Vauban, T04 68 35 19 91.
Mon-Sat 0730-1930, Sun 0730-1300 and 1530-1930.
Map: Perpignan, p238.
In business for decades, this café serves the best ice cream in Perpignan, as well as breakfast and home-made pastries.

Les Trois Soeurs
2 rue Fontfoide, T04 68 51 22 33.
Mon 1700-0200, Tue-Sat 0900-0200.
Map : Perpignan, p238.
The bar and terrace where all of Perpignan gathers for an *apéro* in the early evening.

Paradis Fouillis
17 rue de l'Ange, T04 68 34 66 32.
Mon 1400-1900, Tue-Sat 1100-2000.
Map: Perpignan, p238.
This fun *salon de thé* serves tea and coffee in the midd-le of a *brocante* (junk) shop, so you can sip and browse at the same time.

Côte Vermeille

Le Neptune €€€€
Rte de Port-Vendres, Collioure, T04 68 82 02 27, leneptune-collioure.com.
Thu-Mon for lunch and dinner.
Not only does the Neptune have some of the best views along the coast, but it also has some of the best food. The young staff are helpful, and the food – lots of seafood from marinated anchovies to grilled lobster, or the grilled duck in Banyuls wine – is beautifully presented. Menus range from €38-82.

La Côte Vermeille €€€
Quai du Fanal, Port-Vendres, T04 68 82 05 71.
Sep-Jun Tue for dinner, Wed-Sat for lunch and dinner; Jul-Aug daily for lunch and dinner.

Stalwartly traditional, this very popular restaurant attracts diners from far and wide for the freshest seafood served with a touch of creativity and class. The favourites are Collioure-style marinated anchovies, seafood salads, and grilled red mullet, or try the sea bass with artichokes and violet crème. The excellent and generous weekday lunch menu is €25. Book in advance.

La Littorine €€
Plage des Elmes, Banyuls-sur-Mer, T04 68 88 03 12, hotel-des-elmes.com.
Jun-Sep Mon-Wed for dinner, Thu-Sun for lunch and dinner; Oct-May Mon-Wed for dinner, Thu-Sat for lunch and dinner.
In a lovely *farniente* setting overlooking a little inlet, chef Jean Marie Patrouix prepares both seafood and landfood with Catalan pizzazz – saffron risotto, monkfish fricasséed with mushrooms or leek cannelloni filled with crab. Fixed menu €28.

Conflent & the Cerdagne

Auberge Saint-Paul €€€€
7 place de l'Eglise, Villefranche-de-Conflent, T04 68 96 30 95.
Easter-Sep Tue-Sat for lunch and dinner, Sun for lunch, Oct-Easter Wed-Sat for lunch and dinner, Sun for lunch.
The place for a blow-out dinner in the Conflent: Patricia Gomez serves gourmet delights (breast of pigeon with onion confit and coriander, pigeon thigh with foie

gras, or grilled prawns and ravioli stuffed with greens) in the lovely courtyard or 13th-century chapel dining room. Excellent cheese and wines, too. Lunch menus start at €19.

Le Canigou €
Place du Génie, Villefranche-de-Conflent, T04 68 96 12 19.
Mar-Dec daily 0800-2300; Jan-Feb Thu-Tue 0800-2300.
A popular bistro with a shady terrace, Le Canigou serves its Catalan specialities such as *escalivada* (mixed grilled vegetables), hams and charcuterie whenever you're feeling peckish. Owner Joël Méné is a volunteer fireman; don't miss his collection of firefighter memorabilia.

Cafés
Café de l'Union
Rue de l'Eglise, Fillols, T04 68 05 63 06.
Open 0800-late.
This tiny village south of Villefranche-de-Conflent is one of the liveliest in the valley. The Café de l'Union serves food from Tuesday-Saturday, including its famous magret and morels, and hosts concerts and jam sessions throughout the year. The nearby **Café de Canigou** is usually buzzing, too.

Entertainment

Perpignan

Clubs & music bars
El Che
Rue Fabrique d'En Nadal, T04 68 64 97 63.
Tue-Sat 1900-0200.
Popular music bar in the centre of Perpignan.

Le Habana Club
5 rue Grande-des-Fabriques, T04 68 34 11 00.
Mon-Sat 1800-0200.
A popular music bar serving excellent mojitos, with a restaurant upstairs. There's great salsa music on Wednesday nights.

Parc des Loisirs Europa
Colline des Loisirs, Canet-en-Roussillon, T04 68 73 31 01.
Open from 2200.
Complex with several clubs/bars/discos open year-round. Linked to Le Castillet in Perpignan (see Eating & drinking, page 237) by the Route 66 buses (see Essentials, page 237).

Gay & lesbian
Uba Club
5 bd Mercader, T04 68 80 44 48, ubaclub.com.
Mid-Aug to mid-Jul Wed-Sat 2300-0600.
Gay, lesbian and straight disco playing a mix of old and new. It's especially popular with those in their 20s and 30s, and there's no cover charge.

Côte Vermeille

Clubs
Indigo
Collioure, D914, Exit 14, T04 68 98 42 42, indigo-collioure.com.
Going strong since 1998, this is the biggest outdoor club on the coast and is played by internationally famous DJs. Out of season, the action moves inside the casino to Vertigo (vertigo-collioure.com).

Listings

Shopping

Art

Galerie de L'Olympe
*8 rue de la Cloche d'Or, T04 68 34
65 75, galerieolympe.com.*
Tue-Sat 1000-1200 and
1400-1900.
Contemporary art gallery in the
pedestrian zone.

Food & drink

Escargots de Roussillon
*9 place de la République,
T04 68 34 47 65.*
Tue-Sun 0730-1215.
More than fresh snails (a huge
local favourite), this shop sells a
wide range of specialities and is
handy for picnic supplies.

Fromagerie du Mas
*9 av André Ampère, Cabestany,
T04 68 34 89 43.*
Tue-Sat 0900-1900.
Over 80 kinds of (mostly
farm-made) cheese from across
Europe. They also do charcuterie
and cheesy lunches.

Marché
Place Cassanyes.
Open 0700-1230.
Perpignan doesn't have a
covered *halles*, but you'll find
luscious fruit, veg, cheeses and
more in this daily market.

Interior design

Sant Vicens
*40 rue Sant Vicens, T04 68 50 02
18, santvicens.fr.*

Pick of the picnic spots

Perpignan's morning market in
Place Cassanyes or the Prades'
market on Tuesday morning are
great sources for picnic fixings.
Eat your olives and anchovies
on the beach at Collioure (see
page 247). In the Cerdagne,
pick up a basket of goodies at
Bernard Bonzom (see Shopping,
opposite) and find a spot in
a high mountain meadow
overlooking the Pyrenees.

Tue-Sat 1000-1200 and
1430-1830, Sun 1430-1830.
East of the centre in an old
farmhouse, Sant Vicens sells
items and antiques for the
home and garden.

Miscellaneous

Maison Quinta
*3 rue Grande des Fabriques, T04
68 34 41 62, maison-quinta.com.*
Tue-Sat 0945-1200 and 1415-1900.
'L'Art de vivre catalan' is the motto,
and they have it all – food,
furnishings, fabrics, tableware,
cookware and toys.

Food & drink

Anchois Desclaux
*Rte D914, Collioure, T04 68 82 05
25, anchoisdesclaux.com.*
Mon-Sat 0900-1200 and
1400-1830.
Anchovies – plus a little anchovy
museum and film. Also sells
regional gourmet goodies
and wines.

Ets Roque
*17 rte d'Argelès, Collioure, T04 68
82 04 99, anchois-roque.com.*
Mon-Fri 0800-1830, Sat-Sun
0800-1200 and 1400-1830.
Since 1870, the Roque family has
been conserving anchovies the
old-fashioned way. They also sell
vinegars, wines, olives and
roquerones (marinated anchovies).

Le Cellier des Templiers
*Rte de Mas de Reig, Banyuls-sur-
Mer, T04 68 98 36 92.*
Mon-Sat 1000-1300 and
1500-1830 (tastings and sales);
Mon-Fri 1430-1800 (visits).
Banyuls' biggest wine
cooperative enjoys a fabulous
setting under 13th-century arches.

Le Croquant à L'Ancienne
*8 rue Berthelot, Collioure, T04 68
98 08 90.*
Mid-Mar to Oct 0800-1300 and
1500-1900, Nov-Dec Thu-Sun
0900-1200 and 1400-1800.
Traditional almond biscuits
baked fresh every morning
according to a 200-year-old
recipe; if you arrive early, you can
watch how it's done.

Food & drink

Bernard Bonzom
*Rte 116, Saillagouse, T04 68 30 14
27, bernard-bonzom.com.*
Easter-Sep Tue-Sun 0800-1230
and 1500-1930, Oct-Easter Tue,
Thu-Sun 0800-1230 and
1500-1930.
Bernard Bonzom and family
win awards for their exquisite

charcuterie made in the Cerdagne. Their shop also sells a huge range of cheeses, breads and other goodies.

Jewellery
Casa Perez
Place de l'Eglise, Prades, T04 68 96 21 03, joyaux-catalans.fr.
Mid-Sep to Jun Tue-Sat 0900-1200 and 1430-1900, Jul to mid-Sep Mon-Sat 0900-1200 and 1430-1900.
Casa Perez makes jewellery in Catalan colours, blood red garnets and gold. Tours of the *atelier* are offered at 1000, 1500, 1615 and 1730.

Activities & tours

Perpignan

Hot-air balloons
Catalan Sports Tours
1 rue Ballanet, Los Masos, T04 68 05 65 29, catalansporttours.com.
Tours from Perpignan airport over the Pyrenees.

Côte du Roussillon

Children
Aqualand
Mas des Capellans, St-Cyprien, T04 68 21 49 49, aqualand.fr/les-parcs,saint_cyprien.

Mid-Jun to early Sep.
A giant water park packed with things to do.

Ferme de Découverte
Rte de Taxo d'Amont, St-André, T04 68 89 16 39, ferme-de-decouverte.fr.
May-Sep daily 1000-1900, Oct-Apr Wed, Sat-Sun 1400-1900, French school holidays daily 1400-1900.
Three hundred animals, including many rare breeds, for children to pet and care for.

Conflent caves.

Culture

The French Tour Co
19 bd Cassanyes, Canet, T06 07 42 16 68, thefrenchtourco.com.
Irish sisters Suzanne and Karen O'Reilly offer bespoke tours of Roussillon; their day wine tour with lunch is the most popular.

Golf

Golf St-Cyprien
Le Mas d'Huston, T04 68 37 63 63, saintcyprien-golfresort.com.
Excellent course (18 holes par 73 and nine holes par 35) by a lake, with views of the Pic du Canigou.

Wellbeing

Thalassol
Av de Thalassa, Port Barcarès, T04 68 86 30 90, thalassol.com.
Thalassotherapy, beauty, anti-stress, and other spa treatments.

Côte Vermeille

Children

La Vallée des Tortues
Rte de La Vallée Heureuse, Sorède, T04 68 95 50 50, lavalleedestortues.com.
Tortoise/turtle breeding centre just in from Argèles-sur-Mer; feeding time mid-afternoon (check the website for hours).

Diving

Réserve Naturelle Marine de Cerbère-Banyuls: Sentier sous-marin
Plage de Peyrefitte, T04 68 88 31 14. Information point at quai Georges Petit, Banyuls-sur-Mer, T04 68 88 56 87, open 1000-1230, 1630-1830.
Jul-Aug 1200-1800.
Scuba through the rich flora and fauna of France's oldest underwater reserve; you can hire all the necessary equipment.

Wellbeing

Thalacap Catalogne
Banyuls-sur-Mer, T04 68 98 36 66, thalacap.fr.
Thalassotherapy treatments that last for a day, a weekend or longer.

Conflent & the Cerdagne

Donkey trekking

La Licorne
Moli d'Oli, Mosset, T04 68 05 03 40, mari-ane.com.
Half-day treks to 15-day excursions.

Golf

Golf de Font-Romeu
*Espace Sportif Colette Besson,
Font-Romeu, T04 68 30 10 78.*
Mid-May to mid-Nov.
A nine-hole par 36 course, high
in the Pyrenees.

Mountain sports

Aventure Grotte et Canyon
*24 rue St-Jean, Villefranche-de-
Conflent, T04 68 05 51 98,
aventuregrottecanyon.com.*
Trained guides for caving,
canyoning, rock climbing and
Via Ferrata.

Exploration Pyrénéenne
*64 rue St-Jean, Villefranche-de-
Conflent, T06-22 45 82 02, ex-pyr.
com.*
Year-round canyoning trips (in
winter in natural hot springs), as
well as caving, adventure
walking and Via Ferrata.

Ozone 3
*40 av Brousse, Font-Romeu,
T04 68 30 36 09, ozone3-
montagne.com.*
Adventures include canyoning,
rafting, kite flying and kite
'mountain board', fishing, rock
climbing, Via Ferrata, treks and
ballooning over the Cerdagne.

Têt Aventure
*Base Eau Vive, Marquixanes,
T06 24 03 80 60, exterieur-nature.
com.*
Near Prades, an adventure park
for ages three and up. Also offers
canyoning, tubbing, hydrospeed,
whitewater rafting, rock
climbing, mountain biking, sea
kayaking, diving, and off-piste
and helicopter skiing.

Trans Pyr 66
*T06 11 87 85 12/T06 88 65 13 26,
transpyr66.com.*
Summer and winter activities in
the Cerdagne, including dog

sledding, sleeping in igloos, rock
climbing and rafting.

Skiing/wintersports

**Font-Romeu/ Bolquère-
Pyrénées 2000**
*Font-Romeu, T04 68 30 68 30,
font-romeu.fr.*
Well-equipped station with 40
pistes, including eight black and
eight red. Also offers snow
shoeing, a surf park, ice skating,
dog-sledding and a children's
snow park.

Les Angles
T04 68 04 32 76, les-angles.com.
Two black, 16 red, six blue and
seven green pistes, and rarely
any queues. There's also cross-
country skiing, snowboarding
and equipment and training
for disabled skiers.

Wellbeing

Bains de St Thomas
*Fontpédrouse, T04 68 97 03 13,
bains-saint-thomas.fr.*
Hot spring a 30-minute walk
from a station on the Petit Train
Jaune: hammam, jacuzzi, exterior
hot pools, and a choice of
treatments including being
coated in chocolate. Children
welcome. No credit cards.

The Vallespir

Golf

Golf du Domaine de Falgos
*St-Laurent-de-Cerdans, T04 68
39 51 42, falgos.com.*
Beautiful 18-hole par 70 course in
the foothills of the Pyrenees.

Five of the best

Canyoning rivers on Le Pic du Canigou

❶ La Lentilla (Finestrêt) For beginners; July-September.

❷ Le Llech The all-round best, with lots of jumps and slides;
May-September.

❸ La Llitera Steep and wild and a two-hour walk to the start;
May-August.

❹ Le Cady Experienced canyoners only; August to mid-September.

❺ Le St Vincent Long, exciting descent; March-September.

Contents

Practicalities

Sète's railway station.

Getting there

From the UK & Ireland

Languedoc-Roussillon has five regional airports: Nîmes, Montpellier, Bézier-Agde, Carcassonne and Perpignan. These are especially well served in summer by **Ryanair**, departing from Birmingham, Bournemouth, Bristol, Cork, Dublin, East Midlands, Edinburgh, Leeds Bradford, Liverpool, London City, London Stansted, Luton and Shannon. There are also direct flights with **EasyJet** to Montpellier from Luton and Gatwick; **Flybe** to Perpignan from Southampton; and **bmibaby** to Perpignan from Manchester. Other flights (also on **British Airways**, **Air France** and **Jet2**) serve airports close to Languedoc, notably Toulouse and Avignon.

Visitors to Roussillon may also want to look into the year-round Ryanair flights to Spain's Girona airport, as Frogbus (frogbus.com) provides direct links from there to Perpignan, Roussillon's beaches and the Pyrenees resorts of Font-Romeu and Les Angles.

From North America

There are no direct flights to Languedoc-Roussillon from America. **Air Canada**, **Air France**, **British Airways**, **Delta** and **United Airlines** fly into Paris Charles de Gaulle International Airport, where you can pick up direct Air France flights to Montpellier or Toulouse. Often the best deal from North

Air Canada aircanada.com
Air France airfrance.com
Bmibaby bmibaby.com
British Airways britishairways.com
Delta delta.com
EasyJet easyjet.com
Flybe flybe.com
Jet2 jet2.com
KLM klm.com
Lufthansa lufthansa.com
Ryanair ryanair.com
United Airlines united.com

America is to fly into Montpellier or Toulouse via Amsterdam, Munich or Frankfurt on **KLM** or **Lufthansa**.

From the rest of Europe

There are direct flights from Paris (both Charles de Gaulle and Orly), Ajaccio, Bastia, Clermont-Ferrand, Rennes, Lyon and Nantes in France, and from Frankfurt, Madrid and Copenhagen to Montpellier. Nîmes, Perpignan and Carcassonne airports also have connections with Brussels (Charloi); Perpignan and Béziers have links from Odense (Denmark) and Düsseldorf Weeze. Other options to look at are the flights from most of Europe to both Toulouse and Marseille – or hop on a train (see below).

Airport information

Aéroport Nîmes-Alès-Camargue (T04 66 70 49 49, nimes-aeroport.fr) is in St-Gilles. A Navette or shuttle (T04 66 29 27 29, €5) coinciding with every flight links the airport to the train station and other points in town.

Aéroport Montpellier Méditerranée (T04 67 20 85 00, montpellier.aeroport.fr) is 8 km from the centre of Montpellier. A regular shuttle bus runs from the airport to the Place de l'Europe, where there's a station serving the city's two tramway lines. Contact Hérault Transport (T08 25 34 01 34).

Aéroport Béziers Cap d'Agde (T04 67 80 99 09, beziers.cci.fr) is located between Béziers and Agde. There are shuttles that run to coincide with the Ryanair flights, going to Béziers' bus and train stations (€3.10) and to Agde (€4); contact the airport desk on arrival.

Aéroport Carcassonne (T04 68 71 96 46, carcassonne.aeroport.fr) is linked by the Navette Agglo'bus Aeroport (T04 68 47 82 22, tickets €5, available on board) to Carcassonne, the train station, the Ville Basse and the medieval Cité. The shuttles run to coincide with each flight.

Aéroport Perpignan-Rivesaltes (T04 68 52 60 70, perpignan.cci.fr) is north of Perpignan in Rivesaltes. The Couriers Catalans shuttle (T04 68 55 68 00, €4.50) runs from the airport to Perpignan's train and bus stations.

Aéroport Toulouse-Blagnac (T08 25 38 00 00, toulouse.aeroport.fr) has shuttle connections (navette-tisseo-aeroport.com, €4) every 20-40 minutes with the centre of Toulouse and the train station.

Rail

Travelling by **Eurostar** (T08 70 51 86 18, eurostar. com) and **TGV** (tgv-europe.com) from London to Nîmes takes about seven hours; a little longer to reach Montpellier. After an easy change in Paris – from Gare du Nord to the Gare de Lyon, take the RER D – it's non-stop. Contact Eurostar and use the TGV website to arrange the journey independently, or contact **European Rail** (T020-7619 1083, europeanrail. com) and let them do it all. Note that with the TGV's Prem's fares you can get big discounts by booking up to 90 days before you travel.

Road

Car

London to Montpellier is just over 1000 km and the drive can be done in a day if you start early. Once you get to Paris, there are three main *autoroutes* south. The most direct is the A10 to Orléans, the A71 to Vierzon and the A75 down to Languedoc (6½ hrs, tolls €40), which includes crossing the magnificent Viaduc de Millau.

For Carcassonne, Narbonne and Perpignan, it's faster to pick up the A20 in Vierzon to Toulouse and then the A61 (7 hrs to Carcassonne, tolls €40). A third option is the *autoroute du soleil* (A6, and then A7) via Lyon and Orange, where you can pick up the A9 to Nîmes (6½ hrs, tolls €50). Be aware though that in August this route can be at a

standstill, especially at weekends.

To bring a GB-registered car into France you need your vehicle registration document, full driving licence and insurance papers (or Green Card), which must be carried at all times when driving, along with your passport. You'll need to adjust or tape the headlamps, and carry a warning triangle and safety vest inside the car (not the boot).

Car hire The lowest rate for seven days' car hire starts at around €170. If you're travelling with kids and a lot of bags, it's probably cheaper to drive and easier to bring your own car. Otherwise, what works best for you depends on the time of year, what fly/drive or rail/drive deals you can find, and whether or not you like long drives.

Bus/coach

Eurolines (T087-1781 8181, eurolines.co.uk) runs from London Victoria to Montpellier several times a week (if you're not starting in London, the add-on fare is only £15) for €162 return. There are often special offers, and discounts for over 65s, under 26s and children. Journey time is 20 hours.

Getting around

If you just want to stick to the main cities, famous sites and beaches, Languedoc-Roussillon's trains and buses are just about good enough to get around. Otherwise, unless you're hiring a canal barge with bicycles or are coming specifically for a walking or riding tour you may well need a car. Every news-stand sells maps of the region – the Michelin or Blay 1:250000 are both good and frequently updated. Trekkers should pick up IGN Série Bleue 1:25000 maps, which can also be bought before arrival (loisirs.ign.fr).

Rail

France's national railway, the **SNCF**, has a very useful online service (voyages-sncf.com) for finding schedules and booking tickets. They also have a toll number, T3635 (€0.34 per min), which can be used throughout France. The website doubles as a tour operator, offering discounts on hotels, ski packages, flights and rental cars, and they'll post tickets outside France. There are a variety of InterRail passes available for all ages (including a France Rail pass that's valid just for France), but they're really only good value if you mean to do several days of long-distance travelling outside the Languedoc-Roussillon region. European residents should visit raileurope.co.uk, if you live outside Europe the website is raileurope.com.

France's sleek trains, **TGV**s (*trains à grande vitesse*), which nip along at 250 kph or more, are very useful for getting to Languedoc-Roussillon (see above). Unless you're in a hurry, however, the regular and regional trains (TER, T08 91 70 09 00, €0.23 per min) are better for everyday travel: they are cheaper, will carry bicycles for free, and you don't have to book in advance. You can even avoid the queues by buying a ticket with your credit card from a machine in the station. These tickets are valid for two months, but like all train tickets in France you must make sure to date-stamp/validate (*composter*) your ticket in the station before boarding or you will be subject to a fine. Travel from Monday afternoons to Friday mornings (*période bleue*) is cheaper than weekends and holidays (*période blanche*). There are discounts for over 60s, under 26s and under 12s. Sometimes on less busy minor routes, SNCF buses run instead of trains.

TGVs run from Paris to Nîmes, from where there are frequent rail connections to Montpellier (30 mins) and Sète, Agde, Narbonne, Béziers, Carcassonne and Toulouse. Other trains from Nîmes serve TER routes to further destinations in the Gard, such as Beaucaire (24 mins), Aigues-Mortes (45 mins) and the beaches of Le-Grau-du-Roi (50 mins). The train route between Clermont-Ferrand and Nîmes (Le Cévenol) is one of the most beautiful in France, and it stops at Florac, Bagnols-les-Bains and La Bastide-St-Laurent-les-Bains. From the latter you can pick up the Translozerien to Mende, Marvejols and Millau on the Clement-Ferrand to Béziers line. Local TER trains link Mende with Nîmes and Montpellier.

Trains link Carcassonne and Narbonne with Toulouse, and Narbonne with Perpignan, Béziers and Montpellier. A few services a day run from Carcassonne to Limoux, Couiza and Quillan (1 hr) and frequent trains link Perpignan to Spain. Local trains serve the Côte Vermeille and travel up the Conflent valley to Villefranche-Vernet-les-Bains to link up with the Petit Train Jaune (see box, page 225). This, in turn, goes to Cerdagne, where there are connections to Toulouse, Andorra and Barcelona.

Road

Bicycle

Although the French have great respect for cyclists, it's always best to avoid the busier roads. Check out route suggestions and maps on bikely.com and bikemap.net. In Montpellier you can hire and drop off a bike in one of 50 locations for €1 for four hours, or €2 for a day with Vélomagg (see Essentials, page 147). Elsewhere, rentals average €10-12 a day, more for a racing or mountain bike.

Mellow Velo (T04 68 43 38 21, mellowvelos.com) in Paraza on the Canal du Midi delivers bikes in the area. Local tourist offices can advise on other hire shops, alternatively check out holiday-bikes.com/fr.

Bus/coach

Bus services in Languedoc-Roussillon are mostly geared towards getting kids to school, so hours are often early and buses run only once or twice a day. This is especially true in the Lozère and the Aude. Mende is linked to Marvejols and Rodez by regular buses; other buses do exist but are generally scheduled for the early morning school trips. Similarly, apart from the frequent buses that run from Narbonne to the beaches, bus services in the Aude are infrequent.

Roussillon, however, stands out in the region for its network of €1 buses that reach most of the towns in the department. Most branch out from Perpignan's Gare Routière; see cg66.fr (T04 68 80 80 80) for routes and schedules.

You can get to the main sights of the Gard (edgard-transport.fr) and the Hérault by bus, and prices are similar to the trains. Regular buses from Nîmes serve the Pont du Gard (45 mins), Uzès (60 mins), Ganges (90 mins), St-Gilles (50 mins) and Sommières (Mon-Sat, 50 mins), which also has a bus to Montpellier. In summer there are frequent departures from Nîmes to Aigues-Mortes, Le Grau-du-Roi and La Grande Motte. The Hérault has buses travelling the main routes four or five times a day from Montpellier or Béziers, but to complicate things many of the departures from Montpellier are from various outlying tramway stations (check departure points and schedules at herault-transport.fr). Services to Pézenas and the beaches (Palavas-les-Flots and La Grande Motte) are especially frequent in summer.

Car

Motoring in Languedoc-Roussillon presents no great difficulties, although in summer the main *autoroute* that crosses the region (the A9) can get very busy, as it's also the main road between Spain and Italy.

Even minor roads in the mountains are well maintained, and most are well signposted, but a good map and/or a Sat Nav are essential. One wrong turn in the sprawl around the cities (especially Montpellier) can be fatal; signs are few and they never seem to be the ones you want. Driving in the city centres, with their traffic jams and one-way systems, can be frustrating, although here at least if you get lost, you can always follow the handy *Toutes directions* signs, which will eventually lead you out to a ring of roads around the city with many useful signs along the way. Parking garages cost €3-5 an hour.

It's always cheapest to fill up with petrol or diesel (*gazole*) at supermarkets, many of which now have 24-hour machines that take credit cards. Petrol stations of any kind are few and far between in the mountains.

Unless otherwise signposted, the speed limits on *autoroutes* is 130 kph. On two-lane D (departmental) roads it's 90 kph, and in towns (once you've passed the white sign announcing the town's name) it's 50 kph. Speeding fines start at €68 and can be as high as €4500 if you fail a breathalyzer test. If you have an accident, you will be asked to fill out a form called a *constat amiable*. If your French isn't up to it, wait for help rather than unwittingly incriminating yourself.

Car hire This is almost always cheaper to arrange before you arrive, and it's essential you book in advance in the summer when cars can be in short supply. Look at the many car rental websites (autosabroad.com, auto-europe.co.uk and comparecarrent.com) and then compare them to the fly/drive or rail/drive packages. You'll need to be at least 21 and have a credit card with the name of driver matching the name on the card. There are supplemental charges for an extra driver or a child seat. Be sure to check the insurance and damage waiver before setting out, and always carry all the papers with you.

Directory

Customs & immigration

UK and EU visitors need a valid passport to enter France. Standard tourist visas for non-EU visitors are valid for 90 days and encompass the whole EU zone.

Disabled travellers

Languedoc-Roussillon claims to be top when it comes to accommodating visitors with special needs; at en.sunfrance.com you can download a complete list of gîtes, campsites, restaurants, parks, sites and activities adapted for people with a range of disabilities. Most trains, and Montpellier's trams, are wheelchair-friendly, or ring for a **Taxi Tram** (T04 67 92 04 98) which provides transport in the city and beyond, as does the region-wide **Ulysse Transport** (ulysse-transport.fr). Alternatively, hire your own transport with **GNS Adaptation** based in Nîmes (T04 66 68 13 90, gnsadaptation.com, website in French). When booking hotel rooms, be sure to ask for a *une chambre adaptée*.

Emergencies

European emergency line T112
Fire service T18
Police T17
SAMU (medical emergencies) T15

Etiquette

The French are very polite. Greet everyone in shops, restaurants and hotels, with a *"Bonjour, Madame/Mademoiselle/Monsieur"* and then an *"Au revoir"* when you depart. They also love to make *les bises* (cheek air kisses) even when first introduced if at least one member of the party is female (man-to-man, a handshake will do).

Families

Languedoc-Roussillon is a great destination for family holidays; people here are fond of children, and there are long sandy beaches and endless things for them to do (see Children's activities, page 69 and Activities & tours in the Around the region chapters). Most restaurants offer a *menu enfant* (usually *steak frites*). High chairs are rarer, but hotels often have family rooms and cots.

Health

Comprehensive travel and medical insurance is recommended. EU citizens should apply for a free European Health Insurance Card or EHIC (ehic.org), which entitles you to emergency medical treatment on the same terms as French nationals. Note that you will have to pay all charges and prescriptions up front and be reimbursed once you return home. If you develop a minor ailment while on holiday, a visit to any pharmacy will allow you to discuss your concerns with highly qualified staff, who can give medical advice and recommend treatment. Outside normal opening hours, the address of the nearest duty pharmacy (*pharmacie de garde*) is displayed in the pharmacy window. The out-of-hours number for a local doctor (*médecin généraliste*) may also be listed. In a serious emergency, go to the accident and emergency department (*urgences*) at the nearest Centre Hospitalier (numbers listed in the Essentials section at the beginning of each chapter) or call an ambulance (SAMU) by dialling T15.

Post office, Villeneuve-lès-Avignon.

Insurance

Comprehensive travel and medical insurance is strongly recommended, as the European Health Insurance Card (EHIC) does not cover medical repatriation, ongoing medical treatment or treatment considered to be non-urgent. Check for exclusions if you mean to engage in risky sports. Keep all insurance documents to hand; a good way to keep track of your policies is to email the details to yourself.

Make sure you have adequate insurance when hiring a car and always ask how much excess you are liable for if the vehicle is returned with any damage. It is generally worth paying a little more for a collision damage waiver. If driving your own vehicle to France, contact your insurers before you travel to ensure you are adequately covered, and keep the documents in your vehicle in case you need to prove it.

Money

The French currency is the euro (€). There are ATM machines in every town, and nearly all hotels, restaurants and shops accept credit cards. Note that many North American cards lack a chip necessary for them to work in toll machines or in 24-hour petrol stations, so check with you bank before you leave. It's also worth asking your bank

for information on how to save money on cash withdrawal charges. It's very difficult these days to find a French bank to change currency or traveller's cheques; try at the airport exchanges or main post offices in big cities.

Police

There are two types of police in France. The Police Municipal handle mostly traffic issues in cities; the Gendarmes take care of everything else. Note that in France you can legally be stopped for ID checks for no reason (usually for belonging to a minority or looking scruffy). If your passport or any other valuables are lost and stolen, visit the *gendarmerie* (police station) for the necessary paperwork.

Post

La Poste is reliable, but recently many rural bureaux have been closed down, or replaced by a counter in shops. Most newsagents and *tabacs* sell stamps (*timbres*) for postcards and letters to Europe (€0.70) but hardly ever for North America (€0.85). Post offices are closed Saturday afternoons and Sundays, and usually for lunch, too.

Safety

Violent crime is rare in France, but there's a healthy amount of petty theft in Montpellier, Perpignan and Nîmes, and you should avoid some of the run-down quarters after dark. Just be as sensible as you are at home, and don't leave tempting items visible in your car, insure your camera and don't carry all your money with you in one place.

Telephone

The French have dispensed with area codes, and all numbers dialled within the country are now 10 digits.

Around the region

If a number begins with 06 it's a mobile phone. The country code is 33; when dialling from abroad, leave out the first 0 (T+332). Directory assistance, T118 218.

Time difference

One hour ahead of GMT; six hours ahead of EST.

Tipping

French bar and restaurant bills nearly always include a 15% service charge so tipping a little extra is discretionary. Taxi drivers appreciate it if you round up the fare or add an extra couple of euros for any help with your bags. Give a guide a euro or two at the end of guided tours.

Tourist information

Languedoc Regional Tourism Board, 'Acropole, 954, avenue Jean Mermoz, 34960 Montpellier, T04 67 20 02 20, en.sunfrance.com.
Gard Tourist Board, 3 rue Cité Foulc, 30010 Nîmes, T04 66 36 96 30, gardtourism.com.
Lozère Tourist Board, 14 rue Henri-Bourillon, 48002 Mende, T04 66 48 48 48, lozere-uk.com.
Hérault Tourist Board, Avenue des Moulins, 34184 Montpellier, T04 67 67 71 71, herault-tourisme.com.
Aude Tourist Board, Avenue Raymond Courrière, 11855 Carcassonne, T04 68 11 66 00, audetourisme.com.
Roussillon Tourist Board, 16 avenue des Palmiers, 66005 Perpignan, T04 68 51 52 53, cdt-66.com.

Voltage

The electrical current in France is 220 volts 50 Hz; Plugs are the standard European round two-pin variety.

Montpellier's tramway.

Language

You'll find that people speak at least basic English in hotels, restaurants and major tourist sites in Languedoc-Roussillon, so don't worry too much if your French is very rusty. Older people in the countryside, however, may not speak a word of English and you may have difficulty understanding their southern French twang, which is a bit different from the Parisian French taught in school. In Roussillon people are more likely to speak Catalan or Spanish, but you'll find English translations everywhere. If tours are only conducted in French, there will nearly always be a hand-out or audio guide in English.

Basics

hello *bonjour*
good evening *bonsoir*
goodbye *au revoir/salut* (polite/informal)
please *s'il vous plaît*
thank you *merci*
I'm sorry, excuse me *pardon, excusez-moi*
yes *oui*
no *non*
how are you?
    comment allez-vous?/ça va? (polite/informal)
fine, thank you *bien, merci*
one moment *un instant*
how? *comment?*
how much? *c'est combien?*
when? *quand?*
where is…? *où est…?*
why? *pourquoi?*
what? *quoi?*
what's that? *qu'est-ce que c'est?*
I don't understand *je ne comprends pas*
I don't know *je ne sais pas*
I don't speak French *je ne parle pas français*
how do you say… (in French)?
    comment dites-vous… (en français)?
do you speak English?
Est-ce que vous parlez anglais?/Parlez-vous anglais?

Occitan phrases

Hello/good morning	*Bonjorn*
Good evening	*Bonser*
Goodbye	*A lèu/Adieu*
How are you?	*Cossí va?*
I'm fine. And you?	*Va plan, mercés. E tu?*
What's your name?	*Cossí te dison?*
My name is…	*Me dison…*
Welcome!	*Benevenguda!*
Please	*Se vos plai*
Thank you	*Mercès*
I don't understand	*Compreni pas*
How do you say…	*Cossí se ditz…*
in Occitan?	*en occitan?*
Cheers!	*A la bona santat!*
I love you	*T'aimi*
Where is the toilet?	*Ont son los comuns?*
Bon voyage	*Bon viatje*

See also page 44.

help! *au secours!*
wait! *attendez!*
stop! *arrêtez!*

Numbers

one	*un*	two	*deux*
two	*deux*	three	*trois*
four	*quatre*	five	*cinq*
six	*six*	seven	*sept*
eight	*huit*	nine	*neuf*

10	*dix*	11	*onze*
12	*douze*	13	*treize*
14	*quatorze*	15	*quinze*
16	*seize*	17	*dix-sept*
18	*dix-huit*	19	*dix-neuf*
20	*vingt*	21	*vingt-et-un*
22	*vingt-deux*		

				when is breakfast?
30	trente	40	quarante	*le petit déjeuner est à quelle heure?*
50	cinquante	60	soixante	can I have the key?
70	soixante-dix	80	quatre-vingts	*est-ce que je peux avoir la clef?/La clef, s'il vous*
90	quatre-vingt-dix	100	cent	*plaît?*
200	deux cents	1000	mille	

Shopping

this one/that one   *celui-ci/celui-là*
less   *moins*
more   *plus*
expensive   *cher*
cheap   *pas cher/bon marché*
how much is it?
   c'est combien?/combien est-ce que ça coûte?
can I have...? (literally 'I would like')   *je voudrais...*

Travelling

one ticket for   *un billet pour...*
single   *un aller-simple*
return   *un aller-retour*
airport   *l'aéroport*
bus stop   *l'arrêt de bus*
train   *le train*
car   *la voiture*
taxi   *le taxi*
is it far?   *c'est loin?*

Hotels

a single/double room
   une chambre à une personne/deux personnes
a double bed   *un lit double/un grand lit*
bathroom   *la salle de bains*
shower   *la douche*
is there a (good) view?
   est-ce qu'il y a une (belle) vue?
can I see the room?
   est-ce que je peux voir la chambre?

Time

morning   *le matin*
afternoon   *l'après-midi*
evening   *le soir*
night   *la nuit*
a day   *un jour*
a week   *une semaine*
a month   *un mois*
soon   *bientôt*
later   *plus tard*
what time is it?   *quelle heure est-il?*
today/tomorrow/yesterday
   aujourd'hui/demain/hier

Days

Monday	*lundi*	Tuesday	*mardi*
Wednesday	*mercredi*	Thursday	*jeudi*
Friday	*vendredi*	Saturday	*samedi*
Sunday	*dimanche*		

Months

January	*janvier*	February	*février*
March	*mars*	April	*avril*
May	*mai*	June	*juin*
July	*juillet*	August	*août*
September	*septembre*	October	*octobre*
November	*novembre*	December	*décembre*

Index

Index

Index

Credits

Footprint credits

Project editor: Felicity Laughton
Text editor: Sara Chare
Picture editor: Rob Lunn
Layout and production: Kelly Pipes
Maps: Gail Townsley
Proofreader: Tamsin Stirk
Series design: Mytton Williams

Managing Director: Andy Riddle
Commercial Director: Patrick Dawson
Publisher: Alan Murphy
Publishing managers:
Felicity Laughton, Jo Williams
Design and images: Rob Lunn,
Kassia Gawronski
Digital Editor: Alice Jell
Marketing: Liz Harper,
Hannah Bonnell
Sales: Jeremy Parr
Advertising: Renu Sibal
Finance & administration:
Elizabeth Taylor

Print

Manufactured in India by Nutech
Pulp from sustainable forests

Every effort has been made to ensure that
the facts in this guidebook are accurate.
However, travellers should still obtain
advice from consulates, airlines etc about
travel and visa requirements before
travelling. The authors and publishers
cannot accept responsibility for any loss,
injury or inconvenience however caused.

Publishing information

FootprintFrance
Languedoc-Roussillon
1st edition
© Footprint Handbooks Ltd
May 2010

ISBN 978-1-906098-95-7
CIP DATA: A catalogue record for this
book is available from the British Library

® Footprint Handbooks and the Footprint
mark are a registered trademark of
Footprint Handbooks Ltd

Published by Footprint
6 Riverside Court
Lower Bristol Road
Bath BA2 3DZ, UK
T +44 (0)1225 469141
F +44 (0)1225 469461
www.footprintbooks.com

Distributed in North America by
Globe Pequot Press